THE JOY
OF
WOKKING

EMPLOYEE BOOK SALE

NOT TO BE RESOLD

"FOOD & SEX ARE HUMAN NATURE"

Martin Yan

THE

JOY of

WOKKING

A Chinese Cookbook

1982

DOUBLEDAY CANADA LIMITED,
Toronto, Ontario
DOUBLEDAY & COMPANY INC.,
Garden City, New York

SECOND EDITION
REVISED & ENLARGED

Library of Congress Catalog Card number 82—45516
Design by Wayne Lum
Illustrations by Chung-Kwong Cheung
Cartoons by Howard Eng
ISBN 0-385-18342-9 (paperback)
ISBN 0-385-18341-0 (hardcover)

Copyright © 1979 By Martin Yan
All Rights Reserved

Including The Right of Reproduction
In Whole or In Part in Any Form

Reprint April 1983
Reprint February 1984
Reprint August 1984

Printed in Canada by Hignell Printing

To my mother and brother Michael who have given me support and encouragement all the way from mainland China. Their love and understanding have helped me along many difficult paths.

CONTENTS

Let's Wrap It Up!

"The fat fellow on the right is me, being a serious student.

I concentrated so hard that I bit my tongue..."

Here's Martin!

Chow mein, chop suey, sweet and sour spareribs and fried rice are familiar dishes to the majority of households when one mentions Chinese cooking, dines at a Chinese restaurant, or orders a meal to be brought home. This limited familiarity with Chinese dishes is unfortunate for it deprives many of us from the wealth of gastronomic delights Chinese cooking has to offer.

Traditional Chinese cooking is more varied and has a sophistication equal to the famed French and Italian cuisines, yet Chinese dishes are generally less complicated and are relatively simple to prepare. The use of a wide variety of vegetables, low-fat types of poultry, fish and red meat and relatively short cooking times should have added appeal to the dietary-minded consumer who is mindful of nutritious meals yet is seeking to avoid excessive amounts of certain food components.

The author, Martin Yan, is exceptionally well qualified to introduce you to the delights of Chinese cookery, as he has many years of formal education and practical experience in preparing Chinese food and in relating his knowledge to consumers. He has earned a Diploma in Chinese cookery in Hong Kong, Bachelor's and Master of Science degrees in Food Science and Technology at the University of California at Davis, and holds a California teaching credential in Chinese cooking. His practical experience includes employment in one of the largest Chinese food companies in Hong Kong, and he has worked as a chef in Chinese restaurants in Hong Kong, and many parts of North America.

Mr. Yan, in addition to his experience and knowledge of foods and Chinese cookery, has taught classes for over ten years, has been the chief demonstrator for a Chinese food and cookware company and was the television host for over 500 shows in Chinese cooking in Canada.

Thus, the author's experiences and communicative skills are combined here to offer you the opportunity to learn, or gain additional knowledge of Chinese cooking, using experience-proven techniques and simple instructions that will enable you to prepare recipes covering the Chinese cuisine from appetizers to desserts. The ultimate reward is the gastronomic pleasures resulting from Chinese cooking.

Dr. Martin W. Miller
Professor of Food Science,
University of California,
Davis, California

尊敬读者、朋友、同好：

"食色性也"此为中国古圣哲之名言，而民"以食为天"则更为中国恒古以来之习俗。可见食对于中国人，是何等的！其实，这又何止中国人，外国人，不是亦然乎？

应生活之要求，中国烹调术——中国菜，就是经越久远的历史的发展，形成以色、香、味俱全的艺术的结合，而各具风格，彼此融通。且越来越受主人们将道及争相品赏和研究的对象，这决不是偶然的。

笔者因幼习厨，且攻读饮食，故长涯于此而感苦学，每赞研考案，略其心得，谨将之整编奉献。一则以尽推广及发扬中国烹调术之微力，再此藉以求攻破引生，抑望就正于前辈贤达。如有同好，不吝赐教，至为感荷。

EMBARKING ON A LONG WOK

Bang the Cymbals! Hit the Drum!
What's Going On?

After about 5000 years of being very civilized people, the Chinese know what's really important in life. It all boils, sautees, steams and stews down to one word: food. For most Chinese, food is not only essential for survival, but it also is a great source of enjoyment and social enrichment. Food brings together family and friends, and it has long been a tradition to extend one's hospitality by inviting guests to share a feast.

The techniques of cooking, its ingredients, and even its philosophy, are very much a part of a people's culture. By understanding Chinese cooking, you may begin to understand the Chinese. Life, when I was a boy in Kwongchow, China, was very different from what I've experienced here, but all people need to eat, and want to enjoy what they're eating. The biggest difference is one of priorities: to take time to enjoy food (and to cook it well). There is really no magic involved in Chinese cooking. Just remember that a meal should be planned to appeal to all the senses, including the sense of humor.

Nowadays, we live in a diet-conscious nation and recognize that our health has a lot to do with what we eat. The ancient Chinese understood this, too, and the principles of Chinese food, with its emphasis on lots of fresh, wholesome vegetables and small amounts of meat, can provide healthy, nutritious meals, stretch our food budgets, and help us maintain ideal weights. (But if the recipes in this book tempt you to eat too much Chinese food, you can get just as fat by eating 100 chocolate-coated candy bars a day!)

In this book, I hope to tell you a great deal about Chinese food, and incidentally, something about Chinese customs and culture. You will find recipes from different culinary regions of China, as well as other parts of Southeast Asia. This is the second edition of *The Joy of Wokking*, and it is completely revised and contains much material that is new. For some of that, I have to thank the many kind readers of the first edition, who wrote and told me what they thought was good—and more importantly, what was bad. I hope that I have taken into account all of their thoughtful criticisms (and can now sleep in peace again without having nightmares about my worst goofs). Because of you, my interest in cooking has graduated from a pleasurable hobby to a delightful career. I owe this to you all and feel a great sense of honor for having had the opportunity to introduce this great cuisine to all of you.

But nobody's perfect (least of all, me!), and you will find a note at the end of this book that tells you how to write to me with all your comments—good and bad. But for now, let us begin. May your stomachs always be full, and your wok never grow cold!

Have a good "wok!"

The Great Gastronomical Adventure

Among the world's great cuisines, the regional cooking of China is perhaps the most difficult to classify. China is a great land with diverse weather and resources. Because many parts of China are isolated, the regional styles of cooking of China are as different as its dialects. Over the centuries, certain special dishes from one region have been adopted and adapted in other regions. Most Chinese cooks are notably inventive and flexible due to the availability of ingredients and new dishes and foods are constantly being incorporated into each region. For such reasons, the best of Chinese cooking is mostly found in large cities where the art is nurtured and stimulated by the gourmets, the rich, the educated and the travelers. For simple identification, we will only discuss the four better-known culinary regions.

The Northern School — Peking (or Mandarin)

Peking, the home of the Imperial courts for many centuries, is the political and cultural center of China. There, anything that was the best of its kind from different regions would be introduced, adapted, and presented in this great city of royal families, high officials and wealthy merchants. Pekingese cuisine is derived mainly from Moslem cooking of Inner Mongolia, the local cooking of Shantung and Hopei, the imperial kitchen of the capital, and the dishes of lower Yangtze region, Fukien, Kwontong and Szechwan. The staple in Peking cooking is wheat flour, and many traditional dishes such as Peking Duck and Mushi Pork are served with pancakes. Sizzling the ingredients in a dish with brown bean paste is also a typical cooking method.

The Eastern School — Shanghai

Red cooked dishes, or cooking foods with soy sauce over slow heat, are characteristics of the eastern region of China, particularly Kangsu and Chekang. Shanghai is often considered to be the culinary center for many of these eastern provinces, and because it is on the coast, a great variety of fish and shellfish are available. Dishes from this area tend to be richer, heavier and more highly seasoned with salt and sugar to "wok and roll" your taste buds; rice dishes are a common accompaniment to red cooked dishes in every day family meals.

The Western School — Szechwan

Szechwan is located in a relatively isolated area in the heart of China, where the climate is hot, humid and muggy. Hot and spicy foods are frequently served in this region, as generous amounts of red chili pepper, garlic and leeks are used. The use of hot pepper is not intended to paralyze taste sensations, but to stimulate the palate. Under such stimulation, the palate becomes more sensitive and capable of appreciating a number of flavors simultaneously. However, as in the more delicately flavored banquet dishes not all dishes from this area are spicy. Szechwan dishes also rely on other seasonings and relishes, and salted meat dishes are common. This school of cooking, along with the Hunan style, has recently gained increased popularity in this country.

The Southern School — Canton

Canton, because of its mild, tropical climate and abundant rainfall, is a rich agricultural region on the southern tip of China, with fresh food available all year round. The Cantonese kitchen is characterized by its vast choice and endless combination of ingredients and textures. Unlike the Eastern school, very little soy sauce is used in cooking to preserve the natural color and flavor of food. Garnishes are carefully selected to add color and appeal, and much effort goes into the artful presentation of each dish. North Americans are most familiar with this southern style of cooking, because the Cantonese were the first to immigrate to North America.

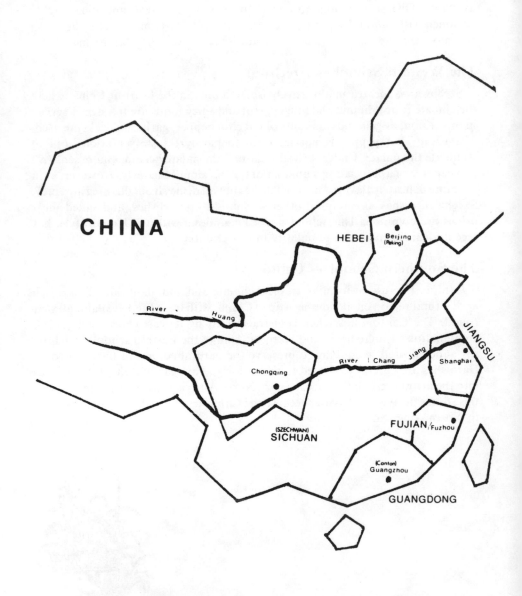

CHINA

HEBEI

Beijing
(Peking)

River   Huang

JIANGSU

River   Chang   Jiang

Chongqing

Shanghai

(SZECHWAN)
SICHUAN

FUJIAN/Fuzhou

(Canton)
Guangzhou

GUANGDONG

Tools of the Trade

If you are worried that you'll need a large warehouse of utensils for Chinese cooking, you can start smiling! Only a few items are essential to perform multiple functions: a wok, a curved spatula, a wok lid and a sharp Chinese cleaver. As far as other utensils you may wish to purchase, how about a set of bamboo steamers, a wok stand (ring), a skimmer (strainer), a heavy cutting board and chopsticks? No, these items are not absolutely necessary, but after you have been wokking for a while, you may find it more exciting and handier with these basic Chinese tools. Otherwise, you may use whatever you can find "hidden" in your kitchen—don't be afraid to improvise!

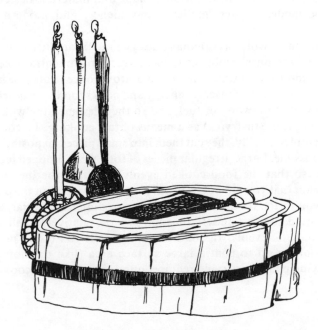

Wokkie Talkie

You can cook Chinese food without a wok. But that's like dancing in workboots—or like playing hockey with a tennis racket—or . . .well, you get the idea. It's just not as much fun. Besides, considering the price of kitchenware these days, the wok, a multi-functional cooking pan, is an incredible bargain. Once you know how to use one, you may still keep your old frying pans, but you will probably use them less.

Woks are available in different dimensions, ranging from 12", 14", 18" to the much larger ones used in restaurants. The 14" wok is the most common and is large enough to prepare meals for 2-8 hungry people. There are three different kinds of woks commonly available on the market, with a significant range in prices:

1. the traditional round-bottomed wok—made from carbon steel (by spinning or hand-hammering), stainless steel (of different thicknesses), or aluminum alloy with or without a specially-treated cooking surface.
2. the flat-bottomed wok (specially designed for cooking on electric burners)— made from the same types of materials as the round-bottomed wok.
   the electric wok—made from stainless steel or aluminum alloy with or without a non-stick surface.

There is one very unique wok which is worth special mention here. The traditional hand-hammered steel wok looks much like its ancestors a thousand years ago. It is not pretty, but unfortunately, there are no 'designer woks.' Anything that departs from this traditional shape and material is essentially a compromise for modern tastes, modern convenience, and modern electric burners.

The round-bottomed wok was originally designed to fit on the Chinese stove, which has no oven and burns wood, coal, hay or certain unmentionable animal by-products. But more importantly, the round bottom concentrates the heat into a small, intense hot spot that conserves energy and cooks food very quickly. The Chinese had very little firewood or fuel, and so they designed the wok (and of course, the technique of stir-frying) as a means of fast cooking. To cook meats and fibrous vegetables quickly, they cut them into small pieces, exposing as much surface area as possible. Large, irregular pieces of food were chopped into small, regular chunks (so that the food cooked evenly). Cutting the ingredients in advance also meant that you did not need different sized pans to fit the pan to the food. Instead, you fit the food to the pan. You also didn't need a large heated area, since you could now toss and stir the food over the relatively small hot spot, and it would still cook evenly. In addition, that meant you didn't need great quantities of cooking oil to coat a large surface area (like the bottom of a conventional frying pan). Stir-frying requires only a minimum of cooking oil.

Not only is a wok ideal for stir-frying, but it's also perfect for steaming. Its high-domed lid turns the wok into a natural steam bath for vegetables, fish and other foods. The depth of the wok and its high sides are equally well-suited for deep-frying, while braising and stewing are another suitable function of the wok.

The problem with most flat-bottomed woks is that while they stay balanced on an electric stove, they lose some of the ease of tossing and stirring. Stainless steel is shinier, but it cannot be 'seasoned', which means that foods tend to stick to its surface. Electric woks usually have a flat bottom and a heating element that's too small to produce the intense heat necessary for stir-frying. Heat control is much more difficult, unless you can find a round-bottomed electric wok which heats up as fast as a regular wok. I cannot tell you which wok to buy, but by now, I think you can tell which wok I use.

Using a Wok:

A traditional round-bottomed wok should stand without too much wobble on a conventional gas burner. If you have a gas stove, you are a lucky cook because you can control your heat very precisely, going from instant high heat to the barest simmer, almost immediately. An electric burner takes time to heat up and more time to cool down. If you have an electric stove, try balancing the wok directly on the burner. A wok ring (or wok stand) may initially feel more secure, but it raises your wok off the burner and takes forever to heat up. If you use the stand, turn it in the direction that allows the wok to sit closest to the heat. When you are ready to cook, place the clean wok on the larger burner turned to its highest heat. When the wok is hot (about 1-2 minutes, depending on whether you are using gas or electric burners), add a small amount of oil (about 1-3 table-spoons) by trickling it down the sides of the wok in a smooth circular movement. When the oil is just about ready to smoke (about 15 seconds or so), it is hot enough, and you can now add the food and avoid sticking. For stir-frying, use the same high heat throughout the cooking process. For steaming reduce heat to medium high or medium once water boils. To deep-fry, heat oil to 375° F, then reduce heat to maintain a constant temperature.

Like anything new and unfamiliar, this procedure may sound strange and difficult. But it really isn't. With a little practice, you will be wokking proudly and cooking up a storm.

A Well-Seasoned Wok:

Most woks on the market are made or rolled (or spun) steel that should be treated ('seasoned') before use to prevent food from sticking to it. Once you have seasoned a wok (metal will be discolored), it should stay that way. And no Chinese cook would ever want to trade a well-seasoned wok for a brand new one, just as a good omelet chef prizes a well-seasoned omelet pan. Like people, they don't get older, they get better.

New woks are generally coated with either rust-resistant industrial grease, or a gummy, shiny coating that must be removed in the seasoning process.

1. Remove the protective coating by scrubbing with cleanser and scouring pads in hot soapy water. For the hard, shiny and gummy coating, you may sprinkle the surface with cigarette lighter fluid (now don't strike a match to get a closer look) before scrubbing. Then fill the wok with water and bring it to a boil; boil for 8-10 minutes. Clean and scrub again.

2. Dry wok over medium to medium-high heat for several minutes. Spread a thin film of cooking oil (about 1½ teaspoons of any vegetable oil) with a paper towel over the entire inner surface. Using a hot pad, move the wok by slowly tilting it in a constant circular motion to get a uniform heating of a large bottom surface. Use paper towel to rub a little bit of extra oil into the wok until the paper towel comes away fairly clean. Continue heating over medium to medium-high heat for 20-25 minutes until wok turns brown. (Be sure to turn on the exhaust.) For best results, repeat this step one or two more times. You can also season a new wok in the oven. Rub it with oil and put it in a preheated oven at 350° F to 375° F for 10-15 minutes. Repeat several times. (Treating the wok in the oven will not produce the same smooth, even browning that is achieved when wok is seasoned over the burner.)

3. Wash the wok in hot water with a soft nylon pad (do not use steel wool or any heavy detergent). For best results, place wok on a hot stove to dry. Now the wok is seasoned and all 'broken in'. It's ready to use.

What's that? You are wondering why your wok looks all discolored? That's ok. It's supposed to look that way, and in fact, it will continue to darken and mellow with use and age. "The blacker it gets, the better it cooks." (No, I don't know who makes up these sayings.) So don't ever spend 5½ hours trying to scrub away the big 'black spot' in the center of your wok.

How to Keep a Seasoned Wok Clean and Happy:

1. When preparing any highly acidic foods, such as sweet and sour or a dish with pineapple or tomato, try to use a saucepan instead of a seasoned wok to make the sauce, then quickly toss the food with sauce in the wok and immediately remove the food from the wok after mixing. Because hot, acidic food is abrasive and destroys the seasoning, you could end up having a tin-metal taste, and the wok might have to be seasoned again.

2. Clean your wok with a sponge, nylon pad or a bamboo brush in hot water. You may use a few drops of mild liquid soap. Rinse and pat dry with paper towels.

3. Place wok over medium-high heat on stove to complete drying, then rub a tiny bit of oil (about ¼ teaspoon) in wok to prevent rusting. Keep inside a paper bag in a cool, dry area. If you use the wok every day (like most Chinese) you will not need to oil the wok after each use.

Those who do not follow these simple instructions, beware. If you do not take care of your wok, it may feel neglected and rust away. And you may end up seasoning the wok every day for the next 20 years!

Pick Up Sticks

Some of my best friends eat with a knife and fork. Of course, no one needs a knife to eat Chinese food because it is already cut up during preparation. As for the fork, I've been known to use one myself. But chopsticks are just right for Chinese food, and they've been used since at least the Shang Dynasty (1766 B.C. to 1123 B.C.). Before that, we used our fingers. Some authorities speculate that originally twigs were used to pick up hot pieces of food, or to seize the choicer morsels. In fact, like any tool, the chopsticks are like an extension of your fingers, and their name, 'Faii Jee', means 'quick little boys'. (I guess the girls still ate with their fingers!) Marco Polo, who was probably the first European to see chopsticks in action, said, "What the heck is this?" (Just kidding!) But another early Italian visitor named Francesco Carletti did say, "With those two sticks, the Chinese are able to fill their mouths, with marvellous agility and swiftness."

In the Chinese kitchen, chopsticks serve a dual purpose—as eating utensils and as cooking tools. During food preparation, chopsticks are used to mix, stir, whip and pick up foods.

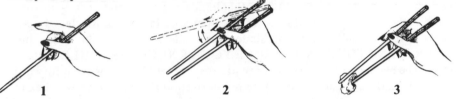

There are even legends and superstitions about chopsticks. If you find at your place setting, a pair of uneven chopsticks, you can be sure that you are due to miss a bus, a train or a plane. Dropping chopsticks will herald bad luck. And so do crossed chopsticks—unless they are crossed by the waiter to indicate that you've paid your bill at a dim sum lunch. Incidentally, a set of ten or more pairs of ivory chopsticks make a very proper wedding present. The chopsticks are given to the bride in hopes that she will quickly give birth to a child.

Chopsticks may be tricky to get used to at first. But with a little practice, it's child's play (I should know—I never saw a fork until I was 17!). All you really need to know is how to grip the chopsticks correctly.

1. Place the first chopstick in between the middle and fourth fingers with the top part anchored between the thumb and index finger. This chopstick is stationary and never moves.
2. Hold the second chopstick as if you were holding a pencil.
3. When using them, move only the second chopstick, keeping the other one straight and motionless. Be sure that the tips of the two chopsticks meet. Otherwise, you might still end up using your fingers.

In these times of inflation, eating with chopsticks is the only way to 'make ends meet'. But if you try to save a few pennies by 'borrowing' your chopsticks from a Chinese restaurant, just don't tell them that I sent you (especially if you get caught!).

Chinese Cleaver Gives You a Big Edge

At first glance, you might think that the Chinese cleaver is clumsy and awkward, as it looks short, squat and heavy. By comparison, a French chef's knife is elegant, lean and rapier-like, but once again, looks aren't everything. The Chinese cleaver is a much more versatile tool. It can be used to cut, slice, shred, chop, mince, press meat and crush garlic. The back of the blade makes a fine meat tenderizer, and the broad face of the blade is handy for transferring the cut-up pieces of food from the cutting board to wherever you want. Except for the occasional use of a small paring knife, a Chinese chef needs nothing but his cleaver.

Like any other razor-sharp knife, however, the cleaver can be dangerous if it is not handled properly. You should first make sure that your cutting board is stable and secure. If the board shifts while you are chopping, you may never play the piano again. Grip the handle firmly, with your thumb touching one side of the blade and your index finger stretched along the other side. Basically, you move the cleaver up and down in the same position, while you move the food into the cleaver's path. To do that, place your other hand on the food to be cut, with your thumb tucked in and your fingers curled slightly under. The knuckles of your fingers should actually guide the blade. The blade touches the knuckles, but NEVER RAISE THE BLADE ABOVE YOUR KNUCKLES WHILE CHOPPING. The blade cuts in short, shallow strokes—never sawing. Move it forward and down; that's all. The blade should be sharp enough that its own weight can pierce the skin of a tomato. As the cutting progresses, move all four fingers gradually backwards, leaving what remains to be cut in place, without changing the original knuckle as a guide. This technique may feel a bit awkward at first. As with learning any new technique, you will improve with practice. Just go slowly at first. After you build your confidence, you will be so fast that you'll amaze your friends and family, and they will all call you the 'human food processor'!

Clay Pot/Casserole:

The Chinese casserole is a covered, earthenware pot with an interior coating of lead-free glaze. Frequently, the exterior will be encased in a wire mesh to protect the fragile clay pot. While these pots can be used both on top of either a gas or an electric range and in the oven, special care must be taken to prevent the pots from breaking:

1. Do not use medium-high to high heat when the clay pot is used directly over and electric or gas burner.
2. Never place an empty clay pot over heat: always have some liquid in it.
3. Never place a hot clay pot on a damp surface or into water until it has cooled.
4. Soak clay pots in water a couple of days before using.

Take care to mind these warnings, otherwise you may end up with a clay pot jigsaw puzzle!

These clay pots can be purchased in most Chinese specialty stores, but while they are fun to use and have the appeal of authenticity, you probably already own a good substitute. Chinese casserole dishes can be cooked just as well in enamel, glass of any other type of casserole dish.

Cutting Board:

A good cutting board is an indispensable tool when preparing Chinese food. You will need a board that can take the abuses of slicing, shredding, chopping and mincing.

The traditional Chinese cutting board is a block of wood made from a cross-section of a hardwood tree. You can purchase these blocks in certain Chinese specialty stores, or you can quite easily make your own. Simply follow these step-by-step instructions:

1. Take your electric saw to your nearby hardwood forest and cut a 2-4 inch cross-section from a likely tree.
2. Season the cross-section with ½ cup oil. Rub the oil over the entire surface and wrap in aluminum foil. (The oil will saturate the wood grain and repel water and prevent cracking.)
3. Unwrap in 2-3 days. Rinse and dry your own personal cutting block.

Always remember to secure your cutting board so that it will not slide off the counter and hit the cat! To prevent slippage, place a damp cloth or damp paper towel between the board and the counter. A good substitute for the Chinese cutting board is a large, 2-inch thick cutting board.

Exhaust Fan:

When you are wokking up a storm, remember to turn on your exhaust fan. The fan will draw up the heat and will prevent the grease from splashing all over you like a tidal wave!

Skimmer (Strainer):

A good size strainer (6-inch diameter) or sieve is a tool I recommend for wokking. Many dishes require that ingredients be removed from hot oil or boiling water. A strainer will save you from burning fingers and will give you better control over the cooking of these types of dishes.

Most Chinese strainers are made of copper wire mesh in the shape of a wide, shallow ladle. I prefer the ones made from stainless steel because they are easier for this humble dishwasher to clean!

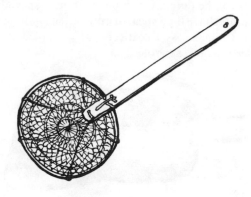

Spatula:

The Chinese spatula has a long handle and is slightly curved to match the curvature of a wok for easy stirring and tossing of food to prevent burning. You may substitute a large kitchen spoon or spatula.

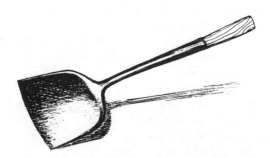

Steamer:

There are two types of steamers on the market today — bamboo and aluminum. The intriguing and traditional bamboo steamers come in a variety of sizes, have no base, and will fit right inside a wok. For a 14″ wok, buy a 13″ steamer. For a 12″ wok, use a 11″ steamer. The bamboo steamer allows slow dissipation of moisture through the lattice top which prevents excessive condensation of steam on your dish. The self-contained aluminum steamer is impervious to moisture, and has a tighter seal which causes more condensation. The aluminum steamer cooks faster, but the bamboo steamer is better for buns and pastries.

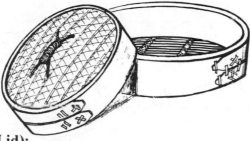

Wok Cover (Lid):

The cover to a wok looks like an inverted bowl. It should fit the wok well and should trap steam. This convex design enables the wok to build up vapor pressure which will increase the temperature in the wok. The traditional concave shape also allows the larger bowls of foods to be placed inside the wok. For the 14″ wok, buy a 13″ lid, for the 12″ wok, use a 11″ lid.

Wok Stand (Ring):

The wok stand or ring is usually designed for round-bottomed woks. It is used to steady the wok on top of the burner. (If your stove has a gas burner, remove the burner grid and set the ring securely over the burner before setting the wok on top.) The ring has several holes around the middle for ventilation. The sloped sides allow you to place the wok at two levels for better cooking control: for slow cooking or simmering, set your wok over the smaller opening, which will slightly lift the wok away from the heat source; for fast cooking, place the wok over the larger opening, bringing the wok closer to the heat source. From personal experience, a wok stand is not needed for stir-frying because the wok without sitting over the ring will be closer to the heat source. Besides, the wok moves a lot easier without the ring.

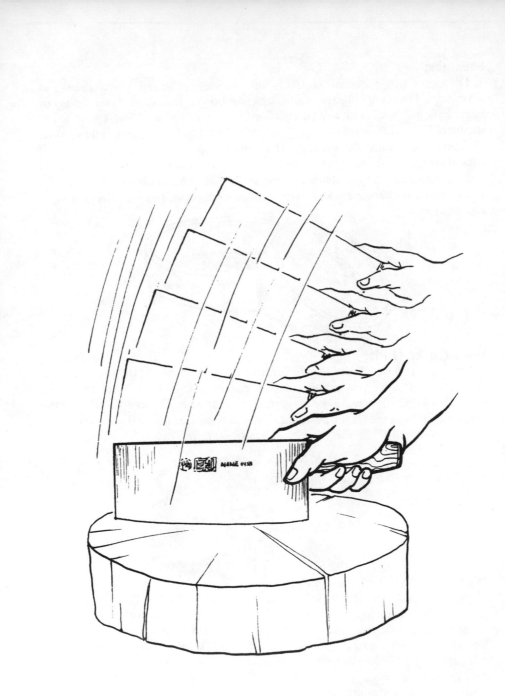

Chop, Chop, Wok and Roll

If you have ever seen an experienced Chinese cook in action, I bet the first thing that caught your eye was his cleaver technique. With a flashing blade and a percussive Chop! Chop! Chop!, and in barely a second or two, the food seemed to fall apart into perfect slices. It's not magic, and you don't have to study on a mountain-top for half your life. With a little experience, patience and some practice, you, too, can master the various techniques of slicing, dicing, and shredding with your cleaver.

Practice makes perfect in other areas, too! Many cooking techniques such as stir-frying, deep-frying, shallow-frying, steaming, stewing, simmering, braising and smoking have been used for centuries by the Chinese, so it's no wonder they are so good at it!

Clever Cleaver Techniques

Being clever with your cleaver really comes in handy in Chinese cooking. Most of the Chinese dishes are comprised of bite-size morsels. This not only allows everything to cook in just a few minutes over high heat, but preserves the natural goodness and color of the ingredients. Best of all, bite-size pieces are a lot easier to pick up with chopsticks (just try cutting a steak with chopsticks, sometime!). The cleaver has very often been the only cutting tool in a Chinese kitchen.

27

Chopping:

Most cleavers are used for slicing and cutting vegetables and meats (if you need to cut through pork and chicken bones, you will need a heavy duty cleaver). In chopping, take a firm hold on the handle and use a straight up and down motion with plenty of force. To prevent damage to the blade and to ensure your safety, never wiggle or twist the cleaver from side to side. Always cut in the center of the cutting board and watch those fingers!! If you aren't strong enough, rest the cleaver on the food to be chopped and hammer down on the blunt edge with the heel of your hand or a small hammer if necessary. When you're doing this, be sure not to chop your cutting board into a dozen pieces.

Crushing:

To crush garlic, place the cloves on the cutting board close to the edge, slap the blade on top of the garlic to flatten. The handle of the cleaver can be used to further crush the garlic with salted black beans: place both the garlic and black beans in a small bowl, and crush both together until a paste is formed.

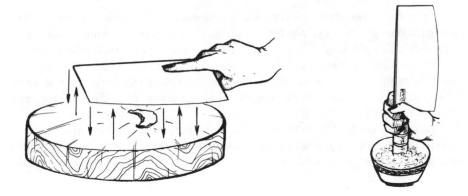

Dicing:

To dice, cut the ingredients lengthwise into long strips, about ¼″ (.75 cm) wide, then cut each strip into small cubes. You can do the same with meat or vegetable.

Mincing:

In order to mince any ingredient with a cleaver, you should first cut it into strips, and then dice it. To mince the diced pieces, hold the handle of the cleaver firmly in one hand, and bring the cleaver up and down to chop. To get an even mincing of your ingredient, pivot the blade on its tip. If you have a large amount of food to mince, simply toss it all into your food processor. In seconds you will have everything chopped up! From personal experience, I prefer the cleaver, because it is the best exercise I can get without spending a fortune in the fitness center.

Parallel (Slanting) Slicing:

Parallel slicing is used to cut thin slices from flat pieces of meat or vegetable. To make slanting cuts, place the ingredients on the cutting board, close to the edge. Hold the cleaver at a slant (the blade should be at an angle of approximately parallel from the cutting board) and move the cleaver back and forth to slice. Be careful of your delicate fingers and never rush.

Roll Cutting (Oblique Cutting):

Roll cutting is perhaps the most distinctly Chinese method of cutting. The advantage of oblique cutting is that it exposes a greater total surface area for faster cooking.

To roll cut, slice a piece off at an angle, then roll the ingredient over a quarter turn and make another cut at the same angle. Continue cutting and turning until you reach the final cut. You can practice this technique best by using a carrot or zucchini. Roll cutting is often applied for dishes with foods cut into larger cubes or bite size chunks. Roll cutting also allows you to cut food into similar size but different shapes thus looks more appealing.

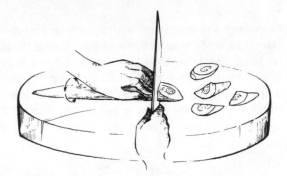

Shredding:

Shredding may be the most common technique of cutting in Chinese cooking. The ingredients are first thinly sliced at an angle (approx. 45°) to the cleaver blade, then each slice is cut into small strips.

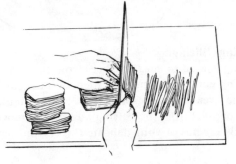

Slicing:

When slicing, place the piece to be cut perpendicular to the blade or at any other angle. The thickness of these slices will vary, depending on the particular recipe used. Pieces which are cut at a slant will have a larger surface area, allowing them more exposure to heat.

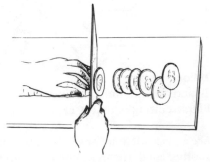

Tenderizing:

Most Chinese cooks and homemakers make use of their cleavers to do most of the tenderizing. To tenderize meat, simply turn the cleaver over to the blunt edge and pound the meat in crisscross patterns. For added excitement, fun, and noise, you can slap the meat with the blade, until you drive everybody up the wall.

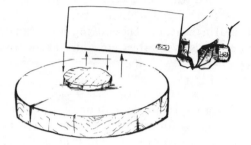

Cooking Techniques

Braising:

Braising can be considered a combined technique of stir-frying and stewing. The ingredients are first stir-fried over high heat for several minutes, then the heat is reduced to finish the cooking in a sauce. Braising allows the seasoning from the sauce to penetrate into the foods.

Deep-frying:

The two important things to remember when deep-frying are: 1) to use enough oil. There should be enough to totally submerge the food to insure uniform cooking; 2) to be sure that the oil is hot enough for frying *before* you add the food for frying. To determine if the oil is hot enough for deep-frying, submerge a pair of clean bamboo or wood chopsticks into the hot oil. If a lot of bubbles appear around the chopstick immediately after contact with the hot oil, it is hot enough for most frying purposes. Another method is to watch for the first trace of smoke (but don't wait until the smoke fills up your kitchen, your dining room, your neighbor's kitchen . . .)

Always drop the food gently into the hot oil or slide it gently down the side of the wok into the hot oil. Turn the food around frequently during frying. The cooking time will vary with the type and size of the ingredients. As a rule of thumb, the food is usually ready when it starts to turn golden brown and begins to float freely on the surface of the oil.

Shallow-frying:

This technique is similar to stir-frying except that more oil is used; the cooking time is also longer because the food is cooked on medium heat instead of high heat. Continuous stirring is not necessary. The food is placed (spread out evenly) in the wok and is turned over only a couple of times during the cooking process.

Simmering:

The light soup stock used when simmering food gives a purity not found in stews. The meat is cooked in a liquid medium over low heat. The pot should have a tight lid or cover to seal in the steam. The cooking liquid can be served as a soup with the meat. The fresh, crisp vegetables are added at the concluding stages of cooking.

Smoking:

This is more of a flavoring technique than one for cooking. To achieve the smoked flavor, brown sugar (with or without tea leaves) is burned in a tightly closed pan that has been insulated with foil. The meat is placed on a rack within the pot and the strong smoke from the burning sugar flavors the food. Fish, chicken and duck can be smoked and are great do ahead dishes.

Steaming:

This method plays an important role in Chinese cooking, both in preparation of foods and in the reheating of leftovers. Steaming food in its natural juice preserves the original flavor and nutritional value without adding extra calories.

The Chinese method of steaming is as unique as the wok itself. Most Chinese kitchens have bamboo steamers, which sit directly in the wok over boiling water. The food is simply cooked by steam, allowing it to cook to perfection without even getting wet! Even better, the bamboo steamer can be stacked to do more than one dish at the same time, saving energy and money.

If you don't have a steamer, simply place 2 pairs of chopsticks tic-tac-toe style over the water in the wok, then rest the plate or bowl of food on the chopsticks. Another method is to place a 6 oz. tin can (both ends removed) in the middle of the wok. Fill the wok with water up to $2/_3$ the height of the can. You can also place your plate of food on a round cake rack in the wok. Be sure the water level is at least 1″ (2.1 cm) below the dish being steamed, otherwise you may end up making soup! Also be sure to keep an eye on the water level while steaming. Add ½ cup boiling water to the wok around the lid every 6-8 minutes. If it boils dry you might end up in a smoky kitchen with a charcoaled steamer and a melted wok. So, once you steam a dish, do not take a vacation.

Stir-frying:

This is the most predominant and widely known method of Chinese cookery. It is simply frying food over high heat with continuous tossing and stirring, using only a small amount of oil (generally 2-3 tablespoons). Most of the stir-fried dishes take relatively short cooking time.

When stir-frying, the sequence of adding ingredients is important to maintain the crisp texture and natural flavor of food — this is the essence of Chinese cooking. Add ingredients to the wok in decreasing order of delicacy. Ingredients requiring a longer cooking time (meats and fibrous or firm vegetables) should be added to the hot oil before those requiring less cooking time. In addition, foods should be of uniform size so that they will cook evenly. The ingredients should be kept to a reasonable amount in each preparation so that the wok is not piled to the ceiling with vegetables and meat which cannot be stirred!

When stir-frying, first heat the wok over high heat for 2-2½ minutes until piping hot before adding oil. Wait for 10-15 seconds before adding food ingredients. The hot oil assures quick cooking of food in a short time and helps seal in the juices and flavors, but it also means that food can stick easily and get burnt. Therefore, it is most important to remember that "stir-frying" means exactly that: stirring and scraping continuously with the spatula to prevent sticking and buring of the food as it fries. Meat, in particular, has a tendency to stick to the piping hot wok, so use the spatula to scrape it off before it turns to carbon! (If something should burn in the wok, be sure to clean it thoroughly before cooking anything else.) Should the food become dry while cooking, add a small amount of soup stock or water to the wok.

It is a general practice to stir-fry the meats and vegetables separately, then mix well before thickening. Prepare all stir-fried dishes in the very last few minutes. If the dish can't be served right away, slightly undercook the vegetables, wrap the dish with aluminum foil and keep in a warm oven for a few minutes.

Roasting:

Roasting is a popular method in restaurant kitchens, but is less common in Chinese homes where kitchens are less well equipped. This slow method of cooking is great for larger cuts of meat and whole fowl. To cut down on cooking time and to avoid dryness, you can slightly pre-cook the meat by browning or frying it in a wok with a small amount of oil. Roasted meat is first rubbed with soy sauce or seasoning, then marinated to give it color and added flavor. The meat is slowly roasted on hooks or on a rack until cooked, then is finally seared by broiling to make the skin crisp. The delicious juices can be collected in a pan below the meat.

Red Cooking/Stewing:

Red cooking is a form of stewing, but less water and vegetables are used. Dark soy sauce is normally used and gives these dishes their red coloring and rich flavor. This method is generally used for cooking larger cuts of meat and poultry which are generally seasoned with pickled, dried or salted ingredients. It is a slow method of cooking. After initially bringing the mixture to a boil, the temperature is reduced and kept low to continue cooking.

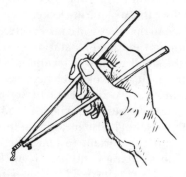

The Bare Necessities

Chinese cooking requires a few ingredients available only in Chinese grocery stores, but the majority of ingredients in the following recipes can be obtained in your local supermarkets.

If you are lucky, and live near a Chinese specialty grocery, you can make regular trips for the freshest and most exotic ingredients. But if you live in the middle of nowhere, you have only two choices — either take a Greyhound, train or plane to the nearest Big City Chinatown and stock up for a 20-year stint of wokking or you can shop long distance by mail order, which is much less fun but cheaper. Either way, with proper storage, most of the exotic Chinese ingredients can be kept for a considerable period of time.

Here is a list of the basics:

CHUNG KWONG(C.K.)

Bean curd (tofu):
Used widely in Chinese cooking since it goes well with most vegetables. Keep in clear water in refrigerator for up to 3-4 days. Be sure to change water every day. Refer to the recipe in this volume for home-made bean curd.

Bean thread noodles:
Used in soup, stir-fried dishes, and when deep-fried it can be used as a garnish. Keep in dry, cool area, and it will last indefinitely.

Black beans, salted:
Used for flavoring. Keep in an air-tight jar in dry, cool area.

Black mushroom, dried:
Used for flavoring, color, and as a vegetable addition to a dish. Keep in an air-tight container in a dry, cool area.

Cornstarch:
Used for thickening, dry coating and in marinades. Used frequently so keep a box handy. When used as a thickening a "cornstarch solution" is made — 1 part cornstarch to 2 parts water. Be sure to stir the mixture just before using.

Ginger, fresh:
Used frequently for flavoring. Buy enough to last a week or two. Keep refrigerated.

Hoisin sauce:
For BBQ meats and sauces. Keep in dry, cool area or refrigerate. Transfer canned sauce to an air-tight jar.

Oyster-flavored sauce:
For flavoring and sauces. Keep refrigerated.

Plum sauce:
Mainly for sauces or dip. Keep in a dry, cool area in air-tight jars. Transfer canned plum sauce into a glass or plastic jar and keep in the refrigerator.

Sesame oil:
For meat marinade and flavoring in cooking. Refrigerate to prolong shelf life.

Soy sauce, dark:
For flavoring or dips. Refrigerate to prolong storage.

Soy sauce, light:
For meat marinade, for flavoring or for dips. Refrigerate to prolong storage. In this volume "soy sauce" refers to *light* soy sauce. Otherwise it will be indicated as *dark* soy sauce.

Star anise:
Used for flavoring in roasting and stewing. Keep in air-tight container.

Szechwan peppercorn:
Used for flavoring. Keep in air-tight container.

Wine:
For meat marinade and flavoring. Chinese rice wine or dry sherry are used most often.

Wonton/Spring roll wrappers:
Keep refrigerated for 3-5 days or frozen for up to 6 months. Wrap well to prevent freezer burn.

There are many, many more, but these should get you on the right track to start "wokking." For anything else "nice" to cook, refer to "Chinese Spice and Everything Nice" in the back of this book.

Let's Get Soy Sauced—A Biography

It may not have been called soy sauce ("Shoyu" in Japanese), but a salty liquid seasoning made from soy beans is known to have been used for centuries in China and Southeast Asia for the cooking and flavoring of foods. It originated in China, and from there it was introduced to the other countries of the Orient. The early sauce was probably cruder in taste and appearance, but with improved fermentation and refining processes, soy sauce is now a polished product that is enjoyed by many and is used both in the kitchen and at the table.

Soybeans, often called "meat from the fields," are rich in fat and provide the soybean oil often used in cooking. Soybeans also have a high protein content that is of special nutritional value. The balance and type of amino acids in the protein is similar to that found in beef and pork. Although we certainly could not consume enough soy sauce to meet our daily protein needs, we can use it as a seasoning, knowing full well that it is a natural, healthful product.

There are two common types of soy sauce in Chinese cooking — light and dark. Light soy, or thin soy is lighter in color, saltier and is used mainly for marinating and seasoning in stir-fried dishes. Dark soy, or black soy, is much darker and sweeter (due to the addition of caramel) and is used mainly in stewing and sauteing to add color. Both types are produced in basically the same way, with different lengths of time in fermentation processing.

Simply stated, soy sauce is produced from the chemical breakdown, during fermentation, of soy beans and wheat by the action of microorganisms in the presence of salt. The fragrance and coloring are from the wheat; the flavor and reddish hues are from the soy beans; the salty taste is, of course, from the salt.

For soy sauce production, the soy beans are carefully selected, washed, and soaked in water for about three hours. Then they are steamed, to soften them and to allow the useful microorganisms to be more easily propagated. The wheat is roasted, allowed to sit overnight, and then cracked.

I must apologize that this sounds so terribly technical, but that's the way this story goes . . . The following information is designed for those who have retired or for those who cannot go to sleep at night and need something to help lull them into the Land of Nod.

The next step is to inoculate the mixture with living mold, (koji molds, mainly *Aspergillus*), which produces specific enzymes to breakdown the protein to amino acids and the starch to various sugars. The mixture ("koji") is kept at a constant temperature to facilitate growth for 3-4 days, and then is removed on the fourth or fifth day.

Next the koji is mixed with the separately prepared salt solution and is put into large stainless steel tanks or cement vats (fitted with steam pipes for temperature control) for brewing and aging. This brewing process goes on for about 3-4 months for light soy and one year for dark soy, with occasional stirring to add oxygen. During the "aerobic (with oxygen) fermentation" process, the action of the enzymes in the koji causes the amino acids and sugar content to increase. As the yeast multiply, the sugars are broken down to alcohols, which give the soy sauce body and aroma. Some organic acids form and combine with the alcohols to form esters which make up the main components of the bouquet. The bouquet of soy sauce is unique and surprising. When analyzed, it was found to have more than 100 total components, including alcohols, aldehydes, ketones, acetals, organic acids, esters and sulphur compounds.

After brewing, the next step is "pressing" which removes the oil. The liquid is then heated and pasteurized, killing the microorganisms and improving the color and fragrance. It is then bottled or canned, producing an exceptional sauce with unlimited uses in cooking.

Ethyl alcohol is one of the components of soy sauce. Besides imparting a pleasant flavor to foods, it also serves to heat food uniformly during cooking, aid in the permeation of flavor and enhance the other flavors present. Several sugars are contained in soy sauce, but glucose, from the breakdown of starch in the wheat, is the most prevalent. If all the salt were removed, the remaining product would be actually quite sweet. The extra sweetness of dark soy is from the addition of caramel.

The salt content of most common brands ranges from 15-18%. For the health-conscious, you may want to use the reduced sodium soy sauce—same flavor, same aroma, but only half the salt (about 7.8%). It may be interesting to know a 15% salt content soy sauce does not taste as salty as a 15% pure salt solution because the amino acids present make it milder to your tongue. The salt is not just added for the taste; it is necessary in the production of the sauce. Without it, the resulting sauce would have a completely different taste. The high amount of salt also serves to preserve the soy sauce, as there are generally no other preservatives added.

Good soy sauce will be translucent with a beautiful reddish-brown hue. The color is the result of a browning reaction that occurs during heating. If left out and permitted to remain in contact with oxygen after opening, the browning will continue, and the flavor will change somewhat. (This is how dark soy sauce is made.) Low temperatures will prevent this reaction, so it is a good idea to keep opened soy sauce containers in the refrigerator.

Soy sauce is often called the "all-purpose" seasoning because of its versatility and universal appeal. It goes well with most dishes, serving to enhance the flavors that are present. Soy sauce, either light or dark, usually darkens the appearance of any food to which it is added, so to retain the natural colors of the food, use salt instead of soy sauce.

One of the appealing qualities of soy sauce is the "roasting aroma" it releases when heated to over 320° F (158° C). This is caused by the reactions of the amino acids and carbohydrates that are present. The aroma is released with heat and is especially intriguing when the food is allowed to soak in soy sauce prior to cooking. If the soaked food is boiled instead of roasted, a different reaction occurs.

Soy sauce is considered a healthful addition to foods. Since it is low in calories — only 4 per teaspoon, compared to butter at 45 — it is a good way to cut down on caloric intake while still adding flavor. And as mentioned previously, the soybeans contain protein which add to the nutritional value. Nevertheless, soy sauce is not consumed for its nutritive value, but rather for its flavor-enhancing properties. If prepared well, it stimulates the secretion of gastric juice from the stomach lining, the same effect a glass of wine has on your appetite. So, along with its superb flavor, soy sauce also serves as an appetizer and helps your digestion.

So, let's get soy sauced!

Wok's the Secret?

While there are cooking shortcuts, there are no shortcuts to becoming a good cook. These rules are not written in stone, but they do sum up the basic procedures, plus a little encouragement. Anything you do for the first time is likely to make you a bit nervous, but you shouldn't be afraid. Think of the pleasurable eating that's ahead for you.

All the recipes in this book were tested on the large burner of a domestic electric stove. If a gas stove is used, cooking time can be slightly reduced. Be sure to read through the entire recipe first. Here is a checklist you can follow that will help your next Chinese feast be absolutely amazing!

The 10 Commandments of Wok Cooking

1. Plan your menu and organize your time. Be realistic about your own skills and experience. Select a few dishes that can be prepared ahead, having no more than 2-3 last-minute stir-fried dishes. Otherwise, you might be serving charcoal at your next dinner party.
2. Gather all the ingredients, seasonings (such as sauces, spices, soup stock, cornstarch solution, etc.), and utensils required, having them within reach. Have a clean wok ready at all times.
3. Wash, cut up, and marinate (if required) all ingredients called for in the recipes. Place ingredients of the same recipe in one plate.
4. Prepare all sauces and soup stock, and measure all seasonings; set aside. Have enough bowls and plates available for cooked foods. Have a warm oven ready for cooked dishes. (Preheat oven by turning to low, let stand for 20 minutes, then turn oven off.)
5. Let the wok heat up before pouring in oil; add food a few seconds later. Stir and toss food constantly to avoid burning of food. Add a small amount of water or soup stock if food becomes dry.
6. If a variety of ingredients are called for in the same recipe, meat and vegetables can be cooked separately to retain their original flavors. Firmer and more fibrous vegetables should be cooked first, because these will take more time to cook.

7. Once you begin stir-frying or deep-frying, give your most undivided attention. When cooking at a high temperature for a short time, every second counts. Over-cooking is the worst mistake in Chinese cooking.
8. Prepare a couple of things simultaneously—try cooking two dishes (or one sauce and one dish) at the same time, if you can handle it. But don't undertake more than you can manage.
9. When a dish is done (particularly stir-fried dishes with green vegetables), remove from heat or transfer to a plate immediately. If it is not to be served right away, cover the plate with foil (punch a few holes on top) and keep it in a warm oven. Always wash the wok with hot water (use a few drops of mild detergent, if necessary) and have it ready to use for the next dish.
10. Don't be intimidated and don't get nervous. Relax and remember that cooking should be fun.

FOOD
FOR THOUGHT

"First, you pluck a duck. . . . ."

Stimulating Starters

Hors d'oeuvres traditionally don't occupy much place in classical Chinese cuisine. When a Chinese family sits down to eat, they don't need any coaxing, and nothing is needed to tease or whet their appetites. Most Chinese restaurants don't list appetizers at all. A common Chinese appetizers menu may offer assorted cold cuts (kind of like Chinese antipasto), cooked seafoods and pickled vegetables. For quite different reasons, a salad of raw mixed vegetables has no place at a proper Chinese table. In China, animal (and sometimes, human) manure is used as fertilizer, and so, for hygienic reasons, all vegetables are cooked, parboiled or pickled before serving.

On the other hand, the traditional Chinese brunch of Dim Sum consists of nothing but appetizers, such as little dumplings and rolls, assorted bits and pieces. When served in larger portions, they can be main courses or you can offer them as hors d'oeuvres before a full-course dinner. The spring roll is one of the world's oldest hors d'oeuvres (So, if you don't get a fresh one, you'll know why!), and you might typically find it being served with a cup of tea at lunch time or mid-afternoon. You can also serve it for starters with a dinner. Some traditions change, too!

Most of the dishes on the following pages will help you make a grand entrance into your Chinese dinner.

B.B.Q. Spareribs CANTON

This is one of my favorites and soon will be your favorite, too! These spareribs are just fantastic! The savoriness of ginger, the spiciness of five-spice powder and the sweetness of hoisin sauce — the delicacy of their flavors will send you back for seconds.

1½ pounds (675 g) pork spareribs

Marinade:
2 teaspoons (10 ml) sugar
¾ teaspoon (3 ml) salt
1 clove garlic, minced
1 teaspoon (5 ml) ginger juice
1½ tablespoons (22 ml) soy sauce
2 tablespoons (30 ml) wine
½ teaspoon (2 ml) five-spice powder
1 tablespoon (15 ml) hoisin sauce
2 tablespoons (30 ml) catsup
few drops red food coloring
   (optional)

3 tablespoons (45 ml) honey
2 tablespoons (30 ml) hoisin sauce

1. Trim excess fat and thin edges of meat from ribs (never cut into individual ribs; leave whole rack of ribs intact for roasting). Save thin edges of meat for other dishes.
2. Place ribs in a large container and marinate for 1 hour.
3. Preheat oven to 375° F (190°C). Place marinated ribs on a rack in a roasting pan. Bake at 375° F (190°C) for 25-30 minutes. Turn ribs over and bake another 10-12 minutes or until meat shrinks from bone.
4. Turn oven to broil. Combine honey and hoisin sauce, baste both sides of ribs with mixture and broil 4 to 5 inches from heat for 1 minute on each side. Serve hot or cold.

Remarks
- *Marinate ribs overnight if desired.*
- *To reheat ribs, wrap them in foil, place in 350° F (180° C) oven and bake for 10-15 minutes.*

Bronzed Eggs

In China, eggs are a symbol of fertility, prosperity and wealth. This particular dish is often served on special occasions, but you don't have to wait for a special occasion! This is a distinctively different choice for a party appetizer.

12 eggs	½ cup (125 ml) dark soy sauce
2 cups (500 ml) soup stock	2 slices ginger
¼ teaspoon (1 ml) salt	dash of five-spice powder
1 tablespoon (15 ml) sugar	(optional)

1. Place eggs in a saucepan, cover with cold water and bring to a slow boil over medium heat. Boil gently for 10 minutes. Cool eggs in cold tap water and remove shells.
2. Combine remaining ingredients in a saucepan and bring to a boil.
3. Carefully place eggs in boiling liquid. Reduce heat to simmer; cover and cook for 1 hour.
4. To serve, cut each egg lengthwise into 4-6 wedges. Serve hot or cold.

Remarks
- *There is a similar dish called Tea Eggs (Shanghai Style). It is prepared in basically the same way except that unpeeled eggs with cracked shells are simmered in a stock of black tea leaves and star anise.*

Cantonese Pickled Cucumber

I hear stories about pregnant women craving pickles, but you don't have to be pregnant to crave this delectable Cantonese pickled cucumber dish. In fact, this can be prepared ahead, kept in the refrigerator, and anytime you have a craving, it's yours for the taking!

2 small to medium-size cucumbers, seeded	2 teaspoons (10 ml) salt
	6 tablespoons (90 ml) sugar
2 small carrots	½ cup (125 ml) white vinegar
1 small Chinese turnip (optional)	

1. Cut cucumbers, carrots and turnip into 2" x ½" x ½" (5 x 1.5 x 1.5 cm) sticks.
2. Combine salt and vegetables in a large bowl; let stand for 1-2 hours. Rinse and drain well.
3. Add sugar and vinegar; let stand for 2-3 more hours. Keep in refrigerator and serve cold.

Remarks
- *The use of sugar and vinegar should be adjusted to your family's, your relatives' or your neighbors' tastes. After all, food is to be shared.*

Chinese Chicken Salad

Salad is not a common dish in Chinese cuisine, particularly in Southern China. Many cold plates with vegetables and meat prevail in Northern regions, however. This versatile dish can be a salad or entree; it is delightfully fresh, simple and convenient to serve.

¾ pound (340 g) boneless chicken
　　breast, scored or pounded

Marinade:

½ teaspoon (2 ml) hoisin sauce
1 tablespoon (15 ml) wine
1 tablespoon (15 ml) soy sauce
¼ teaspoon (1 ml) garlic salt
¼ teaspoon (1 ml) sesame oil
1 teaspoon (5 ml) cornstarch

Dressing:
6 tablespoons (90 ml) white vinegar
2 tablespoons (30 ml) sugar
1 teaspoon (5 ml) Tabasco sauce
¼ teaspoon (1 ml) black pepper
½ teaspoon (2 ml) salt
3 tablespoons (45 ml) soy sauce
1 tablespoon (15 ml) sesame oil
3 tablespoons (45 ml) oil
1½ teaspoons (7 ml) cornstarch
　　solution

½ head of lettuce, cut into
　　bite-size pieces
4 ounces (112 g) bean sprouts
2 stalks green onion, cut into
　　1″ (2.5 cm) strips
1 tomato, cut into ½″ (1.5 cm) cubes
½ cup (125 ml) Chinese pickled
　　vegetables (optional)
4 cups (1 L) oil
2 ounces (56 g) bean thread noodles
2 tablespoons (30 ml) toasted
　　sesame seeds

1. Marinate chicken for 30 minutes.
2. Place vegetables on a large platter or in a salad bowl; set aside.
3. Heat oil in wok to 375°F (190°C). Deep-fry bean thread noodles in hot oil until puffed, approximately 5 seconds. Drain well and break into 2″-3″ pieces. Set aside.
4. Bake marinated chicken in a preheated oven at 375°F (190°C) for 25-30 minutes or deep-fry whole breast in hot oil over medium-high heat for 2½-3 minutes. Turn a few times for even browning. Cut chicken into thin strips.
5. Combine all ingredients for dressing except cornstarch in a saucepan; heat until boiling. Thicken with cornstarch solution. Set aside.
6. Combine chicken strips with vegetables. Add dressing and mix well. Stir in fried noodles and toasted sesame seeds just before serving. Serve cold.

Chinese Pickle Relish

So you're a little tired of Grandma's pickle relish and you would like to try something new and exciting. Here's just the challenge you have been looking for to change those taste buds which are in a rut! This spiced, piquant vegetable dish can be served as an appetizer or as a side dish, accompanying other main dishes.

2 medium cucumbers, seeded and cut crosswise into thin slices
2 teaspoons (10 ml) salt
1 tablespoon (15 ml) sugar
¼ pound (112 g) cooked shrimp (optional)

Pickling Dressing:
1 teaspoon (5 ml) soy sauce
¾ teaspoon (3 ml) sesame oil
3 tablespoons (45 ml) vinegar
2 tablespoons (30 ml) sugar
½ teaspoon (2 ml) ginger juice
½ teaspoon (2 ml) dried red chili peppers
¼ teaspoon (1 ml) ground Szechwan pepper (optional)
dash of Tabasco sauce (optional)

1. Combine cucumber with salt and sugar; mix well. Let stand for 30 minutes. Rinse with water, drain well, and place in a bowl.
2. Add shrimp, cover with pickling dressing, and mix well. Refrigerate until ready to serve.

Remarks
- *Cucumber can be peeled, if desired.*

Golden Shrimp Toast

Shrimp lovers unite! This appetizer is just for you. Elegant and easy, it can be prepared ahead of time, kept warm and easily reheated. Fantastic for cocktail parties and dynamite with a bottle of beer.

8 slices bread
16 medium-size prawns

Marinade:
½ teaspoon (2 ml) wine
dash of white pepper
¼ teaspoon (1 ml) garlic salt
¼ teaspoon (1 ml) ginger juice

3 egg whites, lightly beaten
6 tablespoon (90 ml) finely chopped
  ham
2 dried black mushrooms, soaked and
  finely chopped
1 stalk green onion, finely chopped
⅔ cup (160 ml) flour
¼ cup (60 ml) cornstarch
cornstarch for dry-coating
4 cups (1 L) oil

1. Remove crusts from bread and cut each piece in half (1½" x 3") (4x5.5 cm). Set aside to dry for about 30 minutes.
2. Clean, shell and devein prawns, leaving tail intact. Cut along back side of prawn and flatten slightly. Marinate prawns for 20 minutes.
3. Mix egg whites, ham, mushrooms, green onion, flour and cornstarch in a bowl.
4. Spread 1 teaspoon egg white mixture on one side of each piece of bread. Coat flat edge of prawns with cornstarch. Place one prawn flat on top of each coated piece of bread. Cover each prawn with ¾ teaspoon egg white mixture, making a smooth surface.
5. Heat oil over medium-high (350-375° F, 180-190° C) heat. Deep-fry toast, a few at a time, with prawn side facing down, for 1 minute. Turn and fry for another 30 seconds until golden brown.

Remarks
• *Fried shrimp toast can be reheated in oven at 325° F (170° C) for about 10 minutes.*

Imperial Shrimp Balls

Delicate and delicious, these little gastronomical delights will send you to the ends of the earth. An excellent choice for an appetizer as well as a main dish when garnished.

½ pound (225 g) fresh or frozen prawn
2 tablespoons (30 ml) pork fat (optional)
4 water chestnuts, finely chopped
1 stalk green onion, finely chopped
1 egg white, lightly beaten
1 teaspoon (5 ml) wine
½ teaspoon (2 ml) garlic salt

½ teaspoon (2 ml) sesame oil
1-2 teaspoons (5-10 ml) cornstarch
dash of white pepper
dash of sugar
1 cup (250 ml) fine bread crumbs, for coating
4 cups (1 L) oil for deep-frying

1. Shell, devein and mince prawn. Combine prawn, pork fat, water chestnuts and green onion in blender or food processor and process for 3-5 minutes.
2. Add remaining ingredients except bread crumbs to prawn mixture and blend well. Knead several minutes until slightly elastic.
3. Form 20 "perfectly round" (1¼", 3 cm) balls from the mixture. Roll balls in bread crumbs.
4. Deep-fry prawn balls in hot oil over medium-high heat until golden brown, and they float freely on top of the oil.
5. Serve hot with wine, beer or whatever you are drinking.

Remarks
- *Prawn balls can be made in advance and refried before serving.*

Sesame Toast

Toast is usually a breakfast food, but this combination can be a delight morning, noon or night! The sesame seed coating gives a nut-like flavor, and the strong aroma makes you ask, "What's cooking?"

¼ pound (112 g) fresh or frozen shrimp, washed, shelled and minced

Marinade:
½ egg white
dash of salt
dash of white pepper
dash of sugar
½ teaspoon (2 ml) cornstarch

2 water chestnuts, finely chopped
1 tablespoon (15 ml) finely chopped Virginia ham
½ stalk green onion, finely chopped
5 slices bread, each cut diagonally into 4 triangles
$^1/_3$ cup (80 ml) sesame seeds
4 cups (1 L) oil

1. Marinate minced shrimp for 30 minutes.
2. Mix shrimp, water chestnuts, ham and green onion in a bowl. Process mixture in blender or food processor until well blended.
3. Spread mixture on one side of each bread triangle. Place sesame seeds in shallow dish. Press covered side of each triangle into sesame seeds to coat well.
4. Heat oil over high heat (375° F, 190° C), then reduce heat to medium-high (350° F, 180° C). Deep-fry triangles, coated side down, for 45 seconds, turn, and fry for 30-40 seconds longer. Remove and drain well; serve immediately.

Remarks
- *These are best with ice cold wine or beer — enjoy!*
- *All ingredients must be very finely chopped or they will fall off of the bread during cooking.*
- *Use white or wheat bread, whichever you prefer.*

Subtle but sensational! This delicacy comes wrapped like a special gift, in foil or paper. Cooking in its own juices gives the meat a succulent texture and will be a pleasant surprise for family and guests.

¼ pound (112 g) chicken, prawn, or beef, cut into 2" x 2" (5 x 5 cm) thin slices

18-21 4½" (10 cm) square pieces of aluminum foil

2 stalks green onion, cut into 1" (2.5 cm) pieces

½ small zucchini, cut into 1" x 2" (2.5 x 5 cm) thin slices

¼ cup (60 ml) fresh mushrooms, sliced

4-5 snow peas, halved (optional)

4 cups (1 L) oil

Chicken Marinade:
2 teaspoons (10 ml) soy sauce
1 teaspoon (5 ml) wine
1 teaspoon (5 ml) hoisin sauce
pinch of white pepper
pinch of five-spice powder
1½ teaspoons (7 ml) oil
1½ teaspoons (7 ml) cornstarch

Beef Marinade:
2 teaspoons (10 ml) soy sauce
1 teaspoon (5 ml) wine
1 teaspoon (5 ml) water
1 teaspoon (5 ml) oil
½ egg white, lightly beaten
1½ teaspoons (7 ml) cornstarch
¼ teaspoon (1 ml) five-spice powder

Prawn Marinade:
1 teaspoon (5 ml) wine
½ teaspoon (2 ml) cornstarch
½ teaspoon (2 ml) oil
½ teaspoon (2 ml) salt
¼ teaspoon (1 ml) ginger juice
pinch of white pepper

1. Marinate chicken, beef or prawn for 30 minutes.
2. Slightly brush foil squares with oil. Place one piece of meat of choice, green onion, zucchini, mushroom and snow pea in center of each square. (See illustration) Squeeze envelope to remove excess oil which would prolong cooking time.
3. Deep-fry envelopes (chicken for 2½-3 minutes; beef for 2-2½ minutes; prawn for 1½-2 minutes) over medium-high heat (350°-375° F, 180° C-190° C). Turn several times while frying. Drain well and cool slightly before serving or you will burn your fingers!

Results
- *Parchment paper can be used instead of foil.*
- *Most recipes don't include any vegetables; however, they may keep the final product juicier.*

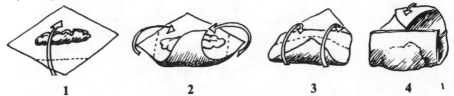

1 2 3 4

Spring Rolls (Egg Rolls)

This recipe is for people who get spring fever. Spring rolls are light, crisp and absolutely delicious. They make an ideal appetizer, as well as a delightful snack.

1 package (1 pound, 450 g) spring roll
   wrappers
1 egg white, lightly beaten
4 cups (1 L) oil

Filling Mixture:
1½ tablespoons (22 ml) oil
1 clove garlic, chopped
2 slices ginger, chopped
½ pound (225 g) boneless pork,
   chicken or BBQ pork, shredded
1½ cups (370 ml) bean sprouts
1½ cups (370 ml) cabbage, thinly
   shredded
½ cup (125 ml) shredded bamboo
   shoots
½ cup (125 ml) thinly shredded carrot
4-6 dried black mushrooms, soaked
   and shredded (optional)
3 stalks green onion, cut into 1″
   (2.5 cm) pieces
1½ teaspoons (7 ml) garlic salt
¼ teaspoon (1 ml) five-spice powder
   (optional)
1 teaspoon (5 ml) sugar
¼ teaspoon (1 ml) white pepper
½ cup (125 ml) soup stock, if needed
2 tablespoons (30 ml) cornstarch
   solution

1. If frozen, defrost wrappers inside the package at room temperature.
2. For filling mixture: Heat wok over high heat with oil, garlic and ginger. Stir in meat and cook for about 2 minutes. Add remaining ingredients, except cornstarch solution, to wok and stir 2 minutes. Moisten with stock if needed. Add cornstarch solution and mix well.
3. Place about 2 tablespoons of filling mixture in the center of each wrapper. Roll up and seal with egg white (or flour paste).
4. Heat oil over high heat (375°F, 190°C), then reduce heat to medium-high (350°F, 180°C) and deep-fry rolls until golden brown and floating freely on top of oil. Serve hot, with or without plum sauce.

Remarks

- *To avoid drying and cracking on edges of wrappers, be sure to defrost inside package. During the wrapping process, take a few out at a time and cover the rest with a damp cloth.*
- *Replace bean sprouts with cabbage; filling will keep better when prepared in advance — less watery.*
- *Spring rolls can be prepared in advance and put in the freezer. Thaw and fry when ready to serve. Leftover spring rolls can also be refried over high heat and served again!*
- *If you leave out the meat, you will have yourself a vegetarian roll.*
- *Spring rolls are often confused with egg rolls. They are similar but differ in ingredients and outer skins.*

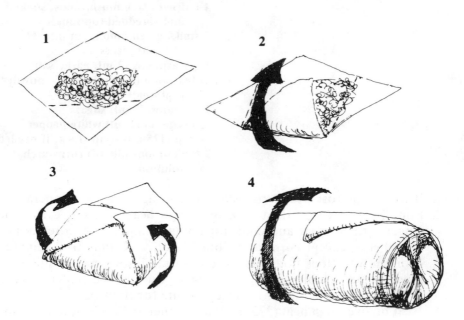

Stuffed Banana Crisp

The only word for this is delectable! If you are creative, you will enjoy this refreshing treat. The sweet banana is filled with tasty shrimp, then covered by a delicate, crispy batter. Wonderful as an appetizer or as a dessert.

6 medium-ripe bananas
2 teaspoons (10 ml) cornstarch
4 cups (1 L) oil
½ cup (125 ml) flour

Filling:
¼ pound (112 g) shrimp, minced
½ ounce (14 g) pork fat, minced
    (optional)
1 teaspoon (5 ml) cornstarch
1 egg yolk, lightly beaten
1 teaspoon (5 ml) wine
dash of salt
white pepper to taste

Batter:
1 cup (250 ml) sifted flour
¾ teaspoon (3 ml) baking powder
1 cup (250 ml) flat beer
½ teaspoon (2 ml) oil
½ teaspoon (2 ml) sugar

1. Slice each banana in half lengthwise, then cut each half crosswise into four pieces. Sprinkle with cornstarch.
2. Combine ingredients for filling in a bowl and blend well. Spread ¼" (0.75 cm) thickness of filling between two matching pieces of banana to form a sandwich. Secure with toothpicks.
3. Combine batter ingredients in a bowl and mix until smooth.
4. Heat oil in wok over high heat (375° F, 190° C) then reduce to medium-high (350° F, 180° C). Dredge banana sandwiches in flour, shake off excess and dip in batter. Deep-fry for 2½ minutes or until golden brown. Turn several times while frying.
5. Remove, drain well, and remove toothpicks. Serve immediately.

Remarks
- *This may be messy to prepare, but you will find the results scrumptious!*

Water Chestnuts Take A Wrap

HAWAII

This classic, well-known appetizer always wins compliments. It is a great choice for a large party.

12 whole water chestnuts, halved

Marinade:
4 teaspoons (20 ml) soy sauce
1½ tablespoons (22 ml) sugar
1 tablespoon (15 ml) honey
2 tablespoons (30 ml) soup stock
1 tablespoon (15 ml) wine
¼ teaspoon (1 ml) garlic salt

12 strips lean bacon
2 stalks green onion, cut into ½″ (1.5 cm) pieces
1 slice cooked ham, cut into 1″ x ½″ (2.5 x 1.5 cm) strips

1. Marinate water chestnut slices for 2-4 hours.
2. Cut each bacon strip in half. Wrap strip around 1 piece each of water chestnut, green onion and ham; secure with toothpicks.
3. Place water chestnut rolls on a rack in a roasting pan. Bake on upper level in preheated oven at 425°F (220°C) for 18-20 minutes. Switch oven to broil, and broil rolls 1-1½ minutes on each side.

Remarks
- *The longer the water chestnuts marinate, the more crunchy the texture will be.*

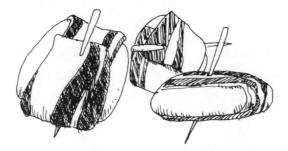

Wonton Delight

This Cantonese delectable delight is so versatile — it can be filled with a number of different fillings and served in soup, as an appetizer or a snack. Surprisingly simple — try it and impress your family and friends.

1 package wonton wrappers (1 pound)
  (450 g)
4 cups (1 L) oil

Filling:
½ pound (225 g) ground pork
¼ pound (112 g) fresh or frozen
  shrimp, shelled and minced
2 water chestnuts, finely chopped
1 dried black mushroom, soaked and
  chopped (optional)
1 stalk green onion, finely chopped
1 egg yolk, lightly beaten
¼ teaspoon (1 ml) cornstarch
1 teaspoon (5 ml) wine
¼ teaspoon (1 ml) garlic salt

Sweet and Sour Sauce:
¼ cup (60 ml) brown sugar
¼ cup (60 ml) white vinegar
¼ cup (60 ml) pineapple juice
dash of garlic salt
¼ teaspoon (1 ml) soy sauce (optional)
¼ cup (60 ml) water
few drops red food coloring (optional)
2 teaspoons (10 ml) cornstarch
  solution

1. Defrost wonton wrappers (if frozen) inside the package at room temperature.
2. In a large bowl, combine filling ingredients. Blend well and let marinate for 30 minutes.
3. Combine all ingredients for sweet and sour sauce, except cornstarch solution, in a saucepan. Bring to a boil, thicken with cornstarch solution and set aside. Keep warm.
4. Place ½ teaspoon filling mixture in center of each wrapper. Moisten edges of wrapper with water or beaten egg white. Fold in half to enclose filling and press edges to seal. Pull the two bottom corners toward each other and moisten one corner; place the other over top. Pinch at overlap (please refer to drawings).
5. Heat oil in wok to 350° F (180° C). Deep-fry wontons in hot oil 8-10 at a time. Stir wontons during frying for even browning. Fry 'til golden brown.
6. Serve with sweet and sour sauce, if desired.

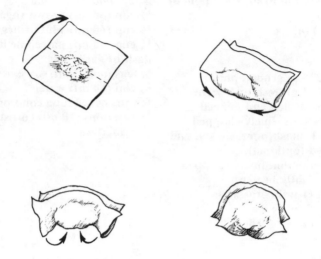

Remarks
- *Ground pork can be replaced with ground beef or minced fresh or frozen shrimp.*
- *Leftover fried wontons can be kept in refrigerator and fried again to serve.*
- *If prepared wontons are not fried immediately, cover with plastic wrap and refrigerate — they will last 1-2 days.*

Souped Up

Is it soup, yet? A recurring question for any child, or adult for that matter. Soup is an integral part of any Chinese meal since it is a common way to quench the thirst or clear the palate. In China one may have soup any time during the meal, depending on the region. It is usually served smack-dab in the middle of the table. For you gluttons, this means more than one serving — seconds and thirds!! One caution — don't try to eat the soup with your chopsticks — or you could be involved in a very long meal.

Most Chinese soups are fundamentally simple. A flavorful soup depends largely on a good basic stock in the company of a good chicken. Once the stock is made you can add any meat, seafood, poultry, vegetables or noodles you have on hand for a scrumptious one-dish meal. This is a great way to use your leftovers (or get rid of any stray animals in the neighborhood! Just joking!) The ultimate character of the soup depends on the particular blend of ingredients involved. The soup can be a very light, clear soup for an everyday meal or the hearty, rich type. The ingredients range widely from everyday, inexpensive ones to exotic and rare ingredients, such as shark's fin or bird's nest.

A Chinese soup is usually made in four basic steps: 1) preparing the basic soup stock, 2) adding dried, salted or other preserved ingredients to give flavor or piquancy, 3) cooking the major ingredients in the broth, such as meat and vegetables, and 4) adding other seasonings and aromatic ingredients. Most Chinese use a touch of sesame oil and white pepper to give an added zest to the soup when served. With all the souper duper variations in this chapter, you're only limited by your creativity and the number of pots you have.

Basic Chicken Stock

Although there are hundreds of soups in Chinese cooking, most begin with a basic stock: meat or poultry bones, vegetables, herbs and spices cooked into a rich broth. In this humble publication, soup stock is also used, instead of MSG, to season dishes. Prepare a large quantity of stock and freeze it for future use.

6-8 cups (1½-2 L) water
2½ pounds chicken bones (legs,
   wings, necks, etc.)
3 stalks green onion

4-5 slices ginger
pinch of white pepper
salt to taste

Bring 6-8 cups of water to a boil over high heat. Add chicken and reduce heat to medium-low. Cover and simmer for 1½ hours. Occasionally skim foam from soup while cooking. Add ginger, green onion and remaining seasonings. Continue to simmer for 20-25 minutes. Strain and discard solid ingredients. Keep stock in refrigerator or freezer.

Creamy Chicken Corn Soup

This is one of the few rich Chinese soups served at banquets and formal dinners. It's simple and economical, yet elegant.

6 cups (1½ L) soup stock
3 tablespoons (45 ml) minced cooked ham
½ stalk green onion, chopped (optional)
2-3 baby corns, sliced into small pieces (optional)
1 can (17 ounces) cream style corn, approximately 2 cups (500 ml)

½ cup (125 ml) minced cooked chicken
1 teaspoon (5 ml) salt
1 teaspoon (5 ml) sugar
$^1/_3$ cup (80 ml) cornstarch solution
¼ teaspoon (1 ml) white pepper
½ teaspoon (2 ml) sesame oil
1 egg white, lightly beaten (optional)

1. Bring stock to a boil; add ham, green onion and baby corn.
2. Add creamed corn and return to a boil. Add chicken and stir well. Stir in salt and sugar. Return to a boil and slowly add cornstarch solution, stirring constantly.
3. Add white pepper and sesame oil. Slowly pour in egg white, stirring constantly. Serve hot.

Remarks
- *This is a creamy soup with a full body. It can be prepared ahead of time and reheated to serve.*
- *For the best flavor, be sure to use ham of superior quality.*
- *Additional cream of corn can be used, if desired.*

Cucumber Soup

This is a very popular and well-known specialty of Peking. The refreshing crispy cucumber with its delightful green color is exceedingly tempting. It is sensational on a hot summer day.

4 ounces (112 g) pork or chicken,
   thinly sliced 1" x 2"
   (2.5 cm x 5 cm)
1 cucumber
7 cups (1¾ L) soup stock
½ teaspoon (2 ml) sesame oil
1 teaspoon (5 ml) salt
1 stalk green onion, chopped

Meat Marinade:
1 teaspoon (5 ml) soy sauce
dash of white pepper (optional)
1 teaspoon (5 ml) wine
1 teaspoon (5 ml) cornstarch

1. Marinate pork or chicken slices for 30 minutes.
2. Cut cucumber in half, lengthwise and remove seeds. Cut each half diagonally into ¼" slices (0.75 cm).
3. Bring soup stock to a boil; add marinated meat, and cook for 1½-2 minutes. Add cucumber, cook for another 30 seconds.
4. Remove from heat; season with sesame oil and salt and garnish with green onion. Serve hot.

Remarks
* *Add cucumber slices right before serving to avoid overcooking. The amount of cucumber used can be adjusted to taste.*

Egg Flower Drop Soup

Delicious for a winter's day, fantastic for a spring celebration, scrumptious for a mid-summer's night and excellent for the days of autumn. A soup which is simple, but one which will be remembered by family and guests.

7 cups (1¾ L) soup stock
1-2 slices ginger
2 ounces (56 g) pork, cut into 2"
    (5 cm) long shreds
¼ cup (60 ml) shredded carrot, 1"
    (2.5 cm) shreds
¼ cup (60 ml) shredded bamboo
    shoots, 2" (5 cm) shreds

dash of sesame oil
white pepper to taste
salt to taste
1 sheet dry seaweed, crumpled and
    soaked in water (optional)
2 eggs, lightly beaten
1 stalk green onion, chopped

1. Combine stock and ginger in a large pot; bring to a boil over high heat.
2. Add shredded pork, reduce heat to medium and cook for 2 minutes.
3. Add carrot, bamboo shoots, sesame oil and pepper. Cook for 1-2 minutes. Add salt to taste. Remove from heat and add soaked seaweed. Stir in beaten eggs. Garnish with chopped green onion to serve.

Remarks
- *In many restaurants, a dry, dark green seaweed with a fishy aroma is used in the recipe. It is available in Oriental stores and sold in plastic bags or in bulk.*

Fish and Spinach Soup

When it comes to soup, there is no limit to the ways of preparing it. Basically, the family style soups are light and clear. Anything can be used in the way of ingredients: red meat, any poultry meats, and seafoods of all kinds. Generally, soup consists of a light broth with a lot of vegetables and a touch of meat or seafood.

This is a simple, down-to-earth recipe for those who treasure nutritious, low calorie ingredients. It only takes a few minutes to prepare and is great any time of the year.

¼ pound (112 g) white fish fillet, cut into ¼" x 1" x 2" slices (0.75 cm x 2.5 cm x 5 cm)

Marinade:
1 teaspoon (5 ml) wine
¼ teaspoon (1 ml) salt
1 teaspoon (5 ml) cornstarch

½ pound (225 g) spinach
8 cups (2 L) soup stock
2 slices ginger
¾ teaspoon (3 ml) salt
¼ teaspoon (1 ml) sesame oil
white pepper to taste

1. Marinate fish for 30 minutes.
2. Thoroughly wash the spinach to eliminate mud or sand left on the leaves. Cut off excessively long leaf stems.
3. Bring soup stock to a boil with ginger. Add fish fillet, spinach, salt, sesame oil and pepper. Reduce heat to medium-low. Cook until spinach is somewhat wilted. Serve hot.

Remarks
• *Watercress is a good substitute for spinach.*

Gourmet Soup Stock

A good stock serves as a base for great soups or a delicious dish. This expensive proposition is worth the price! You will be able to enjoy the best of dishes!

6 cups (1½ L) water
1 whole stewing hen (cleaned and
    trimmed)
2 ounces (56 g) Smithfield ham,
    ½″ (1.5 cm) cubes

4-5 slices ginger
3 stalks green onion
pinch of white pepper
salt to taste

Combine chicken and ham in a large pot. Cover with water and bring to a boil. Reduce heat to medium low and simmer for 1½-2 hours. Skim foam from soup frequently. Add ginger, green onion, pepper and salt and continue to simmer for 1-1½ hours. Strain stock and discard bones and seasonings. Store in refrigerator.

Soy Bean Sprout and Sparerib Soup

Here is a typical Cantonese soup served at home. The crispy soy sprouts give it a little crunch, a hint of ginger in the stock distinguishes the soup from all others, and the inexpensive pork spareribs make it a delectable, nutritious bargain.

$^2/_3$ **pound (300 g) spareribs**
½ teaspoon (2 ml) salt
6 cups (1½ L) soup stock
2 slices ginger
salt to taste
½ pound (225 g) soybean sprouts, rinsed

1 stalk green onion, cut into 1½″ (4 cm) lengths
½ teaspoon (2 ml) sesame oil
pinch of white pepper

1. Trim excess fat from spareribs and cut into 1-1½″ (2.5-4.0 cm) cubes. (Ask your butcher for help!) Sprinkle with salt and let stand for 10-15 minutes.
2. Bring soup stock to a boil. Add ginger and salt to taste. Add spareribs and cook over medium heat for 12-15 minutes. Turn heat to high, add soy bean sprouts and cook for 2 minutes.
3. Add remaining ingredients. Mix well and serve hot.

Remarks
- *Be sure to trim all visible fat from the ribs.*
- *Soybean sprouts are grown from soybeans, not mung beans which are seen in most grocery stores.*
- *Soybean sprouts are not found in most grocery or Chinese food stores. They can easily be grown at home. Just follow the directions in this book for "Sprouting your own beans."*
- *If you have time, remove the roots from the soybean sprouts. This will make the dish more attractive.*

Seafood and Bean Curd Soup

The combination of shrimp, scallops, crab and fish fillet, with the soft texture of bean curd makes this soup a perfect choice for all seasons! The textures and flavors give your palate a real taste sensation.

3 whole fresh or frozen shrimp,
   shelled and deveined
3 scallops
¼ pound (112 g) white fish fillet
1 teaspoon (5 ml) wine
1 teaspoon (5 ml) cornstarch
½ teaspoon (2 ml) oil
8 cups (2 L) soup stock

2 slices ginger
salt to taste
1 square (8 ounces) (225 g) bean curd,
   cut into bite-size cubes
½ teaspoon (2 ml) sesame oil
dash of white pepper
1 stalk green onion, chopped

1. Cut all seafood into small, bite-size pieces. Mix seafood with wine, cornstarch and oil; set aside.
2. Combine soup stock and ginger and bring to a boil. Add salt to taste.
3. Add seafood and bean curd to stock. Reduce heat to medium-low and cook for 3-5 minutes.
4. Add sesame oil and white pepper. Garnish with chopped green onion and serve immediately.

Remarks
* *Seafood has a strong and distinctive flavor and should be served immediately — unless you wish to get rid of some of your guests!*

Singing Rice Soup

You need no introduction for this one! Listen carefully and you will hear the tempting sounds of this soup which is anxiously waiting to be enjoyed by all. A restaurant favorite which can be "sizzling" on your own dinner table.

6 cups (1½ L) soup stock
2 slices ginger, shredded
2 ounces (56 g) pork, thinly shredded
¼ cup (60 ml) button mushrooms,
    sliced
¼ small carrot, shredded
¼ whole zucchini, shredded

1 stalk green onion, chopped
½ teaspoon (2 ml) salt
white pepper to taste
2 cups (500 ml) dried rice crust,
    2″ (5 cm) squares
4 cups (1 L) oil for deep-frying

1. Bring soup stock to a boil. Add ginger and pork and cook for 2 minutes. Add mushroom, zucchini and carrot; continue to cook for 1 minute. Add remaining ingredients except rice crust. Keep warm and set aside.
2. Deep-fry rice crust in hot oil over high heat (375° F, 190° C) just until puffed.
3. To serve, pour soup in tureen and put hot rice crust (immediately after deep-frying) over soup to sing. Serve immediately.

Remarks
- *To make rice crust: after rice is cooked in saucepan, scoop out most of the rice, leaving a layer on the bottom. Continue to heat over low heat until slightly brown and dried. Remove crust. Bake at 300° F (150° C) for about 30 minutes to complete drying. Let cool and store in plastic bag in a dry, cool cupboard.*
- *Two cups (500 ml) dried rice crust is equal to approximately 8 ounces (225 g).*

Winter Melon Soup

Winter melon soup is often prepared in the whole melon with the skin skillfully carved in floral designs. The following is a modified version which everyone can prepare in their own kitchen.

4 ounces (112 g) boneless chicken or pork, diced

Chicken or Pork Marinade:
1 teaspoon (5 ml) wine
1 teaspoon (5 ml) soy sauce
1 teaspoon (5 ml) cornstarch

6 cups (1½ L) soup stock
2 slices ginger
2 dried black mushrooms, soaked and diced
¼ cup (60 ml) diced cooked ham
½ pound (225 g) winter melon flesh, cut into ½" (1.5 cm) cubes
5 water chestnuts, diced
5 button mushrooms, cut in half
¾ teaspoon (3 ml) salt
pinch of white pepper
dash of sesame oil
1 stalk green onion, chopped

1. Marinate chicken or pork for 30 minutes.
2. Bring soup stock to a boil with ginger. Add mushroom, ham, chicken or pork, and winter melon. Cook over medium to medium-high heat for 5-6 minutes.
3. Add remaining ingredients except green onion and cook for 1-2 minutes. Transfer to soup tureen or individual bowls and garnish with green onion. Serve hot.

Remarks
- *Prepare this ahead of time and reheat before serving.*
- *This soup can be prepared inside the scooped-out melon, with all the ingredients cooked in the melon. Steam melon for 3-4 hours over low heat in a gigantic pot.*

Wonton Soup

Wonton, either fried or in soup, is so popular that it has almost become the symbol of Chinese food. This soup is considered to be a meal in itself at lunch. It is also eaten as a snack, but it is never served at dinner.

Filling Mixture:
¼ pound (112 g) ground pork
¼ pound (112 g) fresh or frozen shrimp
2 whole water chestnuts, finely
   chopped (optional)
1 dried black mushroom, finely
   chopped (optional)
1 green onion, finely chopped
1 egg yolk, lightly beaten
¼ teaspoon (1 ml) cornstarch
1 teaspoon (5 ml) wine
¼ teaspoon (1 ml) salt
dash of sesame oil

24 wonton wrappers
8 cups (2 L) soup stock
2-3 whole water chestnuts, sliced
2 tablespoons (30 ml) sliced bamboo
   shoots
dash of white pepper
dash of sesame oil
1 stalk green onion, chopped

1. Combine filling ingredients and mix well. Wrap wonton as illustrated on p. 60.
2. Cook wrapped wontons in boiling water for 2 minutes, drain, and place in a bowl of cold water (to prevent them from sticking together).
3. Bring soup stock to a boil; add water chestnuts, bamboo shoots, white pepper and sesame oil. Cook for 1-2 minutes.
4. To serve, add cooked wontons to hot broth and garnish with green onion.

Remarks
- *The traditional Chinese recipe for wonton filling includes shrimp, pork fat and bamboo shoots. You can use just shrimp, pork or any combination of your choice.*
- *Overcooked wonton may be too soft and fall apart.*
- *When wrapping wontons, only take out a few wrappers at a time and cover the rest with a damp cloth. This will keep them from drying out.*

Sassy Sauces

Sauces make good things taste better and give flavor to some foods that don't have any taste at all. The use of sauces is as indispensable to Chinese cooking as it is in French cuisine. The Chinese have a great variety of sauces and dips, each with its own particular flavor and purpose. Here are a few of the most popular and frequently used combinations that you can prepare ahead of time. So, let's hit the sauce (but not too hard) and tantalize your tastebuds.

A Good Batter Mix

Don't believe that all Chinese dishes are deep-fried. Actually only a limited number of dishes are prepared in this fashion. For those who like crispy, golden fried food, here is a delectable batter. It is puffy, crispy and absolutely sensational!

¾ cup (200 ml) flour
¼ cup (60 ml) cornstarch
½ teaspoon (2 ml) sugar (optional)

¾ cup (200 ml) flat beer (or water)
¾ teaspoon (3 ml) baking powder
¾ teaspoon (3 ml) oil (optional)

Combine all ingredients in a large bowl. Mix well until batter is smooth and light. If water is used, increase baking powder to 1¼-1½ teaspoons (6-7 ml).

Important Message!
It is very common to deep-fry batter foods a second time in order to achieve an extra crispy texture. To do this, deep-fry once, let food cool thoroughly, then deep-fry a second time over high heat for 45 seconds to 1 minute. Serve immediately. This practice will yield a crispy golden brown product and should apply to all deep-fried batter dishes.

Black Bean Sauce

Salted black beans are frequently called for in Chinese recipes. Keeping black bean sauce on hand will save a lot of time when entertaining or fixing quick meals for the family. This recipe makes enough sauce to season many tasty dishes.

8 ounces (225 g) salted black beans
6 medium cloves garlic, finely
   minced

4 tablespoons (60 ml) brown sugar
4½ tablespoons (67 ml) oil

Rinse salted black beans and drain well. Combine black beans and minced garlic in a bowl. Mash until blended. Mix in sugar and oil and steam over high heat for 10-12 minutes. Cool and transfer to a covered jar. It keeps several weeks in the refrigerator.

Bouillon Cubes

They are great when you are in an absolute rush. Bouillon cubes are frequently used by many Chinese homemakers in place of home-made soup stock and are especially helpful in last minute cooking decisions as a fill-in flavor. Most Chinese cooks prefer the Swiss bouillon cubes to the American ones because of their more delicate flavor and softer texture, which make them easier to handle. They are also less salty. Swiss bouillon cubes are normally 3-4 times as big as American bouillon cubes. If the American bouillon cube is used as a seasoning, dissolve 1 cube (1½ cc) of bouillon in 1-1½ cups water for stock; use as needed. For soups, dissolve enough bouillon cubes to adjust to your own taste. I generally use 4 cubes per 6 cups of water.

Ginger Juice

Prepare enough ginger juice for several days. It keeps well in the refrigerator.

4 tablespoons finely chopped ginger

Place ginger in garlic press and squeeze juice into a small bowl or jar, or wrap ginger in a piece of cheese cloth or muslin and squeeze into a small bowl or jar. Sprinkle ginger with 1 tablespoon water and squeeze until you are totally exhausted!

Home-made Plum Sauce

A lot of my students and audiences have requested a recipe for plum sauce, which is commonly used as a dip for egg rolls, barbequed duck and for almost anything else imaginable. Here is a very simple recipe; prepare it and keep it in the refrigerator.

6 ounces (168 g) salted plums
¾ cup (200 ml) applesauce
½ cup (125 ml) apricot preserves
½ cup (125 ml) crushed pineapple
½ teaspoon (2 ml) garlic juice

2 tablespoons (30 ml) sugar
1 tablespoon (15 ml) vinegar
2-3 dried red peppers, cut into halves

1. Discard the solid seeds from solid plums.
2. Combine all ingredients, except red pepper, in blender. Blend for 2 minutes.
3. Transfer everything to a saucepan and cook over medium heat for 3-4 minutes. Let cool and put in a covered jar. Serve cool.

Sweet and Sour Sauce (Traditional)

There are countless versions of sweet and sour sauce. Some are too sweet, others are too sour and most lack character! Here is a well-balanced recipe used by traditional Chinese chefs.

¼ cup (60 ml) vinegar
¼ cup (60 ml) sugar
6 tablespoons (90 ml) water
¾ teaspoon (3 ml) soy sauce
½ teaspoon (2 ml) finely minced
  ginger

1½ teaspoons (7 ml) finely chopped
  green onion
2½ teaspoons (12 ml) cornstarch
1 teaspoon (5 ml) oil, heated

Combine all ingredients in saucepan and bring to a boil. Cook, stirring continuously until thick and smooth. Cover and keep warm. The sweetness and sourness should be adjusted to your own taste.

Toasted Szechwan Pepper Salt

This is another widely used seasoning salt. It is a pungent and aromatic dip which complements many dishes.

2 tablespoons (30 ml) Szechwan
  peppercorns
½ cup (120 ml) salt

Stir Szechwan peppercorns in a dry skillet over medium heat for about 1-1½ minutes until fragrant. Remove and grind with a mortar and pestle or rolling pin. Heat salt in the same skillet until color turns light brown. Remove and mix with toasted peppercorns.

To Get Thick Quick — Cornstarch

Unless you are stewing a dish for hours, the natural juices from the ingredients will be too runny to make a reasonably thick sauce. The French thicken their sauces with a mixture of egg yolks and butter, and occasionally flour. In China, the best chefs sometimes use lotus root flour, but this is hard to find, and it's also expensive. Unfortunately, you cannot use wheat flour because it makes the sauce cloudy, while arrowroot or tapioca starch are too exotic and difficult to get (and sauces of arrowroot starch cannot be reheated). But happily, cornstarch is just perfect. It thickens with a glossy appearance and a satiny smoothness, and it adds no extraneous flavor of its own. Sauces thickened with cornstarch have a clear, translucent appearance, and because it is finer than wheat flour, cornstarch blends more easily with water. It also has twice the thickening power of flour.

To mix a cornstarch solution, use twice as much cold water as starch and stir the mixture until it is smooth. If left standing, the starch and water solution will settle out, so stir again just before using. When adding the cornstarch solution during cooking, slowly pour the cool cornstarch mixture into the hot cooking liquid and stir constantly until it blends smoothly. Make sure the mixture comes to a full boil, but then reduce it back to medium heat; otherwise, cooking over a high heat may cause lumping, particularly when you are preparing a large pot of sauce. With acidic sauces that feature ingredients such as lemon juice, vinegar or tomatoes, these ingredients should be added only after the mixture has already thickened and is removed from the heat. If you add acidic ingredients before or during cooking, the thickening ability of the starch is reduced. Finally, to prevent 'a skin' from forming on cooked sauces, cover the surface of the container with plastic wrap.

Chinese chefs make their batter from a mixture of cornstarch, wheat flour, baking powder and water. Adding more or less water changes the consistency of the batter. The use of cornstarch in a batter gives a firmer and crispier texture.

Frequently, you will see recipes that instruct you to add cornstarch to a marinade for meats before stir-frying. This serves to seal in the natural juices of the meat, to give a smoother and tender texture, and to hold the surface moisture, which should reduce the chances of hot oil splatters during deep-frying. (Otherwise, you might need safety glasses and an asbestos cap!)

Clucks and Ducks

You don't have to be a turkey to get stuffed—you could be a duck or a chicken! In Chinese cooking, the first and most common fowl play is chicken. You can serve it in a variety of dishes—some very simple, while others are more exotic. And some of the most sophisticated Chinese cooking features chicken livers and gizzards—just those parts you might carelessly feed to Fido!

Poultry is nutritious, versatile and lower in calories than most other red meat. Because of its subtle flavor, you can actually present a meal with several chicken dishes, each with its own distinctive taste. Since chicken is comparatively inexpensive, it doesn't always command the status it deserves, but in China, a host trying to impress a guest would serve him chicken and that would be considered a great honor. My mother, who is still a resident of Kwongchow, China, always keeps a few chicks in the patio of our small humble home and only dresses a chicken when I or some other honored guest comes to visit her.

While squab and some other selected wild game are doing fowl plays only at formal banquets, the Chinese always love a duck, and they don't care how he comes—whether fashionably well-trussed or falling to pieces. It's all ducky to them. Peking duck is the most famous banquet dish, while barbeque duck can be seen in the windows of many Chinatown shops. Because the oven is not standard in a traditional Chinese kitchen, the Chinese mainly prepare duck by barbecuing (with an open fire), steaming, deep-frying or simmering. The best part is that however you cook them, you can't fowl up. So don't be an old hen! Try your wings at some of these clucks and ducks.

Almond Chicken Crisp CANTON

Nuts to you and to the chicken, too! A traditional dish for many, it is served at Chinese restaurants across the country. Crispy chicken topped with almonds — something new to try and go nuts with!

1 whole boneless chicken breast
  (about ½ pound) (225 g)
½ tablespoon (7 ml) wine
½ teaspoon (2 ml) garlic salt
¼ cup (60 ml) cornstarch for dry
  coating
½ cup (125 ml) bread crumbs
  (optional)
4 cups (1 L) oil
½ head of lettuce, shredded for
  garnishing
2 tablespoons (30 ml) crushed roasted
  almonds

Batter:
1 cup (250 ml) flour
¾ cup + 3 tablespoons (245 ml) flat
  beer, more if needed
½ teaspoon (2 ml) baking powder
¼ teaspoon (1 ml) oil

Sweet and Sour Sauce:
3 tablespoons (45 ml) white vinegar
¼ cup (60 ml) water
¼ cup (60 ml) brown sugar
2 teaspoons (10 ml) cornstarch
  solution

1. Lay chicken breast flat and slice horizontally to ¼″ (0.75 cm) thickness. Use cleaver to flatten slightly.
2. Marinate chicken with wine and garlic salt for 30 minutes. Dry coat chicken with cornstarch.
3. Mix batter ingredients together until smooth.
4. Dip chicken in batter, then dry coat with bread crumbs. Set aside.
5. Deep-fry coated chicken over medium-high heat (350° F, 180° C) until golden brown. Remove, drain and cut into bite-size pieces. Line platter with shredded lettuce and arrange chicken on top.
6. In a saucepan, bring all of sweet and sour sauce ingredients, except cornstarch, to a boil. Thicken with cornstarch.
7. To serve, pour sweet and sour sauce over chicken. Sprinkle with almonds. Serve hot.

Remarks

- *Pour sauce over chicken just before serving or dish will be soggy. This principle applies to all other dishes of a similar nature.*
- *You may use water instead of beer, but beer makes a crispier coating.*
- *Cooking time depends on the temperature of the oil.*
- *Add a few drops of food coloring (any color you wish) to the sauce if desired.*
- *For extra crispiness, deep-fry chicken once and set aside. Cool, then deep-fry again over high heat for 30-45 seconds.*

Black Bean Wings

This gastronomical adventure will send you somewhere!! Delicate white chicken meat combined with the strong sophistication of bean paste will enhance any dinner or party. It's distinctively different from any other dish you've ever tried.

1 large clove garlic, minced
1½ tablespoons (22 ml) salted black
    beans, rinsed
2 tablespoons (30 ml) oil
12-14 chicken wings
2 slices ginger
2 ounces (56 g) lean ground pork
½ cup (125 ml) soup stock
1 stalk green onion, cut into 1"
    (2.5 cm) pieces

1 tablespoon (15 ml) wine
1 tablespoon (15 ml) soy sauce
¼ teaspoon (1 ml) salt
¼ teaspoon (1 ml) sugar
1 teaspoon (5 ml) cornstarch solution
1 egg white, lightly beaten

1. Mash garlic and black beans in a bowl to form a paste.
2. Heat wok over high heat with 1 tablespoon oil. Add chicken wings and cook for 1½ minutes, stirring continuously. Remove.
3. Add 1 tablespoon oil to wok over medium-high heat; add ginger, black bean mixture and ground pork. Cook for 1½ minutes.
4. Stir in stock, green onion, wine, soy sauce, salt and sugar. Return wings and mix well. Reduce heat to low, cover and simmer for 8-10 minutes. Thicken with cornstarch solution.
5. Turn off heat; slowly pour in beaten egg white. Mix well and serve.

Remarks
- *Stir wings continuously while cooking as black beans burn easily.*

Braised Chicken (or Duck) with a Surprise   CANTON

This is a delightful way to serve a whole chicken — stuffed with ham, bamboo shoots and other delicious ingredients. If you take the time to bone the chicken, you will truly have a dish fit for a king.

1 whole chicken or duck, 2½-3 pounds (1125-1350g) cleaned, dried and boned, if desired

Marinade:
1 tablespoon (15 ml) dark soy sauce
2 teaspoons (10 ml) wine
1 tablespoon (15 ml) sugar
1½ teaspoons (7 ml) salt

3 tablespoons (45 ml) oil

Filling:
¼ cup (60 ml) cooked rice
2 tablespoons (30 ml) Virginia ham, chopped
3 tablespoons (45 ml) diced bamboo shoot
2 tablespoons (30 ml) frozen peas and carrots
2 tablespoons (30 ml) dried Chinese shrimp, soaked (optional)
1 chicken liver, boiled and diced (optional)
3 medium-size dried black mushrooms, soaked and diced

Braising Sauce:
1 cup (250 ml) soup stock
2 tablespoons (30 ml) dark soy sauce
2 tablespoons (30 ml) wine
1 star anise
1½ teaspoons (7 ml) sugar
3 slices ginger
1 stalk green onion, cut into 1" (2.5 cm) pieces
1½ teaspoons (7 ml) cornstarch solution

1. Rub marinade mixture over entire chicken. Marinate for 1 hour.
2. Heat wok with 1 tablespoon oil, add filling ingredients and stir-fry for 1½ minutes over medium-high heat.
3. Stuff chicken (or duck) with filling mixture and close opening by threading with a skewer.

4. Heat wok with 2 tablespoons oil over medium heat. Add chicken and cook for about 3 minutes, turning to brown on all sides. Drain oil and turn chicken, breast side down, in the wok. Pour braising sauce over chicken and cover. Reduce heat to low and braise for 45 minutes or until tender.
5. To serve, remove stuffing and place in the center of a platter. Cut up chicken, and then reassemble it as a whole fowl on top of the stuffing. Thicken ¾ cup of braising sauce with cornstarch solution and pour over chicken. This dish can be prepared ahead & reheated in the oven.

Braised Lychee Chicken   NEW DISCOVERY

These tender morsels of chicken, braised in a generous portion of refreshing lychee sauce are a memorable gourmet experience.

¾ pound (340 g) boneless chicken
    breast, cut into bite-size cubes
1 tablespoon (15 ml) wine
¾ teaspoon (3 ml) salt
2-3 tablespoons (30-45 ml) oil
4 pineapple rings, cut into quarters
12-14 lychees, fresh or canned
1 tablespoon (15 ml) cornstarch solution

Braising Sauce:
2 tablespoons (30 ml) pineapple juice
2 tablespoons (30 ml) lychee juice
2½ tablespoons (37 ml) white vinegar
5 teaspoons (25 ml) sugar

1. Marinate chicken in salt and wine for 30 minutes.
2. Heat wok with oil over high heat and stir-fry chicken cubes for 1½ minutes. Add pineapple pieces, lychees and the braising sauce.
3. Cook chicken over low heat for approximately 10 minutes. Thicken with cornstarch solution and serve.

Remarks
• *This dish can also be placed in a covered baking dish and baked in the oven at 350° F (180° C) for 25-30 minutes.*

Braised Plum-Flavored Drumsticks   NEW DISCOVERY

These drumsticks are just sensational! Would I lie to you? Delicate plum sauce imparts a distinctive flavor to the tender chicken. It forms a velvety glaze over each piece of chicken, making this entree a true gastronomic adventure.

6 chicken drumsticks

Marinade:
1 teaspoon (5 ml) wine
¼ teaspoon (1 ml) salt
1 teaspoon (5 ml) cornstarch
**½ teaspoon (2 ml) finely chopped
    ginger**

2 tablespoons (30 ml) oil
3 tablespoons (45 ml) plum sauce
½ cup (125 ml) soup stock
fresh or canned plums (for garnish)

1. Marinate chicken drumsticks for 1 hour.
2. Heat oil in wok over high heat. Add drumsticks and brown for 1½-2 minutes, turning frequently.
3. Stir in plum sauce and blend well. Reduce heat to medium-low. Add soup stock; cover and simmer for 10-12 minutes, turning occasionally until sauce is slightly thickened and coats the drumsticks. Remove from heat, keep warm and serve anytime.

Remarks
- *Braised Plum-Flavored Drummettes make excellent appetizers, too. Substitute 12-14 drummettes for the 6 drumsticks and decrease the amount of plum sauce to 1½ tablespoons.*
- *If excess sauce remains after simmering, cook over high heat, stirring continuously, until sauce is reduced.*
- *This dish can be prepared ahead of time, reheated, then served.*

Chicken and Cucumber in Wine Sauce   NEW DISCOVERY

Fresh cucumber is generally abundant all year round. Succulent and refreshing, cucumbers can be used in dishes other than salad: quickly fried cucumber imparts a unique character to this dish.

6 ounces (168 g) boneless chicken,
   cut into 1" x 2" (2.5 cm x 5 cm)
   pieces

Marinade:
½ teaspoon (2 ml) salt
1 teaspoon (5 ml) wine
1 teaspoon (5 ml) cornstarch
1 teaspoon (5 ml) oil

1 small cucumber
2 tablespoons (30 ml) oil
1 slice ginger, minced
2 tablespoons (30 ml) wine
1 teaspoon (5 ml) sugar
1 teaspoon (5 ml) soy sauce
½ cup (125 ml) soup stock
2½ teaspoons (12 ml) cornstarch
   solution

1. Marinate the chicken for 30 minutes.
2. Wash and peel the cucumber. Discard any hard seeds. Halve lengthwise and cut into ¼" (0.75 cm) slices.
3. Heat the oil in wok over high heat. Add ginger and chicken and stir for 1½-2 minutes. Add the cucumber slices and stir for another 30 seconds. Stir in the remaining ingredients, except the cornstarch solution. Cover and cook for 1 minute.
4. Thicken with cornstarch solution and serve hot.

Chicken Little

A most unique and delicately spiced dish. It's a great choice for a party because it can be prepared ahead of time. The flavor of five-spice powder blends ideally with the natural juices of the game hen.

2 whole game hens, defrost
    and pat dry

Marinade:
1 teaspoon (5 ml) salt
½ teaspoon (2 ml) five-spice powder
1 teaspoon (5 ml) sugar
1 teaspoon (5 ml) minced ginger
½ teaspoon (2 ml) minced garlic

Dressing Sauce:
2 teaspoons (10 ml) soy sauce
1 teaspoon (5 ml) wine
½ cup (125 ml) soup stock
1 teaspoon (5 ml) honey
¾ teaspoon (3 ml) sesame oil
¼ teaspoon (1 ml) 5-spice powder
1 teaspoon (5 ml) cornstarch
    solution

1. Divide marinade into 2 equal portions, then rub evenly on each of the hens. Let stand for 2 hours.
2. Bring dressing sauce ingredients to a boil in a saucepan. Cook until thickened. Set aside and keep warm.
3. Preheat oven to 350°F (180°C). Place fowls on a rack in a roasting pan (with ½ cup water in the pan). Roast fowls, breast side up, for 25 minutes. Turn over and roast at 375°F (190°C) for 15 minutes. Turn fowls over and broil, breast side up, for 3 minutes or until golden brown.
4. To serve, cut each fowl in half and place on a platter. Pour hot dressing over hens and serve immediately.

Remarks
- *Here's an alternative way, which requires 1 extra step: Pour 2 cups of hot oil over skins of roasted fowls. Continue this procedure until skin is shiny and golden brown. Drain hens well and serve as noted above.*

Chicken Rolls
with Sweet and Sour Sauce

A different and appetizing dish inspired by my love for good food. It takes a few extra minutes to get ready, but it is worth the effort. It might just become one of your favorites!

1 pound (450 g) chicken breast,
  cut into about 12, 1½" x 3"
  (4 x 7.5 cm) thin slices

Marinade:
2 teaspoons (10 ml) soy sauce
1 teaspoon (5 ml) wine
1 teaspoon (5 ml) oil
2 teaspoons (10 ml) cornstarch

Sweet and Sour Sauce:
¼ cup (60 ml) water
3 tablespoons (45 ml) white vinegar
3½ tablespoons (52 ml) packed
  brown sugar
1½ tablespoons (22 ml) catsup
1½ teaspoons (7 ml) cornstarch
  solution

4 ounces (112 g) cooked ham, cut into
  1" x 1½" (2.5 cm x 4 cm) slices
1 Chinese sausage, cut into thin,
  diagonal slices (optional)
½ small zucchini, cut into 1" x 1½"
  (2.5 x 4 cm) slices
3 stalks green onion, cut into 1½"
  (4 cm) lengths
4 cups (1 L) oil
2 tablespoons (30 ml) toasted sesame
  seeds
pineapple slices (for garnish)
red cherries (for garnish)

1. Marinate chicken for 30 minutes.
2. Combine ingredients for sweet and sour sauce, except cornstarch solution, in a saucepan and bring to a boil. Thicken with cornstarch solution. Keep warm.
3. Wrap inside each chicken slice, one piece of ham, Chinese sausage, zucchini and green onion. Secure with toothpicks.
4. Deep-fry chicken rolls in hot oil over medium to medium-high heat (350°F, 180°C) for 2 minutes or until golden brown, turning several times.
5. Arrange fried chicken rolls on a plate. Cover with sweet and sour sauce and garnish with red cherries, pineapple slices and toasted sesame seeds.

Remarks
- *Other ingredients can be used to wrap inside the chicken.*
- *If preferred, bake chicken rolls in a preheated over at 375° F (190° C) for 15-20 minutes instead of frying.*

Chicken Stuffed Pineapple

Designed with the creative person in mind — this dish is for those who are willing to try anything once. This one you may want to try more than once — tender chicken with the sweetness of fresh pineapple. What the heck, I'm ready to go to Hawaii anytime!

½ pound (225 g) boneless chicken breast, cut into ½" (1.5 cm) cubes

Marinade:
½ teaspoon (2 ml) salt
1 tablespoon (15 ml) wine
1 teaspoon (5 ml) cornstarch

½ fresh, medium-ripe pineapple, cut in half lengthwise
2½ tablespoons (37 ml) oil
½ teaspoon (2 ml) sesame oil
2 teaspoons (10 ml) sugar
1 stalk green onion, cut into 1" (2.5 cm) pieces
1½ teaspoons (7 ml) white vinegar
½ teaspoon (2 ml) cornstarch solution

1. Marinate chicken for 30 minutes.
2. Remove the flesh of pineapple with a knife or spoon, preserving pineapple shell. Chop flesh, and set aside.
3. Heat wok with oil over high heat and stir-fry chicken pieces for 1½-2 minutes. Add 1 cup chopped pineapple and remaining ingredients except cornstarch solution; mix well. Thicken with cornstarch solution.
4. Place the stir-fried mixture into the pineapple half and bake at 300°F (150°C) for 8-10 minutes.
5. Serve chicken mixture from baked shell or transfer to a platter. Garnish with additional pineapple rings, if desired.

Remarks
• *Baking the chicken in the pineapple shell gives the meat a great pineapple aroma and flavor.*

Chilled Chicken (or Duck)

Some like it hot, some like it cold! This tender chicken is soaked in a subtle sauce mixture. Rich with good flavors, it can be served anytime as an appetizer or as a main dish.

¾ pound (340 g) boneless chicken

Marinade:
2½ teaspoons (12 ml) salt
1½ tablespoons (22 ml) wine
1½ teaspoon (7 ml) ginger juice
1½ tablespoons (22 ml) finely chopped green onion

Soaking Sauce:
¾ cup (200 ml) soup stock
¾ teaspoon (3 ml) salt
½ teaspoon (2 ml) sesame oil
dash of white pepper
1 teaspoon (5 ml) sugar
1 tablespoon (15 ml) wine
dash of five-spice powder (optional)

1. Clean and dry chicken. Marinate for 2 hours.
2. Bring a pot of water to a boil. Add marinated chicken, reduce heat and simmer chicken for 25 minutes. Remove and cool.
3. Place chicken, whole or cut into bite-size pieces, in a casserole. Combine ingredients for soaking sauce and pour over chicken. Refrigerate for at least 2-3 hours, turning several times. Serve anytime.

Remarks
- *You can also use cut-up chicken pieces which have not been deboned.*

Citrus Pineapple Chicken

This recipe will make your next dinner party unforgettable! Golden chicken with a succulent pineapple-lemon sauce and a sprinkle of sesame seeds add up to out-of-this-world eating!

½ pound (225 g) boneless chicken breast, cut into ½" x 2½" (1.5 cm x 6.5 cm) strips
½ cup (125 ml) cornstarch for dry coating
4 cups (1 L) oil
1 teaspoon (5 ml) toasted sesame seeds

Marinade:
½ teaspoon (2 ml) garlic salt
dash of white pepper
¼ teaspoon (1 ml) sesame oil
1 tablespoon (15 ml) wine
1 egg yolk, lightly beaten

Pineapple Lemon Sauce:
3 tablespoons (45 ml) fresh lemon juice
2 teaspoons (10 ml) lime juice (optional)
2 tablespoons (30 ml) orange juice
¼ cup (60 ml) pineapple juice
2 tablespoons (30 ml) white vinegar
¼ cup (60 ml) packed brown sugar
few drops of yellow food coloring (optional)
½ teaspoon (2 ml) cornstarch solution

1. Marinate chicken for 30 minutes.
2. Dry-coat marinated chicken by dipping each piece in cornstarch. Coat thoroughly and shake off excess.
3. Deep-fry coated chicken over high heat (375° F, 190° C), until golden brown, approximately 2 minutes. Drain well and set aside.
4. Combine lemon sauce ingredients except cornstarch solution; bring to a boil and thicken with cornstarch solution.
5. Simmer fried chicken in lemon sauce for 1-2 minutes.
6. Transfer to serving plate and sprinkle with sesame seeds. Optional ingredients for garnishing include pineapple rings, lemon slices and orange wedges.

Remarks
- *Dry-coated chicken can be kept in a plastic bag and deep-fried just before serving.*
- *To save time, marinate the whole chicken breast. Coat with dry starch and deep-fry entire piece. Cut into bite-size pieces before serving.*

Curry Chicken

This dish makes use of the intriguing flavor of curry, which is a nice change from more subtle seasonings. It is great for the cold icy winter and the hot, muggy summer when you need something pungent to keep you warm or to stimulate your palate.

½ pound (225 g) boneless chicken,
   cut into bite-size thin slices

Marinade:
2 teaspoons (10 ml) soy sauce
1 teaspoon (5 ml) wine
½ teaspoon (2 ml) sugar
½ teaspoon (2 ml) cornstarch

2 tablespoons (30 ml) oil
2 slices ginger, minced
¼ teaspoon (1 ml) crushed red chili
   pepper
1 clove garlic, minced
1½ teaspoons (7 ml) curry powder
   or paste
dash of five-spice powder (optional)
½ medium-size onion, cut into 2"
   (5 cm) thin strips
½ bell pepper, cut into 1" (2.5 cm)
   thin strips
¼ teaspoon (1 ml) salt
½ cup (125 ml) soup stock
½ teaspoon (2 ml) cornstarch solution

1. Marinate chicken for 30 minutes.
2. Heat wok with oil, ginger, red pepper, garlic, curry, five-spice powder and onion over high heat for 1 minute. Add chicken and stir-fry for 1½ minutes.
3. Add bell pepper, salt and soup stock and cook for 1½ minutes. Thicken with cornstarch solution and serve.

Remarks
- *The curry powder available in most supermarkets is spicy and pungent, but not really hot. Indian curry paste is more desirable. If a hot lip is desired, add chili pepper.*

Delectable Liver

Many people don't like the soft texture of liver. I love it because it is easy to digest and is economical and nutritious. Liver is relatively high in cholesterol, but if you are not worried about such matters, try this delicious dish for breakfast, lunch and dinner!

1 teaspoon (5 ml) salt
2 slices ginger
¾ pound (340 g) chicken liver
2 tablespoons (30 ml) wine
3 cups (750 ml) oil

Sweet and Sour Sauce:
2 tablespoons (30 ml) catsup
1 tablespoon (15 ml) Worcestershire
    sauce
1 tablespoon (15 ml) sugar
1 tablespoon (15 ml) white vinegar
3 tablespoons (45 ml) water
1 tablespoon (15 ml) wine
1 slice ginger, finely shredded
¾ teaspoon (3 ml) cornstarch solution

1. Bring 4 cups of water to a boil; add ½ teaspoon salt, ginger and liver. Blanch liver for 1½-2 minutes. Drain well and cut liver into bite-size chunks.
2. Mix liver with ½ teaspoon salt and 2 tablespoons wine in a bowl; let stand for ½ hour, stirring several times. Remove and pat dry with paper towel.
3. Combine all ingredients for sauce, except cornstarch solution, in a saucepan and bring to a boil. Thicken with cornstarch solution and set aside.
4. Heat oil over high heat (375° F, 190° C). Reduce heat to medium (350° F, 180° C) and deep-fry liver until golden brown. For safety, use wok cover to shield spattering oil while frying. Remove liver, drain, and place on a platter.
5. Pour sweet and sour sauce over liver and serve hot.

Remarks
- *This dish should be served immediately. It is absolutely delicious. Just don't tell your guests it's liver!*

Drunk Chicken

Chicken drowned in a pool of wine! It's a great party dish, particularly for those who enjoy alcoholic beverages all the time.

1 whole chicken, approximately 2½ pounds (675 g)	1¾ cup (450 ml) wine ¾ cup (200 ml) soup stock
1½ tablespoons (22 ml) salt	dash of sugar
2 slices ginger	dash of sesame oil

1. Clean and dry chicken. Rub inside and out with salt. Let stand for 2 hours.
2. To flatten the chicken, press down on the backbone until you hear it crack. Cook chicken, salt and ginger in large pot of simmering water for 35-40 minutes or until tender. Cut chicken into 8 pieces.
3. In a large bowl, combine remaining ingredients with chicken. Cover and refrigerate for 1-3 days.
4. To serve, cut chicken into bite-size pieces, and arrange on a platter. Garnish with lettuce and serve cold.

Remarks
- *Since the dish is served cold, it can be prepared a few days ahead.*
- *This dish may be called "Wine Chicken" in some restaurants and cookbooks.*

Fried Five-Spice Chicken

NEW DISCOVERY

If you love the eleven secret spices in Kentucky Fried Chicken, you'll love this. Believe me, it is terrific with a glass of wine or light beer!

1 whole chicken breast,
   approximately ½ pound (225 g)

1 tablespoon (15 ml) cornstarch
4 cups (1 L) oil
lettuce, shredded, for garnish

Marinade:
1 tablespoon (15 ml) wine
½ teaspoon (2 ml) five-spice powder
¼ teaspoon (1 ml) sugar
2 teaspoons (10 ml) soy sauce
½ teaspoon (2 ml) garlic salt
dash of white pepper

1. Debone chicken breast and pound slightly or score the surface of the meat with a knife. Keep the skin intact, if desired.
2. Marinate breast for 30 minutes.
3. Lightly coat breast with cornstarch. Heat oil over medium-high heat (350°F, 180°C). Deep-fry chicken until golden brown, about 4 minutes.
4. To serve, cut chicken into bite-size pieces, and place on top of lettuce.

Remarks
- *Chicken can be prepared ahead and kept warm until time to serve.*
- *If five-spice powder is not available, make your own. Refer to "Chinese Spice and Everything Nice."*
- *For a crispy texture, coat marinated chicken with ½ cup of bread crumbs instead of with cornstarch. Add an extra ½ teaspoon more of five-spice powder as the bread crumbs may mask the flavor.*

Golden Crisp Chicken

A delicately marinated whole chicken—air-dried and deep-fried to perfection. It is more tender, crispier and juicier than you've ever dreamed. A classical choice for Cantonese banquets. If you love Kentucky Fried Chicken, you won't want to miss this one and only finger-licking-good classic Cantonese banquet dish.

1 chicken (3 pounds, 1350 g)
8 cups (2 L) water
1½ tablespoons (22 ml) wine
1 tablespoon (15 ml) salt
3 slices ginger
2 pieces star anise (optional)
4 cups (1 L) oil
fried shrimp-flavor chips (optional)
prepared Szechwan pepper salt

Skin Mixture:
3 tablespoons (45 ml) honey
2 tablespoons (30 ml) vinegar
½ cup (125 ml) hot water

1. Clean and pat-dry chicken. Rub cavity with 1 teaspoon (5 ml) salt; let stand for 1 hour.
2. In a large pot, bring 8 cups water to a boil with wine, remaining salt, ginger and star anise. Add chicken and bring to a second boil. Reduce heat to low, cover and simmer for 50-60 minutes, turning occasionally. Turn heat off; let chicken stand in hot liquid for another 15-20 minutes. Remove, drain well and pat-dry.
3. Combine skin mixture ingredients and brush entire outside surface of chicken with mixture. Tie a string around wings and hang chicken in a well-ventilated place to air-dry for 5-6 hours.
4. Heat 4 cups oil in wok to 350°F (180°C). Carefully dip chicken into wok, basting with hot oil constantly by using a ladle. Deep-fry until skin turns evenly brown and crisp. Turn heat up to 375°F (190°C) for last 3-4 minutes to ensure the browning process. Remove and drain well. (To prevent splattering of oil, have a wok lid on guard.)
5. Cut chicken into bite-size pieces and serve with toasted Szechwan pepper salt. Garnish with fried shrimp-flavor chips.

Remarks

- *If you are entertaining friends, deep-fry chicken in advance. Before serving, deep-fry in hot oil again for a few minutes.*
- *For easier handling, chicken can be cut into two halves, then prepared the same way, but it would be less juicy.*
- *To make toasted Szechwan pepper salt, refer to 'Sassy Sauces' section.*

Heavenly Honeydew Chicken

The sweet and refreshing aroma of honeydew combines with the delicate flavors of chicken in perfect harmony. I was inspired to create this dish by a friend in Los Angeles who runs a restaurant. This is one of my favorite dishes; it is quick, honest and out of this world.

¼ pound (112 g) boneless chicken

Marinade:
¼ teaspoon (1 ml) salt
1 teaspoon (5 ml) wine
¼ teaspoon (1 ml) sugar
1 teaspoon (5 ml) beaten egg white
1 teaspoon (5 ml) cornstarch

1 medium-size firm, ripe honeydew
2 cups (500 ml) shredded lettuce
1 cup (250 ml) finely shredded or
   grated carrot
1½ tablespoons (22 ml) oil
1 slice ginger, chopped
2 teaspoons (10 ml) lemon juice
¾ teaspoon (3 ml) sugar
3 tablespoons (45 ml) water
½ teaspoon (2 ml) cornstarch solution

1. Cut chicken into small, bite-size cubes (¾", 2 cm) and marinate for 1 hour.
2. Peel the honeydew and cut it in half, lengthwise. Remove seeds and carve out the center of one half, forming a ½" (1.5 cm) thick bowl. Place this half on a plate decorated with the shredded lettuce and shredded carrot. From the remaining half, cut 1 cup of ¾" (2 cm) cubes.
3. Heat the oil in a wok over high heat. Put in the ginger, and stir-fry for 10 seconds. Add the chicken and stir-fry for 1½-2 minutes.
4. Add honeydew cubes and stir for 30 seconds. Add the remaining ingredients, except the cornstarch solution. Mix well, then thicken with cornstarch solution.
5. To serve, transfer the chicken and honeydew into the prepared honeydew half and serve hot.

Remarks
- *Cantaloupe or papaya can be used as a substitute for the honeydew.*
- *Carve wedges around top edge of honeydew for a special garnish.*
- *Eat the whole thing — melon, lettuce and all.*
- *If you have more people to serve — double the recipe and use two melons.*

Hot and Spicy Chicken

A typical Szechwan dish — harmonious blends of spices and enticing pungency. The spiciness is sure to stimulate everyone's taste buds. A great dish for a chilly winter's day — sure to chase away the grey clouds!

6 ounces (168 g) boneless chicken,
   cut into ½" (1.5 cm) cubes

Marinade:
½ tablespoon (7 ml) soy sauce
1 teaspoon (5 ml) wine
¼ teaspoon (1 ml) salt
¼ teaspoon (1 ml) oil
1 teaspoon (5 ml) cornstarch

Hot Sauce:
½ tablespoon (7 ml) wine
¼ teaspoon (1 ml) sesame oil
1 teaspoon (5 ml) soy sauce
½ teaspoon (2 ml) sugar
¼ teaspoon (1 ml) chili oil
¼ cup (60 ml) soup stock
1 teaspoon (5 ml) hoisin sauce
   (optional)
½ teaspoon (2 ml) salt
¼ teaspoon (1 ml) white pepper

2 tablespoons (30 ml) oil
2 slices ginger, slivered
2 cloves garlic, chopped
2 dry red chili peppers, cut in half
½ cup (125 ml) ½" (1.5 cm) cubed
   bamboo shoots
½ cucumber, cut into ½" (1.5 cm)
   cubes
1 bell pepper, cut into ½" (1.5 cm)
   pieces
1 teaspoon (5 ml) cornstarch solution

1. Marinate chicken for 30 minutes.
2. Combine ingredients for hot sauce and reserve.
3. Heat oil in wok over high heat. Add ginger, garlic and peppers; stir for 15 seconds. Add marinated chicken and stir-fry for 1½ minutes. Remove chicken.
4. Add vegetables; stir for 30 seconds. Pour in sauce mixture. Mix well with continuous stirring for 1 minute. Return chicken to wok and thicken with cornstarch solution.

Remarks
* *To make this dish unbelievably hot, first chop the dry red peppers and cook with oil and ginger, then proceed with the recipe. It will burn your tongue! Adjust to your own taste.*

Hot Pot Lemon Chicken CANTON

Lemon chicken is a delectable way to serve chicken with a different twist. The savory sauce delights anyone who loves lemon and gives the dish a snap of freshness!!

Sauce:
1 tablespoon (15 ml) wine
1 tablespoon (15 ml) brown sugar
1 teaspoon (5 ml) oyster-flavored
    sauce (optional)
dash of sesame oil
¼ cup (60 ml) soup stock
1½ teaspoons (7 ml) salt
1½ teaspoons (7 ml) cornstarch
    solution

2 tablespoons (30 ml) oil
2-3 slices ginger
1 whole chicken (with bones), cut
    into bite-size pieces
1 large or 1½ medium-size lemons,
    sliced and seeded
2 stalks green onion, cut into 1½"
    (4 cm) pieces

1. Combine sauce ingredients and set aside.
2. Heat wok or frying pan with oil and ginger over high heat. Add chicken, stirring continuously for 1½-2 minutes.
3. Add lemon, green onion, and sauce. Stir for another 1½-2 minutes.
4. Transfer mixture to a clay pot (if available) or a saucepan. Cover and simmer on low heat for 15-18 minutes. Thicken remaining liquid with cornstarch solution if desired.

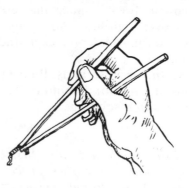

Jeweled Chicken

The contrasting colors of chicken and ham, combined with shiny green vegetables, make this dish a perfect choice for banquets. It has a supreme flavor combination and eye appeal.

12 ounces (340 g) chicken breast,
    lightly pounded on thicker end
½ teaspoon (2 ml) salt
1 cup (250 ml) broccoli flowerets
½ teaspoon (2 ml) oil
2 cups (500 ml) water
8 ounces (225 g) cooked Virginia ham,
    1"x2" (2.5 cm x 5 cm) pieces

Sauce:
1¼ cups (310 ml) soup stock
1 teaspoon (5 ml) salt
2 teaspoons (10 ml) sugar
1 teaspoon (5 ml) oil
2 slices ginger, slivered
1 stalk green onion, slivered
2 teaspoons (10 ml) cornstarch solution

1. Sprinkle ½ teaspoon salt over chicken breast. Steam over medium-high heat for 13-15 minutes. Remove and cut into ¼" x 1" x 2" (0.5 cm x 2.5 cm x 5 cm) pieces. Keep warm.
2. Bring 2 cups water to a boil with ½ teaspoon oil. Blanch broccoli for 3 minutes. Drain well and arrange around edges of serving platter.
3. Bring sauce ingredients to a boil in a saucepan until thickened. Arrange chicken and ham alternately with blanched broccoli around them on a platter. Pour sauce over and serve hot.

Remarks
- *Traditionally whole chicken is used in this recipe. When served, it is cut up and arranged as a whole chicken. This recipe is a simplified version of the original one, but it tastes just as good.*

Moo Goo Gai Pan

The intriguing combination of flavors and textures make this dish distinctively superb. Easy to prepare, nutritious and rich with flavor, it's one of the most popular dishes in any Chinese menu.

3 tablespoons (45 ml) oil
6 ounces (168 g) boneless chicken
    breast, skinned and sliced into
    ¼" x 1" x 2" (0.75 x 2.5 x 5 cm)
    pieces
3 slices ginger, slivered
¾ cup (200 ml) soup stock
4-6 dried black mushrooms,
    soaked (optional)
10-12 fresh snow peas (optional)
1 cup (250 ml) fresh mushrooms

¼ cup (60 ml) canned button
    mushrooms (optional)
2 green onions, white part only, cut
    into 1" (3 cm) pieces
1 tablespoon (15 ml) dark soy sauce
1 tablespoon (15 ml) oyster-flavored
    sauce (optional)
1½ teaspoons (7 ml) wine
1½ teaspoons (7 ml) cornstarch
    solution

1. Heat oil in wok over high heat; add chicken and ginger. Cook for 2 minutes, stirring continuously. Remove and set aside.
2. Add stock and black mushrooms to wok, cover and cook over medium-high heat for 2-3 minutes. Add snow peas, fresh and canned mushrooms, and onions; cook for another 1½ minutes.
3. Return chicken to wok. Add soy sauce, oyster-flavored sauce and wine. Thicken with cornstarch solution and serve hot.

Remarks
- *For added flavor, marinate chicken for 30 minutes in your favorite chicken marinade.*
- *Oyster-flavored sauce is optional but it gives a fantastic flavor to the dish. Keep a bottle handy in your refrigerator.*

Peking Duck

Peking duck is probably one of the best known dishes in Chinese banquets in North America. Its reputation rests on the combination of natural flavor, the glazed, crackling skin, and the juicy, tender meat. At first glance, it appears complicated and troublesome to prepare this sensational century-old dish. In reality, it is quite simple.

1 duck (with neck intact), about 5
    pounds (2250 g)
2 tablespoons (30 ml) red wine
    vinegar
3 tablespoons (45 ml) honey or
    malt sugar
1 cup (250 ml) boiling water
14-16 Mandarin pancakes, steamed
½ cucumber, peeled and shredded
6-8 stalks green onion, shredded

Sauce:
2 tablespoons (30 ml) hoisin sauce
1½ teaspoons (7 ml) sugar
1 teaspoon (5 ml) sesame oil

1. ***To prepare duck:*** Cut off wing tips, wash and pat entire duck dry. Remove and discard any excess visible fat around tail cavity. Close tail cavity tightly with a metal skewer (as illustrated). Then pinch and pull the skin to loosen it from duck meat. To inflate duck, use a clean bicycle or ball pump, blowing air through the skin opening around the neck. Tie opening with a string to trap the air just blown in. Bring 10-12 cups (2½-3L) water to a boil and dip entire duck into boiling water, using a ladle to pour water over entire duck for approximately 3-4 minutes. Pat dry. Hang duck to dry for 5-6 hours in a drafty or well-ventilated place (beyond reach of any big or small innocent animals, including your beloved doggie—it can be very tempting!) In a saucepan, combine vinegar, honey and 1 cup water; bring to a boil. Brush mixture evenly over air-dried duck. Hang duck to dry for an additional 4 hours, until skin looks light brown and dry. (You can prepare this a day ahead)

2. ***To roast duck:*** Preheat oven to 400° F (200° C); place duck on a rack in a roasting pan, lined with aluminum foil (the higher the rack from the bottom of the pan, the better). Roast duck, breast side up, for 20 minutes. Turn over (breast side down); reduce heat to 350° F (180° C) and cook for 30 minutes. Roast duck for another 30 minutes, turning duck a couple of times. Increase heat to 375° F (190° C); continue to roast duck for 15 minutes, turning occasionally. (Remove oil from roasting pan, if too much accumulates while cooking duck).

3. In a saucepan, combine sauce ingredients and bring to a boil. Transfer to a saucer and set aside.
4. Arrange pancakes, shredded cucumber and green onion on small plates; set aside.
5. *To serve:* Carve off skin with a thin layer of meat; arrange on a large serving platter. Let your guests help themselves by spreading ½ teaspoon (2 ml) sauce on the steamy pancake, then add a few pieces of cucumber, shredded green onion and 1-2 pieces of duck. Roll into a cylinder and eat with fingers.

Remarks
- *Traditionally, leftover duck meat will be hand-shredded and stir-fried with bamboo shoot, cabbage and black mushrooms, as a second dish.*
- *The duck carcass can be used to prepare a soup which is served after all the skin and pancakes are gone!!*
- *To prepare Mandarin pancakes, follow instructions on pages 244-245 in THE YAN CAN COOK BOOK.*

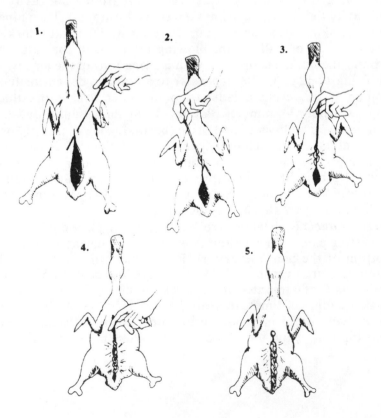

Pie-Pa Duck (Cantonese Roast Duck)

This is a very Cantonese way to prepare a duck—opened on breast side, flattened, then barbecued. It is named after a Chinese musical instrument which is flat and is called "Pie-Pa".

1 fresh frozen duck (4-5 lbs, 2000 g), washed and dried
1½ teaspoons (7 ml) salt

Skin Treatment Mixture:
1 cup (250 ml) hot water
2½ tablespoons (37 ml) red wine vinegar
3 tablespoons (45 ml) honey
1 tablespoon (15 ml) wine

Basting Sauce:
1 tablespoon (15 ml) brown bean paste
2 teaspoons (10 ml) hoisin sauce
2 teaspoons (10 ml) sesame paste or oil
2 teaspoons (10 ml) wine
1 teaspoon (5 ml) sugar
1 clove garlic, crushed
2 teaspoons (10 ml) soy sauce

1. Remove excess fat from duck (around opening). Sprinkle 1½ teaspoons salt over entire cavity of duck; let stand for 1-2 hours.
2. In one of the largest pots you can find, bring about 8 cups (2 L) of water to a vigorous boil; put the entire duck into water and parboil for 2 minutes, turning frequently. Hang and air-dry duck in a well-ventilated area for 5 hours or place in refrigerator overnight, without covering.
3. Cut open duck from breast side; press duck to flatten with palm. Brush skin with skin treatment mixture; air-dry for 4 hours.
4. Coat cavity of duck with basting sauce mixture; let stand for 30 minutes. Roast in a preheated oven at 400° F (200° C) on a rack, over a pan of water. Roast for 20 minutes, skin side up. Turn duck over, reduce heat to 350° F (180° C) and roast for 25 minutes. Continue to roast duck at 350° F by turning it on both sides occasionally for another 30 minutes. Broil duck, skin side up, for 1½ minutes (watch out—it browns easily!)
5. To serve, cut duck into bite-size pieces. Arrange on a platter, in the shape of the original pressed duck. Serve hot or cold.

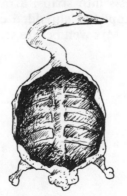

Pon-Pon Chicken

It's a funny name for a not-so-funny dish. This is a spicy and appetizing cold meat plate, easy to prepare and easy to serve. It originated in the Lo Shan area of Szechwan. Pon-Pon refers to the noise generated when a stick is used to pound the meat to tenderize it. The chicken available in North America need not be pounded.

Dressing:

2 teaspoons (10 ml) chopped green
   onion
1 teaspoon (5 ml) chopped garlic
¾ teaspoon (3 ml) toasted
   Szechwan peppercorn
1½ tablespoons (22 ml) sesame paste
   or sesame oil
1 teaspoon (5 ml) hot chili oil
¼ teaspoon (1 ml) salt
2 teaspoons (10 ml) soy sauce
1 teaspoon (5 ml) sugar
1 tablespoon (15 ml) white vinegar
1½ tablespoons (22 ml) oil
½ teaspoon (2 ml) cornstarch
   solution

1 deboned chicken breast, 8 ounces
   (225 g)
2 cucumbers
¼ teaspoon (1 ml) salt
10 bean thread sheets (optional)

1. Combine dressing ingredients except cornstarch solution in a saucepan. Bring to a slow boil, stirring constantly. Add stock or water, if needed. Thicken with cornstarch solution. Transfer dressing to a container and store in refrigerator until needed.
2. Bring a pot of water or soup stock to a boil over high heat. Add the chicken and reduce heat to medium-low. Simmer 12-15 minutes or until done. Remove and let cool. Shred or cut chicken into matchstick-size strips. Set aside.
3. Wash and peel cucumbers; cut into matchstick strips. Toss with salt; mix well and set aside.
4. Cut bean thread sheets into strips; arrange on a platter and place cucumber strips on top. Put shredded chicken over cucumber and pour dressing on top. Mix well before serving.

Pretty Poached Poultry

This is perhaps the most popular and authentic way to serve chicken in Southern China. Simple and down-to-earth, you can serve it hot or cold.

1 whole chicken, approximately 3-3¼ pounds (1462 g)
10 cups (2½ L) water
2 whole star anise
1½ tablespoons (22 ml) salt
2 teaspoons (10 ml) used oil

Chicken Dip A:
1 tablespoon (15 ml) oyster-flavored sauce
5 tablespoons (75 ml) soup stock
1 teaspoon (5 ml) dark soy sauce
½ teaspoon (2 ml) sugar
¾ teaspoon (3 ml) cornstarch solution

Chicken Dip B:
3 tablespoons (45 ml) hot oil
1 stalk green onion, finely shredded
2 tablespoons (30 ml) fresh ginger, finely shredded
½ teaspoon (2 ml) salt

Chicken Dip C:
3 tablespoons (45 ml) hot oil
2 tablespoons (30 ml) chopped green onion
½ teaspoon (2 ml) salt

1. Clean chicken, remove and discard all fat.
2. In a large pot, bring water to a boil; add star anise and salt. Slowly lower chicken into pot, turning once or twice. When water comes to a boil again, let stand for 5-10 seconds. Remove immediately and cool with running tap water for 2 minutes.
3. When water boils again, go through same boiling and cooling process. Repeat process 4 or 5 times.
4. At the end of the fifth time, bring water to a boil again, turn heat to medium-low, and let chicken cook for 20 minutes. Turn frequently. Turn off heat; let chicken stand in hot water, covered, for another 10 minutes, turning occasionally.
5. Remove chicken and cool under running tap water again until completely cooled off. Dry chicken, then rub with 2 teaspoons used oil. Set aside.
6. A. ***To make Chicken dip A***: Combine all ingredients for dip A in a saucepan; bring to a boil and cook until thickened. Keep warm until ready to serve.
   B. ***To make Chicken dips B and C***: Mix together ingredients for dips B and C respectively; set aside until ready to serve.
7. To serve, cut chicken into bite-size pieces (approximately 1" x 2½", 2.5 cm x 6.25 cm, bones included) and serve with your choice of dips, A, B, or C.

Remarks
- *The repeated short cooking and cooling process helps to prevent the skin from breaking and firms up the texture of the skin and meat.*
- *To tell whether the chicken is done, poke a chopstick through the thigh and if bloody red juice comes out, it is NOT done. Cooking time will depend on the size of the chicken, the amount of water and the original temperature of the chicken.*

Sassy Sauce Chicken

This is a popular, traditional Cantonese dish. The whole chicken is prepared in a scrumptious soy sauce mixture which can be repeatedly used for months. It's easy to make in advance and can be served hot or cold; it's great for anyone who is too busy to cook every night.

1 chicken (3 pounds, 1350 g)
1½ teaspoons (7 ml) salt
1 tablespoon (15 ml) rendered
    chicken fat (optional)
1 tablespoon (15 ml) sesame oil
    (used last)

Sauce Mixture:
1½ cups (370 ml) dark soy sauce
3 cups (750 ml) water
¾ cup (200 ml) brown sugar
¼ cup (60 ml) wine
2 stalks green onion
1-2 whole star anise (optional)
1 small stick cinnamon (optional)

1. Wash and pat-dry chicken; rub chicken cavity with salt.
2. Combine sauce mixture in a wok or a large pot; bring to boil. Add chicken, breast side down, and bring to a boil again. Reduce to low heat; cook, uncovered, for 5-6 minutes.
3. Turn chicken to another side, a quarter turn, and cook for 5-6 minutes. Repeat this until all sides have been evenly cooked, for a total of 20-25 minutes. Then put in chicken fat, cover and simmer for 35-40 minutes; turn occasionally. Turn off heat and let chicken stand in liquid for an additional 15-20 minutes, turning occasionally.
4. Remove chicken and brush with sesame oil. Let cool and cut into bite-size morsels. Serve hot or cold.

Remarks
- *The cooking medium can be kept in the refrigerator and reused again several times. If it becomes a bit too salty, dilute with extra water.*
- *Cooking time of chicken varies according to size of fowl.*

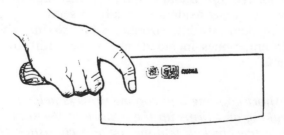

Sea and Sky

Chicken wings are inexpensive and versatile. You can create a great variety of appetizers and entrees with a little imagination and a few wings. This dish can be easily prepared ahead. It is great food for nibblers!

2 tablespoons (30 ml) oil
3-4 slices ginger
12 chicken wings
2 stalks green onion, cut into
    1" (2.5 cm) pieces
1 tablespoon (15 ml) dark soy sauce
1 tablespoon (15 ml) wine

2 tablespoons (30 ml) oyster-flavored
    sauce
¼ cup (60 ml) soup stock
¾ teaspoon (3 ml) sugar
1 whole star anise (optional)
1 teaspoon (5 ml) cornstarch solution

1. Heat wok with oil and ginger over high heat. Add wings and stir-fry for 1½ minutes until brown, turning chicken wings constantly to prevent sticking.
2. Add remaining ingredients except cornstarch solution; reduce heat to low, cover and simmer for 10-12 minutes. Stir several times to prevent sticking. Thicken with cornstarch solution.
3. Arrange on a platter. Serve hot or cold.

Remarks
- *Wing tips may be cut off of chicken wings. Save them for soup stock.*

Spicy Szechwan Chicken

If you are tired of chicken, try this spicy variation. It will change your mind and be a treat for your taste buds. The special seasonings and luscious green broccoli make an excellent combination.

2 cups (500 ml) broccoli flowerets
½ teaspoon (2 ml) salt
2½ tablespoons (37 ml) oil
1 clove garlic, minced
4 slices ginger, slivered
¾ pound (340 g) boneless chicken,
   cut into bite-size pieces
¼ teaspoon (1 ml) toasted, ground
   Szechwan pepper (optional)

2 stalks green onion, cut into 1"
   (2.5 cm) lengths
1 tablespoon (15 ml) wine
1 tablespoon (15 ml) soy sauce
¾ teaspoon (3 ml) sugar
¾ teaspoon (3 ml) sesame oil
2 teaspoons (10 ml) hot bean paste
   or chili sauce
2-4 tablespoons (30-60 ml) soup stock
½ teaspoon (2 ml) cornstarch solution

1. Blanch broccoli in boiling water with ½ teaspoon (2 ml) salt and ½ teaspoon (2 ml) oil for 2-3 minutes. Remove and set aside.
2. Heat wok with 2 tablespoons (30 ml) oil, garlic and ginger over high heat for 10-15 seconds. Add chicken, stirring for 2-2½ minutes.
3. Add remaining ingredients except broccoli and cornstarch solution, and stir for 1 minute. Thicken with cornstarch solution and place in the center of a platter.
4. Garnish the chicken with the blanched broccoli and serve immediately.

Remarks
- *Traditionally, the Chinese hot bean paste (Dao Ban Jiang) is used in this dish. If you cannot find it at your local Chinese grocery, substitute regular chili sauce.*

Stuffed Chicken Breast

This is a Taiwanese dish that was adopted by the Cantonese.

1 whole chicken breast, boned and
   cut into two, 1/8" (0.35 cm) slices
2 tablespoons (30 ml) cornstarch
4 cups (1 L) oil
Tomato slices (for garnish)

Chicken Marinade:
1 teaspoon (5 ml) wine
¾ teaspoon (3 ml) garlic salt
½ teaspoon (2 ml) ginger juice
½ egg white, lightly beaten
dash of white pepper
dash of sesame oil

Stuffing Mixture:
3 ounces (84 g) fresh or frozen
   shrimp, minced
2 water chestnuts, finely chopped
2 tablespoons (30 ml) carrot,
   finely chopped or grated
2 dried black mushrooms, soaked
   and finely chopped
¼ teaspoon (1 ml) salt
¼ teaspoon (1 ml) sugar
¼ teaspoon (1 ml) wine

1. Marinate chicken breast for 30 minutes.
2. Combine all ingredients for stuffing in a bowl, blend well and set aside.
3. To stuff: slightly pound chicken breast to flatten and dust each half with 1 tablespoon cornstarch. Spread stuffing mixture $1/3$" (1 cm) thick on one side of the chicken.
4. Heat oil in wok over medium-high heat (350°F, 180°C). Deep-fry chicken breast, stuffed side down, for about 1 minute or until golden brown. Turn and cook 1½ minutes more or until golden brown. Remove and drain well.
5. To serve, slice browned breast into bite-size pieces and garnish with tomato slices.

Remarks
- *This dish can be prepared ahead of time and kept in the refrigerator or freezer. Refry over medium-high heat for 1-2 minutes to serve.*
- *Sweet and sour sauce is a good complement to this dish.*
- *Place stuffing mixture in a blender or a food processor to get a nice smooth paste.*

Succulent Steamed Chicken

The pleasing flavor of this dish is just perfect for your next celebration. Cooking in its own natural juices makes this dish seductively succulent, light and nutritious. Excellent for a one dish meal — just serve it over rice and savour.

¾ pound (340 g) boneless chicken,
   cut into bite-size chunks
6 dried black mushrooms, soaked
   and halved
1 stalk green onion, cut into 1"
   (2.5 cm) pieces
1 Chinese sausage, sliced (optional)
2½ teaspoons (12 ml) oil

2 teaspoons (10 ml) shredded ginger
2 teaspoons (10 ml) wine
2 tablespoons (30 ml) dark soy sauce
¼ teaspoon (1 ml) salt
½ teaspoon (2 ml) sesame oil
½ teaspoon (2 ml) sugar
1 tablespoon (15 ml) cornstarch

1. Place all ingredients in a mixing bowl; mix well.
2. Spread mixture evenly in a shallow pie pan. Steam over high heat for 12-15 minutes or until chicken is tender.

Remarks
- *For faster steaming, spread chicken in a thin layer over pan.*
- *Chicken can be prepared ahead of time and reheated just before serving.*
- *Keep skin on chicken as it gives the dish a nice texture.*

Sweet and Sour Drummettes CANTON

The aroma of these drumsticks is enough to make your mouth water, and after tasting it you'll never touch ground again! An excellent choice as an appetizer as well as for the dinner menu: attractive, appetizing and very appealing. The cooking time is minimal and preparation can be done ahead of time.

12 chicken wing drummettes

Marinade:
½ teaspoon (2 ml) salt
1 teaspoon (5 ml) soy sauce
½ teaspoon (2 ml) ginger juice
1 teaspoon (5 ml) wine

½ cup (125 ml) cornstarch for dry coating
4 cups (1 L) oil

Batter Mix:
1 cup (250 ml) flour
¾ cup plus 2 tablespoons (230 ml) flat beer
½ teaspoon (2 ml) baking powder
¼ teaspoon (1 ml) oil
dash of salt
dash of sugar

Sweet and Sour Sauce:
5 tablespoons (75 ml) white vinegar
¼ cup (60 ml) water
¼ cup (60 ml) packed brown sugar
2 tablespoons (30 ml) pineapple juice
1 tablespoon (15 ml) cornstarch solution
6-8 drops red food color (optional)

1. Marinate chicken drummettes for 20 minutes. Dry coat wings and set aside.
2. In a large bowl, blend batter ingredients until smooth; set aside.
3. Combine all sweet and sour sauce ingredients except cornstarch solution in a saucepan. Bring to a boil and thicken with cornstarch solution. Keep warm.
4. Heat oil over medium-high heat (350° F-375° F, 180° C-190° C), then dip drummettes in batter and deep-fry in hot oil until golden brown. Drain well and set aside.
5. Arrange drummettes on a large platter and serve with sweet and sour sauce. Garnish with pineapple rings and orange wedges, if desired.

Remarks
- *Refer to illustrations on how to prepare drummettes for cooking.*
- *Sweet and sour sauce can be cooked ahead of time and rewarmed over low heat in a covered pan.*

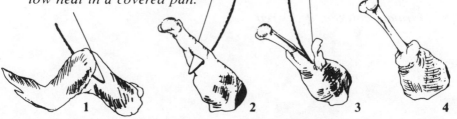

Tender Chicken in a Nest

A classical choice for a formal dinner party or special celebration. Tender pieces of chicken nestled in a nest of potato. It's sure to make you a bird lover.

Bird's Nest: (prepare ahead)
1 potato
½ teaspoon (2 ml) cornstarch
_____

4 cups (1 L) oil
1 clove garlic, minced
2 slices ginger, finely shredded
6 ounces (168 g) boneless chicken
    breast, cut into thin strips
½ celery stalk, cut diagonally into
    ¼″ (0.75 cm) slices

¹/₃ cup (80 ml) sliced carrot
¼ cup (60 ml) sliced bamboo shoots
½ teaspoon (2 ml) salt
½ teaspoon (2 ml) sugar
¼ cup (60 ml) soup stock
½ teaspoon (2 ml) cornstarch solution
¼ cup (60 ml) roasted cashew nuts
    (optional)
1 teaspoon (5 ml) wine

1. *To make Bird's Nest:*
   Peel and shred potato into 2″-2½″ (6 cm x 7.5 cm) julienne strips. Toss with cornstarch. Lay potato strips in a thin layer inside a long-handled stainless steel strainer. Top with another smaller strainer. Heat oil in wok over medium-high (350°F, 180°C) heat. Slowly lower strainers into hot oil, pressing strainers together. Deep-fry until golden brown. Remove to a platter. Now you have a nest! Tap handle of strainer lightly against edge of counter to loosen nest, if it sticks.
2. Heat wok with 2 tablespoons oil, garlic and ginger over high heat. Add chicken and stir-fry for 1½ minutes. Stir in celery, carrot, bamboo shoots, salt, sugar and soup stock. Mix well. Cover and cook for 1 minute.
3. Thicken with cornstarch solution. Add cashews and wine. Place mixture inside the potato nest. Garnish with lettuce or whatever is available.

Remarks
- *Potato bird's nest can be prepared in advance and kept in a dry, cool place for a couple of days. You may have to experiment with a few to get a perfect nest.*
- *Any meat and vegetables combination can be stir-fried and put in the nest. One very popular Cantonese dish is stir-fried shrimp with vegetables.*
- *Marinate chicken, if desired.*

Three Cups Chicken
SZECHWAN

Ready, set, go! Not only will this dish help you win the rat race after a long day at work, it is fun to prepare as well. Convenient and delicious, it's an excellent choice for those who need more than 24 hours in a day!

2 tablespoons (30 ml) oil	3 tablespoons (45 ml) brown sugar
2 cloves garlic, chopped	4 slices ginger
6 chicken thighs	1 clove garlic, sliced
1¼ cup (310 ml) soup stock	1 stalk green onion, cut into 1½″
1 cup (250 ml) wine	(4 cm) pieces
1 cup (250 ml) dark soy sauce	1 whole star anise (optional)
1 teaspoon (5 ml) sesame oil	1½ teaspoons (7 ml) cornstarch solution

1. Heat wok with oil and chopped garlic over medium-high heat. Brown chicken thighs 2-3 minutes, turning to brown evenly. Set aside.
2. In a large saucepan, combine 1 cup of soup stock and remaining ingredients, except cornstarch solution; bring to a boil. Add chicken. Reduce heat to low, cover and simmer for 40 minutes or longer if you are out shopping.
3. Place cooked chicken on a platter. Combine ¼ cup of the sauce with remaining ¼ cup of soup stock and thicken with cornstarch solution. Pour over chicken.

Remarks
- *Chicken wings, drumsticks or a whole cut-up chicken can be substituted for thighs.*
- *This dish can be served hot or cold. Reheating does not affect the quality.*
- *Leftover sauce can be refrigerated and used as a dip for other chicken dishes.*
- *This is a good choice for a dinner party, which may be prepared ahead of time.*

Beefing Ewe Up

Don't be a cow-ard. Just get moo-ving and steak out a few of these recipes. For the Chinese, though, beef is not common in their daily diet and certainly not as widely consumed as chicken or pork. It was believed that Confucius was greatly disturbed to hear the sound of the slaughter of the farmer's best companion (actually, the water buffalo, which was used as a 'work-horse' by peasants). Confucius felt that the people should be kind and merciful and spare the poor buffalo after his life-long loyalty. And later, the introduction of Buddhism reinforced the sacred status of the water buffalo.

However, that has all changed—especially for the Chinese in North America, and many new recipes combine beef with vegetables to produce a scrumptious dish. The secret of Chinese beef cookery is to marinate the meat with seasonings prior to cooking to seal in the juices and to increase flavor. When marinated, the beef becomes more tender, so less expensive cuts can be used to give satisfying results. Flank steak is often the preferred type of beef for use in most Chinese stir-fried dishes. It is lean, and since all of the fibers run the same way, it is easy to cut across the grain, producing tender morsels. This process is made easier by cutting the slices when the meat is partially frozen. As for other cuts of meat, veal is too expensive and relatively bland for Chinese tastes, but sirloin, chuck, tenderloin and round steak are possible choices. Little lambs are usually safe because of their strong aroma. Although rarely used, lamb does find its way into some dishes when masked by braising with plenty of powerful scallions and other pungent ingredients. On the other hand, you will find finely sliced mutton in Mongolian hot pots and barbeques. When Mongols are around, the little lambs are never safe!

Ewe can beef up your experiences by cooking with beef and lamb. Come on now, don't be an old goat about it!

A Measure of Beans

A new way to measure things — use your bean! Yard long beans are an unusual vegetable. They look like green leather whips when raw, but they become crisp and tasty after cooking. This is a quick and sensational meal for you and your family.

6 ounces (168 g) yard long beans
6 ounces (168 g) beef flank steak

Marinade:
1 teaspoon (5 ml) soy sauce
1 teaspoon (5 ml) wine
1½ teaspoons (7 ml) cornstarch
¼ teaspoon (1 ml) sesame oil

2 tablespoons (30 ml) oil
2 slices ginger, shredded
1 tablespoon (15 ml) soy sauce
½ teaspoon (2 ml) sugar
¼ teaspoon (1 ml) salt
½ cup (125 ml) soup stock
1¼ teaspoons (6 ml) cornstarch solution
1 teaspoon (5 ml) wine

1. Wash the yard long beans and cut them into 3″ (7.5 cm) pieces.
2. Cut the flank steak into 1″ x 2″ (2.5 cm x 5 cm) thin slices and marinate for 30 minutes.
3. Heat the wok over high heat. Add the oil and the ginger and sauté for 10 seconds. Add the beef and stir-fry for 1-1½ minutes. Remove the beef from the wok and set aside.
4. Add the yard long bean pieces and the remaining ingredients, except cornstarch solution and wine, to the wok. Cover and cook over medium-high heat for 3½-4 minutes.
5. Return the beef to the wok and thicken with cornstarch solution. Drizzle in the wine and remove wok from heat.

Remarks
- *Yard long beans are only available seasonally in Chinese food stores. If you can't find this exotic vegetable, substitute another exotic Chinese vegetable: snow peas. When using snow peas, reduce the cooking time to 2-2½ minutes.*

Ants Climbing Up the Tree

SZECHWAN

Stir-fried ground beef, served over cellophane noodles has an exotic symbolic Chinese name. Simple, yet nutritious — it's a good choice for lunch.

½ pound (225 g) lean ground beef

Marinade:
2 teaspoons (10 ml) soy sauce
1 teaspoon (5 ml) oil
1 teaspoon (5 ml) wine
1 teaspoon (5 ml) cornstarch
dash of white pepper

2 ounces (56 g) cellophane noodles
4 cups (1 L) oil
1-2 dried red chili peppers, crushed
2 stalks green onion, chopped
¾ cup (200 ml) soup stock
1 teaspoon (5 ml) sesame oil
1½ teaspoon (7 ml) soy sauce
½ teaspoons (2 ml) garlic salt
¾ teaspoon (3 ml) sugar
½ teaspoon (2 ml) hot bean paste
or chili sauce

1. Marinate ground beef for 15-20 minutes.
2. Separate cellophane noodles inside a plastic bag. Deep-fry over high heat a few seconds or until puffed. Remove, drain and set aside.
3. Heat 1 tablespoon oil over high heat. Add red chili peppers and green onion. Stir-fry for 15 seconds over high heat. Add marinated ground beef and stir-fry for 1½ minutes.
4. Add remaining ingredients and fried cellophane noodles, mix well and simmer for 1½-2 minutes over low heat. Serve hot.

Remarks
* *Cellophane noodles absorb a great deal of liquid. Be sure to have some extra stock on hand.*
* *Cellophane noodles are long, elastic and hard to break. Crumble them inside a plastic bag so they don't fly all over your living room and backyard!*
* *This creation is quite filling and very tasty. It is best served with a light side dish.*

B.B.Q. Beef and Pork Union

This is a unique combination for an indoor or outdoor barbeque. Boy, is it delicious! These tasty tidbits are perfect appetizers at a cocktail party, too. Your guests will certainly come back again!

½ pound (225 g) flank steak, cut
    into 2″ x 3″ x ¼″ (5 cm x
    7.5 cm x .75 cm) slices
½ pound (225 g) pork tenderloin,
    cut into 2″ x 3″ x 1/8″
    (5 cm x 7.5 cm x 0.35 cm) slices
2 stalks green onion, cut into 2″
    (5 cm) long pieces
10-12 bamboo skewers
1 teaspoon (5 ml) oil
1 teaspoon (5 ml) sesame oil

B.B.Q. Braising Sauce:
1½ tablespoons (22 ml) hoisin sauce
1 tablespoon (15 ml) catsup
¼ teaspoon (1 ml) five-spice powder
1 tablespoon (15 ml) soy sauce
½ teaspoon (2 ml) salt
¾ teaspoon (3 ml) sugar
½ teaspoon (2 ml) sesame oil
1 teaspoon (5 ml) Worcestershire sauce
dash of ginger juice
dash of garlic juice
2 tablespoons (30 ml) oil

1. Marinate beef and pork separately with B.B.Q. sauce for 30 minutes.
2. Alternate beef and pork slices with green onion pieces on bamboo skewers. Brush everything with 1 teaspoon oil and sesame oil.
3. Preheat oven to broil. Place skewers on broiler pan and broil for 1½ minutes on each side, basting them with B.B.Q. sauce. Broil for an additional 1½ minutes on each side.

Remarks
- *Slice the pork thinner than the beef for faster cooking.*
- *This dish can be prepared ahead of time and reheated just before serving.*
- *Brush meat with oil if it looks dry during cooking.*

Bean Sprouts and Pepper Beef CANTON

This is a down-to-earth family favorite. It's quick, economical, and refreshing.

6 ounces (168 g) beef, cut into 2″
   (5 cm) thin strips

Marinade:
1 teaspoon (5 ml) soy sauce
1 teaspoon (5 ml) wine
2 teaspoons (10 ml) water
1 teaspoon (5 ml) oil
pinch of white pepper

2 tablespoons (30 ml) oil
2 dried black mushrooms, soaked
   and shredded (optional)
½ bell pepper, cut into 2″ (5 cm)
   thin strips
4 ounces (112 g) bean sprouts
¼ cup (60 ml) bamboo shoots,
   shredded (optional)
¼ teaspoon (1 ml) garlic salt
¼ teaspoon (1 ml) sugar
¼ cup (60 ml) soup stock
1 teaspoon (5 ml) soy sauce
1½ teaspoons (7 ml) cornstarch solution

1. Marinate beef for 30 minutes.
2. Heat wok with oil over high heat. Add beef, stirring for 1-1½ minutes. Remove and drain well. Set aside.
3. Add mushrooms to wok and cook for 30 seconds. Add bell pepper and stir-fry for 30 seconds. Add the bean sprouts and remaining ingredients except cornstarch solution. Mix well, cover and cook for 1 minute.
4. Return cooked beef to wok and mix well. Thicken with cornstarch solution. Serve hot.

Shredding technique

Beef and Broccoli with Oyster Sauce NEW DISCOVERY

North American broccoli is not found in mainland China. Instead, there is Gai Lohn (Chinese kale), also known as Chinese broccoli, yet there is no resemblance in appearance or flavor. The North American broccoli has a mild flavor, fantastic green color and a crunchy texture that goes well with any meat or seasoning. Use it often!

6 ounces (168 g) flank steak, cut
    into ½″ x 2″ (1.5 x 5 cm) slices

Marinade:
1 tablespoon (15 ml) soy sauce
1½ teaspoons (7 ml) wine
1 teaspoon (5 ml) cornstarch

½ pound (225 g) broccoli
2 tablespoons (30 ml) oil
1 slice ginger, minced
1 clove garlic, minced
1 tablespoon (15 ml) oyster-flavored
    sauce
½ teaspoon (2 ml) sugar
¾ cup (200 ml) soup stock or water
1½ teaspoons (7 ml) cornstarch solution

1. Marinate beef for 30 minutes.
2. Trim broccoli and cut into bite-size chunks.
3. Heat wok with oil, ginger and garlic; stir for 10-15 seconds over high heat. Add beef and stir-fry for 1½ minutes. Remove and set aside.
4. Put broccoli in hot wok, stirring for a few seconds. Add oyster sauce, sugar and soup stock. Cover and cook over medium-high heat for 2-2½ minutes.
5. Return beef to wok. Mix well and thicken with cornstarch solution.

Remarks
- *If you wish to shorten the preparation time, blanch the broccoli chunks in boiling water for 2-2½ minutes in advance. Keep in refrigerator until ready to use.*

Beef and Leek

Making ordinary ingredients into something surprising can be fun and challenging. In this dish, the combination of beef, a simple sauce, and a less familiar ingredient, leek, is superb.

½ pound (225 g) flank steak, cut
   into 2″ (5 cm) thin slices

Marinade:
1½ teaspoons (7 ml) wine
½ teaspoon (2 ml) salt
2 teaspoons (10 ml) soy sauce
½ teaspoon (2 ml) sugar

3 tablespoons (45 ml) oil
2-3 stalks leek, cut into 2″ (5 cm)
   pieces
¼ cup (60 ml) soup stock
½ teaspoon (2 ml) cornstarch solution

1. Marinate beef for 30 minutes.
2. Heat wok with 2 tablespoons oil and stir-fry beef over high heat for 1½-2 minutes. Remove and set aside.
3. Stir in leek with remaining tablespoon oil; add soup stock, cover and cook for 1-2 minutes over medium-high heat. Return beef to wok and thicken with cornstarch solution. Serve hot.

Remarks
- *Improvise with ordinary green onions, if leeks are unavailable.*
- *To thoroughly wash dirt from leeks, slice lengthwise and rinse with running water. Discard the hard core.*

Beef and Lobok

This popular family-style dish is quick and refreshing. Lobok, also known as daikon, Chinese white radish or turnip, can be found in most supermarkets and all Chinese stores, when in season. It goes well with beef, pork or ribs, and is good in soups, stews and stir-fried dishes.

6 ounces (168 g) flank steak, cut
    into 1" x 2" (2.5 cm x 5 cm)
    thin slices

Marinade:
1 teaspoon (5 ml) soy sauce
1 teaspoon (5 ml) wine
1 teaspoon (5 ml) cornstarch

¾ pound (340 g) lobok
2 tablespoons (30 ml) oil
2 teaspoons (10 ml) oyster-flavored
    sauce
½ teaspoon (2 ml) sugar
1 teaspoon (5 ml) dark soy sauce
1 cup (250 ml) soup stock
2 stalks green onion, cut into 1½"
    (4 cm) lengths
½ teaspoon (2 ml) cornstarch solution

1. Marinate beef for 30 minutes.
2. Wash and peel lobok. Cut in half and slice into ¼" (0.75 cm) pieces.
3. Heat the oil in a wok over high heat. Add the beef, stirring for 1-1½ minutes. Remove beef and return meat juices to wok. Set beef aside.
4. Add lobok to wok and stir-fry for 30 seconds. Add remaining ingredients, except beef and cornstarch solution; mix well. Cover and cook over medium heat for 12-13 minutes, or until tender.
5. Return the beef to the wok and stir-fry for another 10-15 seconds. Add green onions and thicken with cornstarch solution.

Remarks
* *Pork spareribs can be substituted for the beef. If the pork spareribs are used, cook the ribs with the lobok for 15 minutes over medium heat.*

Beef Liver in Wine Sauce

This exotic dish is rarely served in restaurants. The distinctive texture and aroma of liver is not universally appreciated. Considering current rising food costs, however, liver is a nutritious, low-cost choice. When prepared in a delicate wine sauce, it is delicious.

2½-3 cups (625-750 ml) water
½ pound (225 g) beef liver, cut into
   narrow 2" (5 cm) slices
5-7 slices ginger
2 tablespoons (30 ml) oil
2 cloves garlic, minced
½ onion, cut into bite-size pieces

2 stalks green onion, cut into 1"
   (2.5 cm) pieces
¼ cup (60 ml) wine
1 tablespoon (15 ml) soy sauce
½ teaspoon (2 ml) brown sugar
¾ teaspoon (3 ml) cornstarch solution

1. Bring water to a boil, add liver and 2 slices ginger. Return water to a boil. Remove liver and set aside.
2. Heat oil, garlic and remaining ginger in wok over high heat; stir for 45 seconds. Add onion and green onion; stir-fry for 1 minute.
3. Add liver and stir for another minute. Add wine, soy sauce and sugar and mix well. Thicken with cornstarch solution. Discard ginger slices and serve hot.

Remarks
- *Parboiling liver allows it to cook faster in the wok and prevents scum formation.*
- *With a little bit of alcohol and pungent ginger, liver becomes a great tasting dish.*

Broiled Beef Shish Kabobs

This simple and delicious dish is great for indoors and outdoors. Everybody can participate and cook up a storm.

¾ pound (340 g) beef steak, cut
  into 1″ x 2″ x ¼″ (2.5 cm
  x 5 cm x 0.75 cm) pieces

Marinade:
1½ tablespoons (22 ml) wine
1 tablespoon (15 ml) soy sauce
1 tablespoon (15 ml) water
¼ teaspoon (1 ml) ginger juice
¼ teaspoon (1 ml) sugar
¼ teaspoon (1 ml) sesame oil
1½ teaspoons (7 ml) cornstarch

2 stalks green onion, white part
  only, cut into 1″ (2.5 cm) pieces
12 cherry tomatoes
½ onion, cut into bite-size pieces
6-10 bamboo skewers
lettuce (for garnish)

1. Marinate beef for 4 hours.
2. Place steak, green onion, tomato and onion alternately on the skewers. Brush with marinade.
3. Preheat oven to broil for 3 minutes (or use outdoor BBQ grill). Broil for 2-2½ minutes, turn and broil for an additional 2-2½ minutes on the other side.
4. To serve, place skewers on top of lettuce leaves on a platter.

Remarks
- *For more tender meat, use ½ teaspoon (2 ml) meat tenderizer in the marinade.*
- *Move oven rack closest to the heat to broil.*

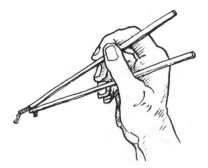

Cantonese Beef Casserole

The stewing of meats is a universal practice — you will find such dishes in every cuisine. Lamb, pork and beef are frequently stewed with spices and soy sauce. When you expect company, prepare this dish ahead to blend the flavors. Reheat and serve when everybody's hungry.

1 pound (450 g) beef brisket
1 tablespoon (15 ml) oil
3 cloves garlic, chopped
4 slices ginger, chopped
1 pound (450 g) fresh Chinese
   turnips, cut into bite-size
   pieces (optional)

Stewing Sauce Mixture:
2 tablespoons (30 ml) wine
2 tablespoons (30 ml) soy sauce
1 tablespoon (15 ml) sugar
2 whole star anise
2 tablespoons (30 ml) oil
dash of black pepper
½ cup (125 ml) beef stock
1 tablespoon (15 ml) hoisin sauce
   (optional)

1. Cover beef with water in a saucepan and bring to a boil. Cook over low heat for 30 minutes. Remove and cut into bite-size chunks.
2. Heat oil, garlic and ginger in wok or saucepan over high heat for 15 seconds. Add boiled beef and stir-fry for a few seconds.
3. Prepare the stewing sauce mixture and add to beef; mix well.
4. Place turnips and beef with sauce in a casserole dish. Cover and bake at 325° F (160° C) for 1½ hours. Serve hot.

Remarks
- *This dish can be reheated anytime without degrading the quality. In fact, it can be reheated several times and tastes better each time.*
- *Fresh Chinese turnip is a long white turnip available in Chinese stores and some supermarkets. The Japanese call it "daikon." The taste and texture is similar to a radish.*
- *If you have a gang of people to feed, double or triple the recipe and keep it in the freezer.*
- *Leftover sauce is sensational over rice or noodles.*

Cellophane Noodles
with Peppered Beef

This unique dish is economical and simple to prepare. Cellophane noodles make it very filling, so accompany it with light dishes. It is similar to "Ants Climbing up the Tree" except the cellophane noodles are not deep-fried.

½ pound (225 g) ground beef

Marinade:
2 teaspoons (10 ml) soy sauce
1 teaspoon (5 ml) oil
1 teaspoon (5 ml) wine
1 teaspoon (5 ml) cornstarch
dash of white pepper

4 ounces (112 g) cellophane noodles
2 tablespoons (30 ml) oil
2 slices ginger, shredded
2 stalks green onions, chopped
1-2 dried red peppers, crushed
1½ cups (370 ml) soup stock
1 teaspoon (5 ml) sesame oil
1 tablespoon (15 ml) soy sauce
1 teaspoon (5 ml) sugar
½ teaspoon (2 ml) salt

1. Marinate ground beef for 30 minutes.
2. Soak cellophane noodles in warm water for 15-20 minutes. Remove and cut into 4-5″ (10-12.5 cm) lengths.
3. Heat oil in wok over medium-high heat. Add ginger, green onions and red pepper. Stir for 15 seconds. Add ground beef and stir for 1½ minutes.
4. Add soaked cellophane noodles; stir for 30 seconds. Put in remaining ingredients and mix well. Reduce heat to low. Cover and simmer for 5 minutes. Stir several times while cooking. Add extra soup stock if mixture gets too dry. Serve hot.

Remarks
• *Cellophane noodles absorb a tremendous amount of liquid. Be sure to have extra soup stock on hand to add as needed.*

Crispy Beans and Beef

This is a classic example of an everyday Chinese dish and a creative way to use the old standard hamburger. The cellophane noodles and green beans make this dish a pleasant change for a quick week-day meal.

1 ounce (28 g) cellophane noodles
4 cups (1 L) oil
1 pound (450 g) green beans, snap ends off and cut into 2" (5 cm) pieces
1 clove garlic, minced
2 slices ginger, chopped
½ pound (225 g) lean ground beef
1½ tablespoons (22 ml) wine

1 tablespoon (15 ml) soy sauce
½ teaspoon (2 ml) sugar
¼ teaspoon (1 ml) five-spice powder (optional)
¼ teaspoon (1 ml) salt
dash of black pepper
¼ cup (60 ml) soup stock
½ teaspoon (2 ml) cornstarch solution

1. Deep-fry cellophane noodles over high heat (375° F, 190° C) until puffed, about 3-5 seconds. Place on a platter.
2. Parboil green beans for 3-3½ minutes. Drain well on paper towels.
3. Deep-fry parboiled green beans, one half at a time, over medium heat (325° F, 160° C) for 4 minutes. Set aside.
4. Heat 1 tablespoon oil, garlic and ginger in wok over high heat. Add beef and stir-fry for 2 minutes.
5. Return fried green beans to wok and mix well. Stir in remaining ingredients, except cornstarch solution. Cook over low heat for 2 minutes. Thicken with cornstarch solution.
6. Pour green beans and beef mixture over fried noodles and serve.

Green Pepper Beef

Delight your guests with this elegant and elaborate dish. You may consider this the twin sister of "Bean Sprouts and Pepper Beef" with an even simpler and stronger taste due to the exotic oyster flavor.

½ pound (225 g) flank steak, cut
    into 2″ (5 cm) thin slices

Marinade:
1 teaspoon (5 ml) soy sauce
2 teaspoons (10 ml) oyster-flavored
    sauce
1 teaspoon (5 ml) wine
1 teaspoon (5 ml) oil
1 teaspoon (5 ml) cornstarch

2 tablespoons (30 ml) oil
½ medium-size onion, cut into
    bite-size pieces
1½ bell peppers, cut into bite-size
    pieces
¼ cup (60 ml) soup stock
1 tablespoon (15 ml) dark soy sauce
½ teaspoon (2 ml) sugar
1 tablespoon (15 ml) oyster-flavored
    sauce
1½ teaspoons (7 ml) cornstarch solution

1. Marinate beef for ½-2 hours.
2. Heat wok with oil over high heat; put in beef and stir-fry for 1-1½ minutes. Remove and drain well. Set aside.
3. Add onion to wok and stir-fry for 30 seconds; add bell pepper and soup stock. Cover and cook over high heat for 1½ minutes.
4. Return beef to wok and add soy sauce, sugar and oyster-flavored sauce. Mix well and cook for 1 minute.
5. Thicken with cornstarch solution and serve.

Mongolian Beef

This is a favorite in Northern China. It is basically simple; however, lots of green onion and a few pieces of red chili pepper make it a unique, spicy dish.

½ pound (225 g) flank steak, thinly
   sliced

Marinade:
1½ teaspoons (7 ml) wine
1 teaspoon (5 ml) oil
1½ teaspoons (7 ml) wine
½ teaspoon (2 ml) cornstarch

4 cups (1 L) oil
2 ounces (56 g) cellophane noodles
4 stalks green onion, cut into 1"
   (2.5 cm) strips
4-5 dried red chili peppers, chopped
   (or 1½ teaspoons (7 ml) crushed
   red chili pepper)
1½ tablespoons (22 ml) soy sauce
½ teaspoon (2 ml) sugar
1 teaspoon (5 ml) sesame oil
dash of white pepper
dash of salt
½ cup (125 ml) soup stock
1¾ teaspoon (8 ml) cornstarch solution

1. Marinate beef for one hour.
2. Deep-fry cellophane noodles, one half at a time over high heat (375° F, 190°C) until puffed. Drain on paper towels and set aside.
3. In the same oil, deep-fry beef over high heat for 45 seconds. Remove beef, drain well, and set aside. (Deep-frying allows more control over the cooking, but the beef may also be stir-fried in 2 tablespoons (30 ml) oil, for 1½-2 minutes.)
4. Remove oil from wok. Add 2 teaspoons oil to wok over high heat. Take a deep breath and add the chili and green onion. Stir for 5 seconds, add the remaining ingredients, except cornstarch solution and bring to a boil. Thicken with cornstarch solution. Add the beef and stir for 15 seconds. Serve over cellophane noodles.

Remarks
- *When deep-frying noodles, don't cook too many at one time or you will find them all over your kitchen.*
- *This dish provides good exercise — just try dividing a pack of cellophane noodles!*
- *Be sure to hold your breath when adding the chilis. Don't come complaining to me if you don't!*

Oyster-Flavored Beef and Eggplant   CANTON

Here is an easy family dish from Canton. If you don't like eggplant, a taste of this special preparation will change your opinion!

½ pound (225 g) flank steak, thinly
    sliced

Marinade:
1 tablespoon (15 ml) soy sauce
1 tablespoon (15 ml) wine
1 tablespoon (15 ml) water
1½ tablespoons (22 ml) oil
2 teaspoons (10 ml) cornstarch

1 small eggplant, cut into bite-size pieces
3 tablespoons (45 ml) oil
2 cloves garlic, chopped
3 slices ginger, chopped
1 tablespoon (15 ml) oyster-flavored
    sauce
2 teaspoons (10 ml) dark soy sauce
½ teaspoon (2 ml) sugar
¼ cup (60 ml) soup stock
2 stalks green onion, cut into 1"
    (2.5 cm) pieces
1 teaspoon (5 ml) cornstarch solution

1. Marinate beef for 1 hour.
2. Blanch eggplant in boiling water for 3 minutes. Remove and drain well. Set aside.
3. Heat oil, garlic and ginger in wok over high heat. Add beef and stir for approximately 2 minutes. Remove and set aside.
4. Add parboiled eggplant, oyster-flavored sauce, soy sauce, sugar and stock to wok. Cover and cook for 2 minutes over medium-high heat.
5. Add beef and green onions, mix well, and thicken with cornstarch solution. Serve hot.

Remarks
- *Try salted black beans instead of oyster-flavored sauce. You will have a new dish!*
- *Add a pinch of salt to the boiling water when blanching eggplant.*
- *If you are using the smaller Chinese eggplant, use 2 or 3, depending on their size.*
- *Peel the eggplant, if desired.*

Sauteed Beef with Snow Peas

This is one of the most popular Chinese dishes in many Chinese restaurants. It should only be made when young, garden fresh snow peas are available and never with overmature or frozen snow peas.

½ pound (225 g) flank steak, cut
    into thin slices

Marinade:
1 tablespoon (15 ml) soy sauce
1 teaspoon (5 ml) cornstarch
1 teaspoon (5 ml) wine

2-3 tablespoons (30-45 ml) oil
1 clove garlic, chopped
2 slices ginger, finely shredded
½ pound (225 g) snow peas, with
    ends snapped off
5-6 mushrooms
½ cup (125 ml) soup stock
2 teaspoons (10 ml) oyster-flavored
    sauce
1 teaspoon (5 ml) cornstarch solution
1 teaspoon (5 ml) wine (optional)

1. Marinate beef for 30 minutes.
2. Heat wok with oil, garlic, and ginger for 10-15 seconds over high heat. Add beef and stir-fry over high heat for 1½-2 minutes. Remove and set aside.
3. Add snow peas and mushrooms to wok; stir-fry for 30 seconds. Add stock and oyster-flavored sauce; cover and cook for 2 minutes.
4. Return beef, mix well, and thicken with cornstarch solution. Stir in wine and serve immediately.

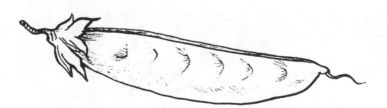

Spicy Ginger Beef

This was developed for curious and educated appetites. The heavy use of ginger and five-spice powder will be an exciting experience for your taste buds.

¾ pound (225 g) flank steak, sliced
    into ½″ x 2″ (1.5 x 5 cm)
    strips

Marinade:
1 tablespoon (15 ml) wine
1 tablespoon (15 ml) water
½ teaspoon (2 ml) oil
¾ teaspoon (3 ml) cornstarch
2 teaspoons (10 ml) soy sauce
½ teaspoon (2 ml) five-spice powder
1 teaspoon (5 ml) ginger juice

3 cups (¾ L) oil
6-8 slices ginger
2 stalks green onion, cut into 1″
    (2.5 cm) pieces
¼ teaspoon (1 ml) cornstarch
    solution
1 teaspoon (5 ml) wine
2 pineapple rings (for garnish)

1. Marinate beef for 2-4 hours.
2. Heat oil with 3-4 pieces of ginger in wok over high heat (375°F, 190°C). Reduce heat to medium-high (350°F, 180°C) and deep-fry beef for 3 minutes. Remove beef and ginger, drain and cool. Discard ginger. Deep-fry beef again over high heat (375°F, 190°C) for an additional 1-1½ minutes until brown; drain well. Set aside. Remove oil from wok, reserving 2 teaspoons (10 ml). Clean wok.
3. Heat reserved oil in wok over high heat. Add remaining 3-4 slices ginger and green onions. Stir for 30 seconds. Return fried beef to wok and stir for another ½ minute. Add soup stock and thicken with cornstarch solution. Stir in wine and serve promptly. Garnish with pineapple rings.

Spicy Shredded Vegetables and Beef   SZECHWAN

Chung King is the capital city of Szechwan province where hot and spicy dishes prevail. This dish is typical; the beef is dry, chewy and full of flavor, the carrot and celery are crispy, and most of all, the dish is HOT. If you are looking for hot lips, this is a perfect choice.

½ pound (225 g) flank steak or
    other steak, finely shredded

Marinade:

2 teaspoons (10 ml) soy sauce
1 teaspoon (5 ml) wine
½ teaspoon (2 ml) sugar
2 teaspoons (10 ml) cornstarch
2 teaspoons (10 ml) oil
1 teaspoon (5 ml) egg white, lightly
    beaten
2 cups (500 ml) oil
2 slices ginger, shredded
1 carrot, finely shredded
1½ stalks celery, finely shredded
2 whole dry red chili peppers,
    chopped (or ½ teaspoon (2 ml)
    chili oil)

Spicy Sauce:
¼ teaspoon (1 ml) salt
dash of white pepper
1 teaspoon (5 ml) sesame oil
2 tablespoons (30 ml) soup stock
2 teaspoons (10 ml) white vinegar
¾ teaspoon (3 ml) sugar

1. Marinate shredded beef for 1 hour.
2. Heat wok with oil over high heat (400°F, 200°C). Add beef and deep-fry for 2 minutes, stirring constantly to prevent sticking. Remove beef and drain. Decrease heat to 375°F (190°C). Return beef and deep-fry again, stirring for 1½ minutes. Remove, drain and set aside.
3. Remove oil, reserving 1 tablespoon (15 ml) and clean wok.
4. Heat reserved tablespoon of oil in wok with shredded ginger for 10 seconds. Add carrot, celery and chili pepper (or chili oil). Add sauce mixture and cook for 1 minute, stirring continuously.
5. Return fried beef to wok; stir 30 seconds until most of the liquid has evaporated. Serve immediately.

Remarks
- *Adjust spiciness to suit your own taste.*

Spicy Szechwan Beef

Hot and spicy dishes are becoming increasingly popular in North America. The hot seasoning sauce is typical of Szechwan style cooking.

½ pound (225 g) beef flank steak,
   thinly shredded

Marinade:
1 tablespoon (15 ml) soy sauce
1 teaspoon (5 ml) cornstarch
2 teaspoons (10 ml) oil
2 teaspoons (10 ml) wine
2 teaspoons (10 ml) cornstarch
¼ teaspoon (1 ml) sesame oil

Hot Sauce:
1 tablespoon (15 ml) hot bean paste
   or chili sauce
2 teaspoons (10 ml) soy sauce
½ teaspoon (2 ml) sugar
1 tablespoon (15 ml) vinegar
½ teaspoon (2 ml) sesame oil
¼ teaspoons (1 ml) white pepper
¼ teaspoon (1 ml) cornstarch solution

3 tablespoons (45 ml) oil
2 slices ginger, thinly shredded
2-3 cloves garlic, chopped
1 small carrot, thinly shredded
2-3 wood ears, soaked and shredded
   (optional)
1 stalk celery, thinly shredded
3 tablespoons (45 ml) soup stock

1. Marinate beef for 30 minutes.
2. Combine hot sauce ingredients. Mix well and set aside.
3. Heat oil, ginger and garlic in wok over high heat for 10 seconds. Add beef and stir-fry for 1-1½ minutes. Add shredded carrot, wood ear, celery and soup stock. Stir one minute.
4. Add hot sauce, stirring for 30 seconds. Add meat and stir well. Thicken with cornstarch solution. Serve hot.

Remarks
- *Never serve more than one hot dish at a meal or you may end up with heartburn and a hot lip!*
- *Hot bean paste is a northern-style chili paste available only in Chinese stores. If it is not available, use regular chili sauce.*

Stuffed Lettuce Leaves
(Chinese Lettuce Taco)

You can't imagine how delightful this is until you try it. Fresh spring lettuce with lots of tasty ingredients wrapped inside is delicious and nutritious. This exotic recipe is often served for the Chinese New Year's in Canton.

½ pound (225 g) lean ground beef

Beef Marinade:
1 teaspoon (5 ml) soy sauce
½ teaspoon (2 ml) sugar
1 teaspoon (5 ml) cornstarch
½ teaspoon (2 ml) wine
1 teaspoon (5 ml) oil

1 ounce (28 g) cellophane noodles
3 cups (¾ L) oil
2 slices ginger, finely shredded
2 cloves garlic, minced
1 stalk celery, finely chopped
1 small carrot, finely chopped
½ zucchini, finely chopped (optional)
2 stalks green onion, cut into 1"
    (2.5 cm) pieces
1 teaspoon (5 ml) sesame oil
½ teaspoon (2 ml) sugar
¼ cup (60 ml) soup stock
1 teaspoon (5 ml) cornstarch solution
¼ cup (60 ml) sweet bean paste or
    hoisin sauce
6-8 lettuce leaves

1. Marinate ground beef for 30 minutes.
2. Deep-fry cellophane noodles in hot oil. Drain well and crumble. Reserve 1 tablespoon oil and clean wok.
3. Heat reserved 1 tablespoon oil in wok over high heat; stir in ginger and garlic. Add ground beef and stir-fry for 1½ minutes over high heat. Remove and drain well.
4. Add celery, carrot, and zucchini to wok, stirring for ½ minute. Add green onion, sesame oil, sugar and soup stock. Mix well, cover and cook for 1 minute. Return beef to wok. Thicken with cornstarch solution. Turn off heat; add deep-fried cellophane noodles and mix well.
5. To serve, spread ½ teaspoon hoisin sauce in center of lettuce leaf. Top with 1½-2 tablespoons of vegetable/meat mixture, wrap like a burrito and eat up a storm.

Remarks
- *Any combination of stir-fried meat and vegetables can be used; season to your own taste. Traditionally, squab meat or dried chopped oysters are used.*
- *Be sure to use lean beef or mixture will be too oily.*

Tomato Beef

Whether you're Chinese or a Westerner, this will be a favorite. It is often served in a typical Chinese meal. Lots of succulent strips of beef smothered in a delicate sauce of tomatoes, peppers and pineapple. Beef up any menu with this dish!

½ pound (225 g) flank steak, thinly
    sliced across the grain into 2"
    (5 cm) strips

Marinade:
1 teaspoon (5 ml) soy sauce
1½ teaspoons (7 ml) wine
1½ tablespoons (22 ml) water
½ teaspoon (2 ml) oil
¼ teaspoon (1 ml) sesame oil
½ teaspoon (2 ml) cornstarch

2 tablespoons (30 ml) oil
2 cloves garlic, finely chopped
2-3 firm tomatoes, peeled and cut
    into 8 wedges
½ bell pepper, cut into bite-size chunks
    (optional)
2 pineapple rings, cut into bite-size
    chunks (optional)

Sauce:
¼ cup (60 ml) hot catsup
1 teaspoon (5 ml) sugar
1 teaspoon (5 ml) white vinegar
¼ teaspoon (1 ml) Tabasco sauce
dash of white pepper
salt to taste
½ teaspoon (2 ml) cornstarch solution
½ teaspoon (2 ml) oil

1. Marinate beef for 30 minutes.
2. Heat wok or skillet with 2 tablespoons oil and garlic for 10-15 seconds over high heat. Stir in beef and cook for 1½-2 minutes.
3. Add tomato wedges, bell pepper and pineapple; stir for 30 seconds. Add sauce mixture, mix well and cook until thickened. Serve immediately.

Remarks
- *Serve immediately or it will become watery since salt draws the liquid from the succulent tomatoes.*
- *If desired, add ½ of a yellow onion, cut into strips along with the tomatoes.*
- *This is an excellent one dish meal when served over rice or noodles.*

"Sometimes the best-laid woks of rice and chow mein go awry. . ."

Porking Out

Don't make a pig of yourself at the dinner table, but do make a pork dish for dinner! In China and many parts of the Orient, pork is so much more common than any other meat that the words "meat" and "pork" are used synonymously.

Pork has a more delicate flavor than beef, a less coarse grain, and is consequently more adaptable for an infinite variety of dishes. The method of cooking this meat is different in each region so one can almost tell where a man lives by the pork dish he orders.

Pork is frequently cooked in relatively large pieces, then sliced, shredded or ground up. When pork is prepared in large pieces, such as in red-cooked dishes, it is cooked first, then cut into smaller pieces and re-fried in combination with fresh or preserved vegetables.

This little "Piggy" loves to pork out and so will you with these fantastic recipes — try not to "hog" the whole dish

Chinese B.B.Q. Pork (Roast Pork)   CANTON

When you pass by a Chinese store or restaurant in Chinatown in New York, San Francisco, Vancouver or Toronto, you will most likely notice many shiny meat products such as BBQ pork hanging on skewers, and roast duck or chicken on specially-designed hooks. They look tempting and delicious. All have distinctive Chinese flavors. This dish is exotic and traditional.

**2 pounds (900 g) boneless pork
shoulder, cut into 8″ x 2½″ x ½″
(20 x 6.5 x 1.5 cm) pieces**

Basting Sauce:
**1 tablespoon (15 ml) hoisin sauce
¼ cup (60 ml) honey**

Marinade:
**2½ teaspoons (12 ml) sugar
¾ teaspoon (3 ml) salt
1 clove garlic, minced
½ teaspoon (2 ml) ginger juice
2 tablespoons (30 ml) catsup
2 tablespoons (30 ml) soy sauce
2½ teaspoons (12 ml) wine
½ teaspoon (2 ml) five-spice powder
(optional)**

1. Marinate pork for 2-4 hours, or overnight if you wish.
2. Preheat oven to 375°F (190°C) and place marinated pork on a rack over a roasting pan filled with ½ cup of water. Bake for 20 minutes at 375°F, basting occasionally with remaining marinade. Turn and bake another 17-20 minutes.
3. Switch oven to broil. Baste both sides of pork with basting sauce and broil for 1 minute on each side.
4. Let pork cool and cut into thin slices. Serve hot or cold. Keep in tightly-sealed container in refrigerator or in freezer if not served right away.

Remarks
- *Reheating the pork will not degrade the quality, but be sure to use a bit of water in the roasting pan, or wrap it inside foil before reheating in oven.*
- *To bake: place on rack on top shelf of oven, hang pork strips with hooks onto rack, place pan beneath rack to catch drippings (refer to illustration).*
- *If pork is cooked horizontally in an electric oven, place about 3″ from top heating element.*

Garlic-Flavored Pork

This dish has an exotic taste that will win acclaim at any social function. Once served to honored guests, they will not dare to complain about a thing!

1 pound (450 g) side of pork, cut into
   1″ (2.5 cm) thick large pieces
3-4 slices ginger
¼ cup (60 ml) sugar
1¼ cup (310 ml) water
1 tablespoon (15 ml) oil
5-6 cloves garlic, finely minced
½ teaspoon (2 ml) cornstarch
   solution
1 stalk green onion, chopped

Garlic Sauce:
½ teaspoon (2 ml) garlic salt
1 tablespoon (15 ml) soy sauce
1½ teaspoons (7 ml) sugar
1½ tablespoons (22 ml) wine
1 teaspoon (5 ml) white vinegar
½ teaspoon (2 ml) hot chili oil or
   crushed red pepper (optional)
½ teaspoon (2 ml) sesame oil
3 tablespoons (45 ml) soup stock

1. Bring a large sauce pan of water to boil over high heat. Add pork and ginger slices; boil for 2 minutes. Reduce heat and simmer for 30 minutes. Remove pork and cut into ¼″ x 2″ x 2″ (0.75 x 5 x 5 cm) slices.
2. In a large bowl, dissolve sugar in water. Soak cooked pork in solution and store in refrigerator for 2-3 hours.
3. Combine ingredients for garlic sauce and reserve.
4. Heat oil and garlic in wok over medium-high heat for 10 seconds. Stir in garlic sauce mixture and blend well. Stir in cornstarch solution to thicken.
5. Drain pork and place on a platter. Cover with the garlic sauce. Garnish with green onion, if desired.

Remarks
* *Leftovers make a delicious snack, hot or cold.*

Happy Family with Golden Crown PEKING

This is the twin sister of Mushi Pork. While the ingredients and preparation are similar, the presentation differs.

6 ounces (168 g) lean boneless pork,
   cut into 2″ (5 cm) thin strips

Marinade:
1½ teaspoons (7 ml) soy sauce
½ teaspoon (2 ml) sesame oil
1 teaspoon (5 ml) cornstarch

2½ tablespoons (37 ml) oil
2 stalks green onion, cut into 1½″
   (4 cm) thin strips
1 small carrot, shredded into 1½″
   (4 cm) thin strips
¼ cup (60 ml) soup stock
4 ounces (112 g) cabbage, shredded
4 ounces (112 g) bean sprouts
1 teaspoon (5 ml) salt
2 tablespoons (30 ml) hoisin sauce
1½ teaspoons (7 ml) cornstarch solution
2 teaspoons (10 ml) oil
2 medium-size eggs, lightly beaten
12 flour pancakes (see Mushi Pork
   recipe)

1. Marinate shredded pork for 30 minutes.
2. Heat 2 tablespoons (30 ml) oil over high heat. Add green onion and stir-fry for 5 seconds. Add pork and stir-fry for 2-2½ minutes. Remove and set aside. Clean and dry wok.
3. Heat ½ tablespoon (7 ml) oil in wok. Stir-fry shredded carrot for 30 seconds. Add soup stock, cabbage, bean sprouts, salt and hoisin sauce, cover and cook for 1 minute. Return cooked pork, thicken with cornstarch solution and set aside.
4. Place 2 teaspoons oil and beaten eggs in a small skillet and make a thin omelet. Slice omelet into strips and place on top of pork mixture.
5. To serve, place the pork mixture in the center of a pancake, wrap it up and eat it with your hands.

Remarks
- *You can use any vegetable combination.*

Hoisin-Flavored Spareribs

The savory subtlety and the succulent smoothness of pork, with a slight sweetness of hoisin sauce is sensational. If this doesn't tempt you, nothing will! Hoisin sauce is an excellent seasoning to use on almost any type of meat.

1 pound (450 g) spareribs

Marinade:
2 teaspoons (10 ml) wine
¼ teaspoon (1 ml) salt
2 teaspoons (10 ml) cornstarch
½ teaspoon (2 ml) sesame oil

1 tablespoon (15 ml) oil
¼ cup (60 ml) soup stock
4-5 teaspoons (20-25 ml) hoisin sauce
½ teaspoons (2 ml) wine
Lettuce for garnish

1. Trim excess fat from spareribs and cut into 1½" (4 cm) cubes. (Ask your butcher for assistance.) Marinate for one hour.
2. Heat oil in wok over medium-high heat. Add spareribs, stirring for 2-2½ minutes. Drain excess oil from wok.
3. Pour in soup stock and reduce heat to medium-low. Cover and simmer for 8-10 minutes, stirring occasionally, until liquid is reduced enough to just cover the ribs.
4. Add hoisin sauce; cook over medium-high heat until ribs are well-coated; then stir in wine. Garnish with lettuce. Serve hot or cold.

Remarks
• *You can also use whole pork chops for this dish.*

Honey Garlic Ribs

This is one of several "exotic" American-style Chinese dishes. The luscious taste of honey, combined with garlic will make you want to lick the bones clean.

1 pound (450 g) pork spareribs, cut
    into 1" (2.5 cm) pieces

Marinade:
1 teaspoon (5 ml) garlic salt
1 teaspoon (5 ml) wine

1½ tablespoons (22 ml) oil
1 slice ginger, finely minced
4 cloves garlic, finely minced
¼ cup (60 ml) soup stock
4 teaspoons (20 ml) honey
2 tablespoons (30 ml) wine
1 teaspoon (5 ml) dark soy sauce

1. Marinate ribs for 2 hours.
2. Heat wok with oil over medium-high heat. Stir in ginger and garlic. Add spareribs and stir-fry for 2 minutes.
3. Add stock, cover and cook ribs over medium heat for 5-6 minutes, adding extra stock, if needed.
4. Remove lid, return heat to high and continue to stir until most of the liquid has evaporated. Add remaining ingredients and stir for another 2 minutes, or until honey is slightly caramelized.

Remarks
- *Like all sweet things, honey burns quickly. Watch carefully when cooking this dish to avoid smoking ribs.*
- *Ask the butcher to cut the ribs across the bones, so you won't have to chop your cutting board into 5,000 pieces.*

Imperial Pork Chops

This royal recipe will make dinner at your castle a special feast. The spicy braising sauce adds the final jewel to the crown. Try it to-knight!

¾ pound (340 g) pork chop or
  spareribs, cut into ¼" x 2" x 2"
  (0.75 x 5 x 5 cm) pieces

Marinade:
2 teaspoons (10 ml) wine
1 teaspoon (5 ml) soy sauce
2 teaspoons (10 ml) cornstarch

4 cups (1 L) oil
1 slice ginger, minced
2 pineapple slices (for garnish)
1 tomato (for garnish)

Braising Sauce Mixture:
1½ tablespoons (22 ml) hot catsup
1 teaspoon (5 ml) Worcestershire
  sauce
1½ teaspoons (7 ml) sugar
1 teaspoon (5 ml) H.P. or A-1 sauce
  (optional)
1½-2 tablespoons (22-30 ml) soup stock
1 teaspoon (5 ml) white vinegar
dash of sesame oil
dash of chili oil

1. Marinate pork for 2 hours.
2. Heat oil in wok over medium-high heat. Deep-fry marinated pork until brown, about 4-5 minutes, stirring constantly. Remove and drain well; set aside. Remove oil reserving 1 teaspoon (5 ml) and clean wok.
3. In the same wok, heat reserved oil and minced ginger over high heat. Add braising sauce mixture and the fried pork, stirring until sauce is reduced slightly, about 1 minute. Serve hot, garnished with pineapple and tomato slices.

Remarks
- *This particular dish has become one of the most popular choices in Cantonese restaurants.*

Oriental Pearls SZECHWAN

This is a rare, exotic dish from the western region of China. There is a story behind it, but it is much too long to tell in this small space. Try the dish anyway!

½ cup (125 ml) short grain rice, uncooked
¾ pound (340 g) lean ground pork
2 water chestnuts, minced
2-3 tablespoons (15-30 ml) dried shrimp, soaked and minced (optional)
1 stalk green onion, chopped
½ teaspoon (2 ml) minced ginger

2 tablespoons (30 ml) chopped carrot
2 teaspoons (10 ml) soy sauce
4 teaspoons (20 ml) cornstarch
1 egg white
¾ teaspoon (3 ml) sugar
¾ teaspoon (3 ml) salt
pinch of white pepper

1. Soak rice in warm water for 1½-2 hours. Drain well and set aside.
2. Mix pork with the remaining ingredients in a bowl. Form into 14 meatballs: take a fistful of the mixture and squeeze out a meatball between your thumb and index finger. Use a wet soup spoon to remove meatballs from your fist.
3. Roll the meatballs in the soaked rice until evenly coated. Gently press rice into meatballs.
4. Steam over high heat for 25-30 minutes. Add more water to the steamer, if necessary. Serve with soy sauce, if desired.

Remarks
• *Pearls can be kept in the refrigerator and resteamed.*

Pork Cashew Nut Surprise

Succulent meat, crunchy nuts, and lots of wholesome vegetables make this dish an all-time favorite! It is colorful, delightful and refreshing.

6 ounces (168 g) pork, diced

Marinade:
1 teaspoon (5 ml) soy sauce
1 teaspoon (5 ml) wine
1 teaspoon (5 ml) cornstarch

3 tablespoons (45 ml) oil
2 cloves garlic, chopped
3 slices ginger, chopped
1 small carrot, peeled and diced
1 stalk celery, diced
1 small zucchini, diced
$^1/_3$ cup (80 ml) soup stock
½ bell pepper, diced
¾ teaspoon (3 ml) salt
½ teaspoon (2 ml) sugar
1 teaspoon (5 ml) sesame oil
1¼ teaspoon (6 ml) cornstarch solution
½ cup (125 ml) unsalted,
    roasted cashew nuts

1. Marinate the pork for 30 minutes.
2. Heat oil in wok over high heat. Add garlic and ginger; stir for 10 seconds. Add pork and stir-fry for 2-2½ minutes. Remove and drain well. Set aside.
3. Put carrot, celery and zucchini in wok; stir-fry for a few seconds over high heat. Add stock, cover and cook for 1½-2 minutes. Add bell pepper and continue to cook, covered, for 1 minute. Stir several times to mix well.
4. Add pork, salt, sugar and sesame oil to wok; mix well. Thicken with cornstarch solution. Stir in cashews and serve immediately.

Remarks
- *If salted cashews are used, you may want to reduce the amount of salt used in the dish.*

Pork Steak Cantonese

You may not realize that you need a new recipe for pork chops until you've tried this one. It will surely become one of your favorite dishes.

4 small pork chops, approximately
  ¾ pound (340 g)

Marinade:
1½ tablespoons (22 ml) wine
1 tablespoon (15 ml) soy sauce
1½ teaspoons (7 ml) cornstarch
2-3 tablespoons (30-45 ml) water
½ egg white, lightly beaten

Braising Sauce:
1½ tablespoons (22 ml) soy sauce
1½ teaspoons (7 ml) sugar
2 teaspoons (10 ml) fresh lemon juice
½ teaspoon (2 ml) chili sauce
2½ tablespoons (37 ml) catsup
¼ cup (60 ml) soup stock
1 teaspoon (5 ml) cornstarch solution

flour for dry-coating
4 cups (1 L) oil
½ onion, cut into strips

1. Pound surface of pork chops with the blunt edge of a cleaver to flatten slightly. Let marinate for 2 hours. Dredge chops in flour and shake off excess.
2. Heat wok with oil over high heat (375° F, 190° C). Reduce heat to medium–high (350° F, 180° C) and deep-fry pork for 1½ minutes on each side. Remove and drain well. Remove oil, reserving 1 tablespoon (15 ml).
3. Heat reserved oil in wok over high heat. Add onion, stir for 30 seconds.
4. Return pork to wok with braising sauce ingredients, except cornstarch solution. Reduce heat to low, cover and simmer 2-3 minutes, turning pork chops once or twice. Thicken with cornstarch solution and serve over lettuce leaves, if desired.

Remarks
• *Dredging the chops in flour will prevent splashing of hot oil.*

Ribs to Remember

Salted black beans flavor dishes at family meals in many regions of southeastern China. They have a strong and distinctive aroma and flavor. If you enjoy exploring new tastes, you will want to try them in this dish.

1½ pounds (675 g) spareribs, cut into 1″ (2.5 cm) pieces

Marinade:
½ teaspoon (2 ml) salt
2 teaspoons (10 ml) cornstarch
1 teaspoon (5 ml) oil

2 tablespoons (30 ml) oil
1½ tablespoons (22 ml) salted black beans, rinsed and mashed to a paste
1 stalk green onion, chopped
2 cloves garlic, finely chopped
¼ cup (60 ml) soup stock
¼ teaspoon (1 ml) sugar
1 teaspoon (5 ml) soy sauce
¾ teaspoon (3 ml) cornstarch solution

1. Marinate ribs for 30 minutes.
2. Heat 1 tablespoon oil in wok over high heat. Add spareribs and brown for 2 minutes, stirring constantly. Remove and set aside.
3. Add 1 tablespoon oil, mashed black beans, onion and garlic to wok and stir-fry over high heat for 30 seconds.
4. Return spareribs to wok and mix well. Add stock, sugar and soy sauce. Reduce heat to medium-low, cover and cook for 3-5 minutes.
5. Thicken with cornstarch solution and serve hot.

Remarks
- *Use a minimum amount of oil in this dish as there will be oil from the spareribs, too.*
- *Before using the salted black beans, rinse the beans in water, drain well and crush to a paste. Since they can burn easily over high heat, have some broth on hand to add to the wok if needed. Black beans will keep if stored in an air tight container or plastic bag.*
- *To save the edge of your knife blade, ask your butcher to cut the spareribs for you.*

Royal Lion's Head

To many Chinese the lion symbolizes strength, dignity and security and is thought to ward off evil spirits. Stone and brass carvings of lions are often seen at the main entrance to temples, the royal palace and, of course, banks. This Szechwan delicacy is a favorite in northern-style Chinese meals. It got its name because the meatballs are so gigantic that they look like lion heads (baby lions, of course).

¾ pound (340 g) lean ground pork
2 water chestnuts, chopped
2 tablespoons (30 ml) chopped ham
   (optional)
2 dried black mushrooms, soaked
   and finely chopped

4 cups (1 L) oil
2 cloves garlic, minced
1 head cabbage, approximately 1 pound
   (450 g), cut into large pieces
1½ tablespoons (22 ml) soy sauce
½ cup (125 ml) soup stock
1½ teaspoons (7 ml) cornstarch solution

Marinade:
1 egg yolk, lightly beaten
2 teaspoons (10 ml) wine
½ teaspoon (2 ml) salt
1 teaspoon (5 ml) sugar
1 teaspoon (5 ml) cornstarch
dash of white pepper
dash of sesame oil

1. Combine ground pork, water chestnuts, ham, mushrooms and marinade in a bowl. Marinate for 30 minutes. Shape into 6 gigantic meatballs, approximately 2″ (5 cm) in diameter.
2. Heat oil for deep-frying in wok over high heat (375° F, 190° C). Turn heat to medium-high (350° F, 180° C) and deep-fry meatballs for about 2½ minutes or until golden brown. Remove, drain, and set aside.
3. Heat wok with 1 tablespoon oil over medium-high heat and add garlic and cabbage. Stir-fry for 30 seconds then add soy sauce and soup stock. Mix well.
4. Arrange meatballs on top of the cabbage, cover, and simmer over low heat for 16-18 minutes. Add extra soup stock, if the dish gets too dry. Thicken with cornstarch solution and serve.

Remarks
- *Spinach can be used in place of the cabbage.*
- *Be sure to add more liquid to the wok while simmering, unless you like dehydrated cabbage with juicy meatballs.*

Spiced Minced Pork with Bean Curd   SZECHWAN

This is a popular and spicy Szechwan dish which will leave you with "hot lips"! You can adjust the hotness to your own taste, however.

2 squares (1 pound) (450 g) soft
    bean curd
1 clove garlic, minced
1 tablespoon (15 ml) oil
1 slice ginger
½ teaspoon (2 ml) Szechwan pepper,
    browned and crushed (optional)
½ teaspoon (2 ml) crushed red
    pepper
6 ounces (168 g) ground pork

¼ medium-size onion, cut into ¼"
    (0.75 cm) cubes
½ teaspoon (2 ml) chili oil
4 teaspoons (20 ml) soy sauce
½ teaspoon (2 ml) soy sauce
½ teaspoon (2 ml) sugar
½ teaspoon (2 ml) salt
2 tablespoons (30 ml) soup stock
1 teaspoon (5 ml) cornstarch solution
1 egg white, beaten (optional)

1. Dice bean curd into ½" (1.5 cm) cubes and drain in colander for 10 minutes.
2. Heat oil in wok over high heat. Add garlic, ginger, both kinds of pepper, and pork. Reduce heat to medium-high and stir-fry for 1½ minutes.
3. Add onion; stir-fry for 30 seconds. Add bean curd; stir-fry for another 2 minutes.
4. Stir in remaining ingredients except cornstarch solution and egg white. Thicken with cornstarch solution.
5. Turn off heat and slowly stir in egg white. Serve immediately.

Remarks
- *If Szechwan pepper is used, lightly stir-fry over low heat, crush to a powder and set aside.*
- *Ground beef can be substituted for the ground pork.*
- *This dish can be prepared ahead of time and reheated before serving. If the bean curd makes the dish too watery, add a small amount of cornstarch solution to thicken when reheating.*
- *Soft bean curd is best for this dish, but any bean curd can be used.*

Steamed Ground Pork Patty CANTON

When I was a child, my mother prepared this dish at least once a week. It is a family favorite among the Cantonese.

¾ pound (340 g) lean ground pork
3 water chestnuts, chopped
3 dried black mushrooms, soaked
    and chopped (optional)
1 teaspoon (5 ml) soy sauce

½ teaspoon (2 ml) wine
¼ teaspoon (1 ml) sugar
½ teaspoon (2 ml) salt
1 tablespoon (15 ml) cornstarch
1 stalk green onion, chopped

1. Place all ingredients in a bowl. Mix well and transfer to an 8″ (20.5 cm) pie pan. Press lightly to form a ½″ (1.5 cm) thick patty.
2. Steam over high heat for 15-16 minutes. Cooking time depends on the thickness of the mixture. Add more water to the steamer, if necessary.

Remarks
- *When properly cooked, this dish has a smooth, tender texture and is a good alternative to stir-fried dishes. Be sure to add water during steaming or you may end up with a smoked pork patty.*
- *Regular ground pork available in the supermarket contains too much fat which will make the dish greasy. Ask your butcher to grind ¾ pound of lean pork.*

Steamed Spareribs with Black Bean Sauce   CANTON

A traditional family favorite in southern China. My mother fixed this dish every other day. I hate it so much that I must share the recipe with you!

1 pound (450 g) pork spareribs,
   cut into 1" (2.5 cm) cubes

Marinade:
1 teaspoon (5 ml) soy sauce
¼ teaspoon (1 ml) sugar
4 teaspoons (20 ml) cornstarch
1 teaspoon (5 ml) wine
¼ teaspoon (1 ml) salt

2 cloves garlic, minced
1-2 tablespoons (15-30 ml) salted black
   beans, rinsed and crushed
1 stalk green onion, cut into ½"
   (1.5 cm) pieces
½ teaspoon (2 ml) crushed red chili
   pepper (optional)
1 slice ginger, slivered

1. Marinate spareribs for 30 minutes.
2. Combine spareribs with remaining ingredients in a large bowl. Mix well.
3. Transfer mixture to a shallow pie pan, spreading out to a single layer.
4. Steam ribs over high heat for approximately 12-14 minutes or until cooked through.

Remarks
- *Count cooking time from the moment the water starts to boil. Check the water during steaming and add more if necessary.*
- *A bamboo steamer is not necessary; use racks or sticks to support the dish.*
- *These ribs are good reheated. Microwave ovens are ideal for such a job, if you have one.*

Stuffed Mushrooms

The Chinese, as well as people of other nationalities, have taken a fancy to mushrooms. Unlike many favorite foods, mushrooms will never make you fat: they have only about 127 calories per pound! Oriental dried black mushrooms are expensive, but if you enjoy them, here is an offbeat way to make elegant hors d'oeuvres.

16 (2-3 ounces) (56-84 g) dried black mushrooms of uniform size
¾ cup (200 ml) soup stock
¼ teaspoon (1 ml) sugar

Pork Mixture:
¼ pound (112 g) lean ground pork
¼ pound (112 g) fresh or frozen shrimp, finely minced
1 stalk green onion, finely chopped
2 water chestnuts, finely chopped
¾ teaspoon (3 ml) garlic salt
1 teaspoon (5 ml) wine
1 teaspoon (5 ml) cornstarch

3 tablespoons (45 ml) cornstarch for dry-coating
1-2 tablespoons (15-30 ml) oil
2 tablespoons (30 ml) oyster-flavored sauce
dash of white pepper
½ teaspoon (2 ml) cornstarch solution, if needed

1. Soak mushrooms in warm water for 30 minutes; remove stems. Simmer mushrooms with ½ cup (125 ml) soup stock and ¼ teaspoon (1 ml) sugar for 30 minutes. Remove, squeeze out liquid, drain well and set aside. Save the liquid for braising mushrooms later.
2. Combine ingredients for pork mixture; place in blender and whip several minutes or until smooth.
3. To stuff mushrooms, dry-coat cavity of each mushroom with ¼ teaspoon (1 ml) cornstarch, and fill with 1-1½ teaspoons (5-7 ml) of pork mixture.
4. Heat oil in a skillet over medium-high heat. Place stuffed mushrooms, meat side down, in skillet. Brown for 1½ minutes. Add remaining ¼ cup (60 ml) stock, liquid from mushrooms, oyster-flavored sauce and pepper. Cover and simmer over medium-high heat for 6-8 minutes.
5. Remove mushrooms with spatula and arrange on a platter, meat side up. If juice remains, thicken with cornstarch solution; pour over mushrooms.

Remarks

- *Prepare mushrooms ahead and store in freezer. To serve, cover with foil and reheat in the oven.*
- *Large fresh mushrooms or bell peppers can be stuffed, too. You do not need to soak them.*
- *The amount of pork mixture used depends on the size of the mushrooms.*
- *Use any leftover pork mixture in soups or in other dishes.*

"You can star in your own food production—
you are as good as you think."

Stuffed Pork Rolls and Broccoli   NEW DISCOVERY

Dishes of this nature are not usually served in restaurants because they can be very time consuming. A lot of the preparation can be done ahead of time, however, so you can serve it and still enjoy the dinner. It is a unique treat — worth the effort to prepare about once every ten years.

½ pound (225 g) pork loin, trimmed
    of fat and cut into 2" x 4"
    (5 cm x 10 cm) slices

Marinade:
¼ teaspoon (1 ml) salt
1½ teaspoons (7 ml) wine
1 egg, lightly beaten
½ teaspoon (2 ml) cornstarch

¾ cup (200 ml) broccoli flowerets
½ teaspoon (2 ml) salt
½ teaspoon (2 ml) oil
4 dried black mushrooms, soaked
    and cut into 2" (5 cm) pieces
2 slices cooked ham, cut into 1" x 2"
    (2.5 cm x 5 cm) slices
2 stalks green onion, cut into 2"
    (5 cm) pieces
cornstarch for dry-coating
4 cups (1 L) oil

Sauce:
1 tablespoon (15 ml) soy sauce
¾ cup (200 ml) soup stock
½ teaspoon (2 ml) sugar
dash of white pepper
2 teaspoons (10 ml) cornstarch
    solution

1. Marinate pork for 1 hour.
2. Blanch broccoli flowerets in boiling water with ½ teaspoon salt and ½ teaspoon oil for 2-2½ minutes, remove, plunge into cold water, and set aside.
3. Place 1 piece mushroom, ham and green onion in center of each pork slice, roll up and close with a toothpick. Dredge pork·rolls in corn-starch and set aside.
4. Heat oil in wok over high heat (375° F, 190° C). Reduce heat to medium-high (350° F, 180° C) and deep-fry pork rolls for 2-2½ minutes, stirring constantly. Remove from oil and drain well.
5. Combine sauce ingredients and bring to a boil. Add fried pork rolls and simmer for 3-5 minutes, stirring occasionally.
6. Remove toothpicks and arrange pork rolls on a platter. Garnish with broccoli.

Remarks
- *Another way to prepare the broccoli is to stir-fry it with soy sauce, sugar, sesame oil and salt. Sprinkle with stock if it becomes too dry. Cook covered for 3 minutes.*
- *Double recipe if unexpected guests show up.*

Stuffed Sunrise Tomatoes

This highly attractive meal will impress everyone and will add a unique touch of color to your table. It takes a little extra time to prepare, but the results are sensational!

4 medium-size tomatoes

Pork Mixture:
½ pound (225 g) ground pork
3 shrimp, minced
1 dried black mushroom, soaked and
   finely chopped (optional)
1 tablespoon (15 ml) chopped ham
1 tablespoon (15 ml) green onion,
   chopped
1 tablespoon (15 ml) wine
1 egg, lightly beaten
½ teaspoon (2 ml) salt
dash of sesame oil
white pepper to taste
2½ tablespoons (37 ml) cornstarch

3 tablespoons (45 ml) oil
½ cup (125 ml) soup stock
3 tablespoons (45 ml) catsup
1½ teaspoons (7 ml) vinegar
1 teaspoon (5 ml) sugar
½ teaspoon (2 ml) cornstarch
   solution

1. Blanch tomatoes for a few seconds in boiling water to loosen skins. Peel and halve. Remove seeds and some flesh to form a cavity. Sprinkle cavity with cornstarch and set aside.
2. Combine ingredients for pork mixture in a bowl and blend well.
3. Stuff tomato with pork mixture and level the meat with the top of the tomato.
4. Heat a flat, non-stick frying pan to medium-high with oil. Carefully place stuffed tomatoes, meat side down on a spatula and slide them into the pan.
5. Brown for 1½-2 minutes, swirling pan occasionally to prevent sticking. Add ¼ cup (60 ml) soup stock to pan, cover and reduce heat to medium-low. Simmer for 8-10 minutes. Remove tomatoes and arrange meat side down on a platter.
6. Mix catsup, vinegar and sugar with remaining stock in a saucepan. Thicken with cornstarch solution and pour over stuffed tomatoes.

Remarks
- *For an exotic touch, sprinkle tomatoes with chopped cilantro, Chinese parsley, before frying.*
- *Tomatoes can be stuffed ahead of time. Refrigerate until ready to cook.*

Sweet and Sour Pork

When you think about Chinese cooking — sweet and sour comes immediately to mind. It has almost become the trademark of Chinese cooking in many parts of the world. Its color, flavor and aroma make it an appetizing and appealing combination in any season. The sauce is extraordinary!

¾ pound (340 g) boneless pork, cut into ¾" (2 cm) cubes

Marinade:
½ teaspoon (2 ml) salt
½ teaspoon (2 ml) ginger juice
1 tablespoon (15 ml) wine

cornstarch for coating
4 cups (1 L) oil

Batter Mix:
¾ cup (200 ml) flour
¼ cup (60 ml) cornstarch
½ teaspoon (2 ml) sugar
¾ cup (200 ml) flat beer (or water
  —if water is used, increase
  baking powder to 1¼-1½
  teaspoons)
¾ teaspoon (3 ml) baking powder
½ teaspoon (2 ml) oil

Sweet and Sour Sauce:
1 clove garlic, minced
¼ cup (60 ml) packed brown sugar
3 tablespoons (45 ml) catsup (optional)
¼ cup (60 ml) white vinegar
¼ cup (60 ml) water
½ teaspoon (2 ml) soy sauce
½ teaspoon (2 ml) oil
dash of Tabasco sauce (optional)
½ tomato, bite size chunks
2 pineapple rings
6 lychees (optional)
½ green pepper, 1" (2.5 cm) squares
2½ teaspoons (12 ml) cornstarch
  solution

1. Marinate pork for ½ hour.
2. Make batter mix. Coat pork with cornstarch.
3. Dip marinated pork into batter and coat evenly.
4. Heat oil in wok over high heat to near the smoking point (375° F, 190° C); reduce to medium-high (350° F, 180° C). Gently place battered pork in hot oil. Deep-fry up to 12 pieces at a time, until they float freely in oil and are golden brown, approximately 2-3 minutes. Remove and drain well. Repeat with remaining pork.
5. ***To make Sweet and Sour Sauce***: heat garlic with ½ teaspoon oil in saucepan. Add remaining ingredients except cornstarch solution, fruit and vegetables. Bring to a boil. Add fruits and vegetables and cook for 1 minute. Thicken with cornstarch solution and keep warm.
6. To serve, combine pork and sauce, mixing well. Garnish with extra tomato and fruit, and serve hot.

Twice Cooked Pork

SZECHWAN

This pork is cooked in two delectable ways, first it is simmered gently, which keeps it juicy and tender; then it's stir-fried in a piquant sauce, with mouth-watering results! Try this typically Szechwan dish tonight!

1 pound (450 g) pork butt or
    side of pork
2 tablespoons (30 ml) oil
2 cloves garlic, chopped
3 stalks green onion, cut into 1"
    (2.5 cm) pieces
½ pound (225 g) Chinese cabbage,
    cut into bite-size pieces

2-4 red chili peppers, fresh or dried
1 tablespoon (15 ml) hoisin sauce
1 tablespoon (15 ml) wine
1 teaspoon (5 ml) soy sauce
½ cup (125 g) soup stock
$^1/_8$ teaspoon (0.5 ml) salt
1½ teaspoons (7 ml) cornstarch solution

1. Place pork in a saucepan. Cover pork with water and simmer, covered, 35-40 minutes or until tender. When done, cut into thin slices and set aside.
2. Heat oil in wok over high heat. Add garlic and green onion, stir-fry for 30 seconds. Add pork slices and cook another 1-2 minutes.
3. Add remaining ingredients except cornstarch solution and cook for 1 minute.
4. Thicken with cornstarch solution, stirring constantly. Serve hot.

Remarks

- *Spiciness can be varied by adjusting the amount of red chili peppers used. This dish is supposed to be very hot. For maximum hotness, finely chop the dried red chili pepper. Add to wok at Step 2 and cook a few seconds over high heat before adding garlic and onion.*
- *If you can't find Chinese cabbage, use head cabbage instead.*

Fishy Finds

Here's a chance to bait your guests and hook their interest with some fishy business. Thanks to abundant waterways and a long coastline, the Chinese are enthusiastic fish-eaters, and there are many restaurants that specialize in seafood only. The same principles of absolute freshness prevail, and it is common to see vast tanks aswarm with live fish, crabs, lobster and even more exotic sea creatures. You may not like to look eye-to-eye with your potential supper, but that's a lot better than buying a fish that's so old his eyes are opaque from spoilage.

Aside from shellfish, such as scallops, snail, shrimp, clam, crab, lobster and oyster, the Chinese are picky about what kind of fish they will eat. In most Chinese fish stores, you will find cod, perch, grouper, sea bass, red snapper and gray sole. These all have firm white flesh, a general absence of fishy odor, and not too many tiny bones. Fish and other seafood are prepared in a great variety of dishes, from everyday meals to elaborate banquets. They may be steamed, deep-fried, braised, stir-fried or any combination of the above. Fish, in particular, is delicate, nutritious and low in calories. But what are you waiting for? Dive right in and make a whale of a splash!

Authentic West Lake Fish

The beauty of the resort city of Hangchow has been described by many poets and writers. This refreshing dish from West Lake, Hangchow is high in protein and low in calories. It has an appetizing sweet and sour sauce and is great for any occasion.

1 whole fish, approximately
    1 pound (450 g)
½ teaspoon (2 ml) salt
3-4 slices ginger, slivered
2 stalks green onion, slivered

Sweet and Sour Sauce:
2 teaspoons (10 ml) soy sauce
1 tablespoon (15 ml) dark soy sauce
    (optional)
3 tablespoons (45 ml) white vinegar
2 tablespoons (30 ml) sugar (brown
    preferred)
1 tablespoon (15 ml) wine
1 teaspoon (5 ml) sesame oil
¼ cup (60 ml) soup stock
½ teaspoon (2 ml) chili oil
1½ teaspoons (7 ml) cornstarch solution

1. Clean fish, sprinkle surface with salt and let stand for 10-15 minutes.
2. Bring a large pot of water to a boil. Add fish and ginger; return water to a boil. Reduce heat and simmer for 6-8 minutes or until fish flakes and is tender. Remove and place on a platter.
3. In a saucepan, combine all ingredients for sweet and sour sauce, except cornstarch solution. Bring to a boil, then thicken with cornstarch solution. Pour sauce over fish and garnish with green onion. Serve hot.

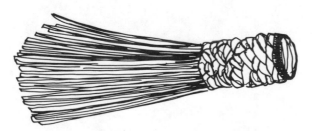

Batter-Fried Fresh Oysters

Many people never try oysters, yet they are a first choice among gourmets the world over. They are delicate, refreshing and extraordinarily tender. In this recipe, the oysters are deep-fried in a crispy batter and are absolutely incredible.

10-12 fresh oysters

Batter:
¾ cup (200 ml) flour
¼ cup (60 ml) cornstarch
1 cup (250 ml) beer or water
¾ teaspoon (3 ml) baking powder
½ teaspoon (2 ml) oil
dash of sugar

2 teaspoons (10 ml) ginger juice
½ teaspoon (2 ml) salt
dash of white pepper
1-2 tablespoons (15-30 ml)
**   cornstarch**
4 cups (1 L) oil
1 lemon, cut into wedges

1. Wash oysters in salted water; drain well. Marinate with ginger juice, salt and pepper for 30 minutes.
2. Place batter ingredients in a bowl; mix until blended. Set aside.
3. Blanch oysters in boiling water for 45-60 seconds. Drain well and sprinkle with cornstarch to absorb excess moisture.
4. Heat oil in wok over medium-high heat (350° F, 180° C). Dip oysters in batter and deep-fry until golden brown, about 1½-2 minutes. Serve hot with lemon wedges.

Remarks
- *Blanching the oysters partially cooks them and seals in the juices. It also firms them, making them easier to handle.*
- *For a crispy crust, deep-fry once, let cool completely, and fry again over high heat for 30 seconds.*
- *Serve with soy sauce and mustard, if desired.*
- *Make sure the oil is not too hot when deep-frying, or the oysters will puff up.*

Braised Oysters

This is an exotic Cantonese dish for seafood lovers: tender, plump oysters cooked to perfection in a ginger and onion-flavored sauce.

½ pound (225 g) shelled oysters, fresh or frozen
4 teaspoons (20 ml) oil
½ teaspoon (2 ml) chopped garlic
3-4 slices ginger, shredded
½ onion, cut into bite-size pieces
2 stalks green onion, cut into 2" (4 cm) pieces

½ teaspoon (2 ml) salt
½ teaspoon (2 ml) sugar
2 tablespoons (30 ml) wine
1 tablespoon (15 ml) oyster-flavored sauce
¼ cup (60 ml) soup stock
½ teaspoon (2 ml) cornstarch solution

1. Blanch shelled oysters in boiling water for 1 minute. Drain well and set aside.
2. Heat oil in wok with garlic and ginger over high heat for 15 seconds. Add onion (except green onion) and stir for 1 minute.
3. Add blanched oysters; stir for 1 minute. Add remaining ingredients, except cornstarch solution. Cover and simmer over low heat for 4-5 minutes, thicken with cornstarch solution and serve piping hot.

Remarks
- *When cooking this delicate seafood dish, be sure not to overcook or you will ruin the whole thing.*
- *The purpose of blanching the oysters is to get rid of the milky substance and to firm the flesh for stir-frying.*

Braised Whole Fish

To many Chinese, fish is a food symbolizing good fortune, or even bon voyage. The Chinese word for "fish" sounds similar to the words for "left over" or "long lasting." To honor a guest, the fish head is always placed towards the direction he is sitting. It sounds fishy, doesn't it?

1 whole fish, approximately
   1 pound (450 g)
½ teaspoon (2 ml) salt
1 egg, lightly beaten
½ cup (125 ml) flour
4 cups (1 L) oil

Braising Sauce:
1 tablespoon (15 ml) dark soy sauce
1 tablespoon (15 ml) oyster-flavored
   sauce
1 clove garlic, chopped
1 slice ginger, chopped
¾ teaspoon (3 ml) sugar
1 tablespoon (15 ml) wine
¾ cup (200 ml) soup stock

3 dried black mushrooms, soaked
   and shredded
2 ounces (56 g) pork, shredded
¼ cup (60 ml) shredded bamboo
   shoots
2 ounces (56 g) ham, shredded
1 stalk green onion, shredded
2 teaspoons (10 ml) cornstarch solution

1. Clean and score fish on both sides by making 3-4 diagonal slashes with a sharp knife about ¼" (0.75 cm) deep. Sprinkle with salt and let stand 30 minutes. Rinse fish with water and pat dry.
2. Coat the fish thoroughly with beaten egg, inside and out. Then sprinkle with flour, coating fish well.
3. Heat oil in wok over medium-high heat (350°F, 180°C). Deep-fry flour-coated fish for 6-8 minutes, turning frequently. Remove and drain well. Set aside. Clean and dry wok.
4. While deep-frying fish, place the braising sauce mixture in a saucepan. Add mushrooms, pork, bamboo shoots, ham and green onion; cook for 3-4 minutes over medium-high heat. Then thicken with cornstarch solution.
5. Return fried fish to wok, pour in hot braising sauce, cover and simmer over low heat for 3-4 minutes. Transfer to a plate and serve immediately.

Remarks
- *You can use white fish fillets instead of the whole fish, if desired. If fillet of fish is used, shorten the cooking time to about 2 minutes.*

Broiled Jumbo Prawns

This is an impressive and flavorful dish for special dinner guests. It has plenty of eye appeal and can be prepared in a flash!

16 jumbo prawns

Marinade:
1 teaspoon (5 ml) wine
¾ teaspoon (3 ml) cornstarch
½ egg white, lightly beaten
dash of salt
dash of white pepper

2-3 stalks green onion, white part only, chopped to 1″ (2.5 cm) pieces
Bamboo skewers
Sesame oil (to brush on prawns)

Sauce:
¼ cup (60 ml) soup stock
½ teaspoon (2 ml) Worcestershire sauce
2 tablespoons (30 ml) wine
1 teaspoon (5 ml) sugar
dash of sesame oil
¾ teaspoon (3 ml) soy sauce
1 teaspoon (5 ml) cornstarch solution

1. Shell and devein prawns, leaving the tails intact. Marinate for 1 hour.
2. Put 2 prawns on each bamboo skewer alternately with green onion. Brush prawns with sesame oil.
3. Preheat broiler for 2-3 minutes. Broil prawns for 2½ minutes on each side.
4. While prawns cook, combine sauce ingredients, except cornstarch solution, in a saucepan over medium-high heat. Thicken with cornstarch solution.
5. To serve, pour sauce over prawns or use as a dipping sauce.

Remarks
- *Flavor the dipping sauce as you like with ketchup, hoisin sauce, chili sauce, etc.*
- *Let your imagination go wild when arranging the prawns on a platter. Try a pinwheel shape, a fan, or a butterfly for a touch of class.*

Crab with Black Bean Sauce

Crabs are absolutely delicious, no matter how they are prepared. Most hard-shell crabs have some of the sweetest flesh. The sweet, delicate flavor of fresh crab combined with the pungent black bean sauce is mouth-watering.

1 live crab, approximately 1½ pounds (675 g)
1 teaspoon (5 ml) salt
2 tablespoons (30 ml) oil
1½ tablespoons (22 ml) salted black beans, rinsed and mashed
1 clove garlic, minced
2 slices ginger
1-2 dried chili peppers, crushed
½ onion, cut into bite-size pieces

1 stalk green onion, cut into 1″ (2.5 cm) strips
1½ tablespoons (22 ml) soy sauce
¾ cup (200 ml) soup stock
¾ teaspoon (3 ml) salt
½ teaspoon (2 ml) sugar
1¼ teaspoons (6 ml) cornstarch solution
1 teaspoon (5 ml) wine

1. *To prepare live crab:*
   A. Place crab in a large bowl of water; add 1 teaspoon salt; let stand for 20 minutes to clean itself.
   B. Cautiously snap off the large claws and crack them with a cleaver or mallet. Beware not to get clawed—somewhat a dangerous act.
   C. Lift and twist off the apron, then pull to separate the body from the crab and back shell. Remove and discard the stomach sac but save the roe.
   D. Remove and discard spongy, feathery gills; rub and rinse off sand and mud, then split the body in half right down the middle.
   E. Cut off and discard the third joints of legs; cut each half into 3 pieces with legs attached to each.
   F. Sprinkle the cut portions with flour and let set for 5 minutes.
2. Heat oil in wok with mashed black beans, garlic, ginger and chili pepper over high heat for 10 seconds. Add crab and stir-fry for 30 seconds.
3. Put in remaining ingredients except cornstarch solution and wine. Cover and cook over medium heat for 6-8 minutes. Thicken with cornstarch solution, then sizzle in wine. Serve hot.

Remarks
- *For texture and colour contrast, onion and bell pepper can be added to this recipe.*

Five-Spice Prawns

Among the many exotic Chinese dishes, this one is among the most popular. Nothing compares with the flavor of five-spice powder.

16 medium-size prawns,
   approximately 6 ounces (168 g)
¼ teaspoon (1 ml) salt
1 tablespoon (15 ml) oil
2 slices ginger, slivered
1 stalk green onion, chopped

¼ teaspoon (1 ml) sesame oil
¼ teaspoon (1 ml) garlic salt
¼ teaspoon (1 ml) five-spice powder
pinch of white pepper
1 teaspoon (5 ml) wine

1. Wash prawns and remove the legs, leaving the tail and shell intact. Sprinkle with salt.
2. Heat the oil and ginger in the wok over medium-high heat for 10 seconds. Add the prawns and green onion and stir-fry for 1½ minutes.
3. Stir in sesame oil, garlic salt, five-spice powder and pepper; cook for 1 minute then drizzle in wine and serve hot.

Remarks
- *These prawns are traditionally served with the shells on. You can remove the shells and prepare the dish in the same fashion.*
- *Fresh prawns are always best for this dish. If fresh ones are not available, fresh, frozen prawns are almost as good.*

Fresh Crab with Ginger and Scallion   CANTON

The delicate, slightly sweet crab meat, combined with the aromatic ginger and green onion is also another favorite among Chinese gourmets.

1 live, Pacific coast crab,
 approximately 1½ pounds (675 g)
2 tablespoons (30 ml) oil
4-6 slices ginger
4 stalks green onion, cut into 2"
 (5 cm) pieces
1 clove garlic, chopped

¾ cup (200 ml) soup stock
½ teaspoon (2 ml) sugar
1 tablespoon (15 ml) oyster-flavored
 sauce or soy sauce
¼ teaspoon (1 ml) salt
1 teaspoon (5 ml) cornstarch solution
1 teaspoon (5 ml) wine

1. Prepare crab as described on page 167.
2. Heat oil in wok over high heat. Add ginger, green onion, and garlic; stirring for 15 seconds. Add crab claws and body; stir-fry for 1-2 minutes.
3. Add back shell of crab and remaining ingredients, except cornstarch solution and wine. Cover and reduce to medium; cook for 6-8 minutes.
4. Thicken with cornstarch solution; sizzle in wine. Serve hot.

Remarks
- *In most Chinese restaurants, crab pieces are deep-fried in hot oil for 1½-2 minutes for quick cooking to achieve even cooking. After deep-frying, you only have to cook the crab for 2-3 minutes.*
- *It is not a great idea to serve crab at a formal dinner party. It's time-consuming to eat and is extraordinarily messy. Therefore, pick this dish when you and your guests can spend a couple of days for a memorable dinner.*
- *If fresh frozen crabs are used, prepare right after defrosting.*

Fresh Gingered Fish

These is nothing more refreshing and delicate than fresh, whole fish, steamed the Chinese way. Its pure and simple beauty is complemented by any sauce served with it. Try this as a unique change from grilled fish fillet or fish and chips.

1 whole fish, approximately 1 pound (450 g)	4 slices ginger, slivered
¾ teaspoon (3 ml) salt	1 tablespoon (15 ml) dark soy sauce
4 green onions, slivered	1 tablespoon (15 ml) hot oil

1. Clean fish and score on both sides by making 3-4 diagonal slashes about ¼" (0.75 cm) deep with a sharp knife. Sprinkle salt over the surface, inside and out.
2. Place half of the slivered green onion on a heat-proof dish. Rinse the salt off the fish and pat dry. Put fish over green onion (used so the fish will not stick to the dish), and sprinkle with ginger.
3. Steam fish over boiling water for 8-12 minutes, depending on the type, size, and thickness of the fish.
4. To serve, transfer the fish to an oval platter. Combine the soy sauce and hot oil and pour over the fish. Garnish with remaining green onion slivers and serve immediately.

Remarks
- *Place fish to steam over vigorously boiling water, then time the cooking of the dish.*
- *Scoring the surface of the fish allows it to cook more quickly and uniformly.*
- *Use of ginger and green onion helps mask the fishy aroma.*
- *Hot oil gives the fish a nice glaze and makes the meat smoother.*
- *Leftover fish deteriorates quickly. Try to finish it in the same meal as it may become very fishy.*

Golden Batter Prawns

This is one of the most popular Chinese dishes known to Westerners, in addition to egg roll, chow mein, and, of course, fried rice. It is great served as an appetizer or as a main dish. The dipping sauce is a refreshing change from the ubiquitous sweet and sour sauce.

12-14 jumbo prawns, shelled and
   deveined
1/8 teaspoon (½ ml) salt
¼ teaspoon (1 ml) wine
Flour for dry coating
4 cups (1 L) oil

Batter Mix:
¾ cup (200 ml) flour
¼ cup (60 ml) cornstarch
¾ teaspoon (3 ml) baking powder
1 cup (250 ml) water (more
   if needed)
dash of salt
dash of sugar
¼ teaspoon (1 ml) oil

Dipping Sauce:
2 teaspoons (10 ml) oil
6 tablespoons (90 ml) white vinegar
6 tablespoons (90 ml) sugar
4 teaspoons (20 ml) lemon juice
2 teaspoons (10 ml) orange juice
½ cup (125 ml) water
few drops of red food coloring
   (optional)
2½ teaspoons (12 ml) cornstarch
   solution
2 teaspoons (10 ml) Worcestershire
   sauce

1. To butterfly prawns, slice lengthwise along the back, almost, but not quite cutting the prawn in half. Keep the prawn intact. (See illustration on p. 181).
2. Sprinkle with salt and wine, then sprinkle the prawns with flour to dry coat.
3. Combine ingredients for batter in a bowl. Mix until smooth and set aside.
4. Heat oil over high heat (375° F, 190° C). Dip prawns in batter and deep-fry 5 or 6 at a time in hot oil over medium-high heat (350° F, 180° C) until golden brown. Turn prawns several times while frying. Remove and drain well. For extra-crispy prawns, cool completely and deep-fry a second time over high heat for 45 seconds.
5. While deep-frying prawns, combine ingredients for dipping sauce in saucepan and bring to a boil, stirring. Cook until thickened.
6. Arrange prawns around a platter. Place sauce in center of platter for dipping or pour sauce over prawns.

Remarks
- *Serve prawns immediately after deep-frying to retain their crispness.*
- *The yellow color in restaurant prawn batter is usually due to food coloring.*

Happy Family Reunion

It is not a common practice in Chinese cooking to have more than one main ingredient in a single dish, but this recipe is an exception. Here is a union of many ingredients, which make a truly delightful dish.

3-4 prawns, shelled and deveined
¼ cup (60 ml) oil
2 slices ginger, shredded
2 ounces (56 g) boneless chicken, cut into bite-size thin slices
2 ounces (56 g) cooked ham, cut into bite-size pieces
4 fresh or frozen scallops
6 snow peas (optional)
4 baby corns, cut in half at a crosswise diagonal
¼ small carrot, sliced

¼ cup (60 ml) sliced bamboo shoots
1 stalk green onion, cut into 1" (2.5 cm) pieces
½ teaspoon (2 ml) salt
½ cup (125 ml) soup stock
1 tablespoon (15 ml) wine
2 teaspoons (10 ml) soy sauce
¾ teaspoon (3 ml) sugar
dash of white pepper
1½ teaspoons (7 ml) oyster-flavored sauce
1¼ teaspoons (6 ml) cornstarch solution

1. To butterfly prawns, see illustration page 181.
2. Heat 2 tablespoons (30 ml) oil in wok over high heat. Add ginger and stir-fry for 15 seconds. Add sliced chicken and cook for 1 minute. Add prawns, ham and scallops. Stir-fry for another 1-1½ minutes. Remove and set aside.
3. Heat same wok over high heat with remaining 2 tablespoons oil. Add all the vegetables; stir for 1 minute. Add remaining ingredients, except cornstarch solution. Reduce heat to medium-high, cover and cook for 1-2 minutes.
4. Return cooked meats to wok. Thicken with cornstarch solution. Serve hot.

Remarks
- *Squid can be included in this recipe. Unfortunately some people won't dare to try it.*
- *Snow peas are optional since they are a seasonal crop and are not always available.*
- *With the combination of all these meats and vegetables, this may turn out to be a jumbo-size dish, so have a gigantic platter on hand.*

Lover's Prawns

(Colorful Prawn Combination)

What a romantic name! It represents the delicious and harmonious combination of two distinctly-flavored prawn dishes. It is a great choice for Valentine's Day or Mother's Day. Try it, and you will love its unique presentation.

3 tablespoons (45 ml) oil
1 onion, sliced
1 cucumber, peeled lengthwise in alternate strips, and sliced diagonally
¼ teaspoon (1 ml) salt
¼ teaspoon (1 ml) sugar
½ pound (225 g) medium-size, fresh or cooked prawns

Sauce for Lover A:
2 tablespoons (30 ml) catsup
1½ teaspoons (7 ml) white vinegar
1½ teaspoons (7 ml) sugar
dash of Tabasco sauce

Sauce for Lover B:
¾ teaspoon (3 ml) sugar
¼ teaspoon (1 ml) sesame oil
¼ teaspoon (1 ml) garlic salt
¼ cup (60 ml) soup stock
¾ teaspoon (3 ml) wine
1 teaspoon (5 ml) cornstarch solution

1. Heat 1 tablespoon (15 ml) oil in wok over high heat. Stir-fry onion for 30 seconds. Add cucumber and stir-fry for another minute. Sprinkle with salt and sugar. Remove and arrange on an oval platter, with the onions in the center surrounded by the cucumber.
2. *To make Lover A:* heat 1 tablespoon oil in wok over medium-high heat, add ¼ pound (112 g) prawns, and stir-fry for 1 minute, or just until they turn pink. Add sauce ingredients for Lover A and mix well, stirring for 1 minute. Remove to one side of the platter.
3. *To make Lover B:* wash and dry the wok. Heat 1 tablespoon oil over medium-high heat and stir-fry remaining ¼ pound of prawns for 1 minute or just until they turn pink. Add sauce B ingredients, except cornstarch solution. Stir for 1 minute, then thicken with cornstarch solution. Remove to other side of platter. Serve hot.

Remarks
- *Traditionally, this recipe calls for spinach instead of cucumber and onion. Use any vegetable that is in season.*
- *English cucumber is a better choice for this dish since it has less seeds, no bitterness and is sweeter.*

Mushroom Abalone in Oyster Sauce

If you've ever been around the West Coast, you have most likely tasted fresh abalone—absolutely terrific! They are usually available in cans in most Chinese stores. It has been a classic choice for formal dinners, even in the most lavish banquets.

8 ounces (225 g) abalone, thinly sliced
   (fresh or canned)
2 teaspoons (10 ml) oil
2 ounces (56 g) dried black
   mushrooms, soaked

Braising Oyster Sauce:
¾ cup (200 ml) soup stock
2 tablespoons (30 ml) oyster-flavored
   sauce
1 tablespoon (15 ml) dark soy sauce
¾ teaspoon (3 ml) sugar
1 teaspoon (5 ml) wine
1½ teaspoons (7 ml) cornstarch
   solution (add at last minute)

2 ounces (56 g) fresh pea pods
   (optional)

1. A. ***To prepare fresh abalone:*** Clean and blanch sliced abalone over hot water for 1-1½ minutes, be sure not to over cook; otherwise you have to chew your jaws off.
   B. ***For canned abalone:*** Slice thinly and set aside.
2. Heat oil in a saucepan; sauté mushrooms for 30 seconds. Add oyster sauce ingredients and bring to a boil. Reduce heat to low and simmer for 15-17 minutes. Keep warm.
3. Snap off ends of pea pods and blanch in boiling water (with ½ teaspoon (2 ml) oil and ¼ teaspoon (1 ml) salt) for 1½ minutes. Remove and set aside.
4. To serve, place abalone on top of mushrooms, with blanched pea pods arranged around them. Pour leftover juice on top and serve hot.

Remarks
- *Traditionally, nothing other than abalone and dried black mushrooms are used. In this recipe, the use of pea pods will add a nice color contrast.*

Poached Fish
with Curried Cream Sauce

Using milk to make a cream sauce for a Chinese dish? You must be kidding! — that's unheard of! But this humble cook and his associates created this delicious cream sauce with milk and an added touch of curry. How extraordinary!

1 whole fish, approximately	*Cream Sauce:*
¾ to 1 pound (340 to 450 g)	**¼ teaspoon (1 ml) salt**
1 teaspoon (5 ml) salt	**2 teaspoons (10 ml) wine**
2-3 slices ginger	**½ cup (125 ml) low-fat milk**
	¼ teaspoon (1 ml) curry powder
	½ teaspoon (2 ml) sugar
	¼ cup (60 ml) soup stock
	2 teaspoons (10 ml) cornstarch solution

1. In a large pot, bring enough water to a boil to cover fish. Add salt and ginger and boil for 10-15 seconds. Reduce heat to low, and poach fish for 7-9 minutes, depending on the type and size of the fish. Remove, drain well, and place fish on a platter.
2. Combine ingredients for cream sauce, except cornstarch solution, in a saucepan and bring to a slow boil over medium heat, stirring constantly. Thicken with cornstarch solution and pour over fish.

Remarks
- *Rex sole or any white fish will do for this dish. If you are looking for a nutritious and fattening fish dish, use half and half instead of low-fat milk.*

Pork and Prawn-Stuffed Fish

CANTON

For the gourmet who enjoys an exciting seafood dish, this recipe is the ultimate experience. Whole fish stuffed with delicately-seasoned ingredients — unsurpassable!

1 whole fish, approximately 1½-2
    pounds (675-900 g)
1 tablespoon (15 ml) wine
½ teaspoon (2 ml) salt
1½ eggs, lightly beaten
3 tablespoons (45 ml) flour

3 tablespoons (45 ml) oil
½ cup (125 ml) soup stock
parsley (for garnish)

Filling Mixture:
2 ounces (56 g) ground pork
2-3 fresh or frozen prawns, minced
1½ teaspoons (7 ml) Virginia ham,
    minced
1 dried black mushroom, soaked
    and minced
1½ teaspoons (7 ml) wine
¼ teaspoon (1 ml) salt
½ teaspoon (2 ml) soy sauce
¼ teaspoon (1 ml) ginger juice
½ teaspoon (2 ml) cornstarch
dash of white pepper
dash of sesame oil

1. Clean and dry fish. Rub whole fish with wine and salt, inside and out. Let stand for 30 minutes. Coat with beaten eggs and 2 tablespoons (30 ml) flour.
2. In a bowl, combine filling mixture ingredients and mix well. Let stand for 30 minutes.
3. To stuff fish, sprinkle 1 tablespoon (15 ml) flour inside cavity. Evenly spread filling mixture over surface of cavity.
4. Heat oil in a wok or heavy skillet over medium-high heat. Carefully place fish in wok; reduce heat to medium and brown for 2 minutes on each side. If using a wok, tilt occasionally so entire fish is browned. Drain oil.
5. Reduce heat to medium-low. Add soup stock, cover and simmer for 10-12 minutes. Turn fish several times during simmering.
6. Transfer fish to a platter and pour remaining juice over fish. Garnish with parsley and serve.

Remarks
- *If not served immediately after cooking, cool, wrap in foil, and store in refrigerator. To reheat, simply brown again in frying pan.*
- *A 10-12 inch fish is a good size to use.*

Scallops in Wine Sauce

Many people enjoy the fine texture and delicate flavor of scallops. With this special wine sauce, it only takes a few minutes to make them into an absolutely heavenly dish.

¾ pound (340 g) fresh or frozen scallops, cut horizontally across the fibrous tissue into two or three thin slices

Marinade:
2 teaspoons (10 ml) wine
¼ teaspoon (1 ml) ginger juice
½ teaspoon (2 ml) garlic juice

3 tablespoons (45 ml) oil
1 stalk green onion, chopped

Wine Sauce:
¼ cup (60 ml) wine
¼ cup (60 ml) soup stock
½ teaspoon (2 ml) garlic salt
½ teaspoon (2 ml) sesame oil
dash of white pepper
¾ teaspoon (3 ml) sugar
¾ teaspoon (3 ml) cornstarch solution

1. Marinate scallops for ½-1 hour, drain and set aside.
2. Heat oil in wok over high heat. Stir-fry scallops and green onion for 1-1½ minutes, or until barely tender. Remove from wok and drain away oil.
3. Stir wine sauce mixture in a saucepan over medium-high heat until thickened. Place in a small serving bowl. Add cooked scallops to sauce, mix well and serve immediately. Serve over a bed of chopped lettuce, if desired.

Seafood Combination Hot Pot CANTON

It is an infrequent practice in Chinese cooking to use more than one type of meat or seafood in a single dish. For many homemakers it is impractical and expensive. Occasionally, you will find a combination of chicken and seafood, or a stir-fried seafood combo. This recipe is a particularly great seafood union.

3 tablespoons (45 ml) oil
2 slices ginger, chopped
1 clove garlic, chopped
5 fresh or frozen prawns, shelled and deveined
3 scallops, sliced
2 ounces (56 g) fresh squid, cut into 1½″ (4 cm) squares
½ onion, cut into 1″ (2.5 cm) squares
3-4 dried black mushrooms, soaked and sliced
3-4 fresh mushrooms, sliced

½ carrot, cut into diagonal slices
3 water chestnuts, sliced
½ bell pepper, cut into 1″ (2.5 cm) squares
1 green onion, cut into 1½″ (4 cm) pieces
2½ teaspoons (12 ml) wine
1 teaspoon (5 ml) soy sauce
½ teaspoon (2 ml) salt
½ cup (125 ml) soup stock
½ teaspoon (2 ml) sugar
1 teaspoon (5 ml) cornstarch solution

1. Heat oil in wok over high heat. Add ginger and garlic, stirring for 10 seconds. Add prawns, scallops, and squid; stir-fry for 1 minute. Remove and set aside.
2. Add onion, mushrooms, and carrot to hot wok and stir for 30 seconds. Add remaining ingredients, except cornstarch solution, mix well and transfer to a hot pot, clay pot or saucepan. Simmer over low heat for 2-3 minutes. Thicken with cornstarch solution. Serve directly from the clay pot.

Remarks
- *This dish is traditionally cooked entirely in the clay pot, but it is easier to stir-fry it in the wok and then transfer to a clay pot before simmering.*

Singing Shrimp Surprise SZECHWAN

Have you encountered a dish that can sing? Many Chinese believe the louder the noise, the better the cook. This is one of the most popular northern Chinese dishes and a good example of how the Chinese create magic out of leftovers. The crusted rice left in the bottom of the pot is dried and broken into bite-size pieces. Traditionally, it is used to make either a sizzling dish or a sizzling soup (refer to the chapter on soups).

¾ pound (340 g) fresh or cooked
  shrimp
4 cups (1 L) oil
4 ounces (112 g) cooked dried rice
  crust, 1½″ (4 cm) squares
1 clove garlic, minced
2 slices ginger, slivered or chopped
¼ cup (60 ml) green peas
1 stalk green onion, chopped

Sizzling Sauce:
1 tablespoon (15 ml) wine
¼ cup (60 ml) hot catsup
2 teaspoons (10 ml) Worcestershire
  sauce
4 teaspoons (20 ml) white vinegar
2 teaspoons (10 ml) sugar
1/3 cup (80 ml) soup stock
½ teaspoon (2 ml) sesame oil
1 teaspoon (5 ml) cornstarch solution

1. Clean, shell and devein shrimp. If using large shrimp, cut into small pieces.
2. Deep-fry rice crust pieces over high heat (375° F, 190° C) until puffed, approximately 10 seconds. Remove, drain well, and place on a large platter.
3. Combine all ingredients for sizzling sauce, except cornstarch solution, and reserve.
4. Heat 2 tablespoons oil, garlic and ginger in wok over high heat for 10-12 seconds. Stir in shrimp and cook for 1 minute. Add sizzling sauce mixture and green peas; cook over high heat for 1½ minutes. Thicken with cornstarch solution.
5. Pour piping hot shrimp mixture over fried rice crust. Garnish with green onion and serve immediately.

Remarks
- *To make rice crust: after rice is cooked in saucepan, scoop out most of the rice, leaving 1/3″ (1 cm) thick layer on the bottom. Keep heating over low heat until slightly brown and dried. Take out and break into 2″ x 2″ pieces for storage.*
- *In Chinatown of San Francisco, Vancouver or Toronto, you may purchase ready-made dried rice crust, which can be stored in dry, cool places for a long time.*

Smoky Fish

This is a delicate and somewhat sweet seafood cold plate from Soochow which is near Shanghai. The fish is not smoked, but is deep-fried. It can be a marvelous appetizer or a main course in a formal dinner. Prepare and freeze. Serve 25 or 30 years later!?

¾ pound (340 g) white fish fillet,
  cut into ½" x 2" x 3" (1.5 cm x
  5 cm x 7.5 cm) pieces

Marinade:
1½ tablespoons (22 ml) dark
  soy sauce
1 tablespoon (15 ml) wine
1 green onion, minced
1 slice ginger, minced

4 cups (1 L) oil
Lettuce or parsley (for garnish)

Dip:
3 tablespoons (45 ml) brown sugar
3 tablespoons (45 ml) dark soy sauce
½ cup (125 ml) water
2 teaspoons (10 ml) oyster-flavored
  sauce (optional)

1. Marinate fish for 3 hours. Drain well and set aside.
2. Heat oil in wok over medium-high (350° F, 180° C) and deep-fry the fish fillet for 3-4 minutes or until light brown.
3. Combine dip ingredients in saucepan and bring to a boil. Immediately dip fried fish in sauce. Set aside and let drain.
4. Deep-fry fish once more over high heat (375° F, 190° C) until dark golden brown, approximately 2½-3½ minutes. If the pieces break apart, do not panic. Remove and let drain over paper towels.
5. Serve over a bed of lettuce or parsley, either hot or cold.

Remarks
• *Prepare this dish in advance and freeze it. Serve it anytime, any place and for any occasion.*

Stir-Fried Prawns

Many favorite Cantonese dishes are seafoods prepared in various ways: deep-fried, stir-fried, steamed, and red-cooked. In Hong Kong's magnificent floating restaurants, many seafood delicacies can be sampled. Here is a gourmet specialty that is also classified as one of the hottest!

1½ tablespoons (22 ml) oil
1 slice ginger, chopped
2 stalks green onions, white part
    only, cut into 1½″ (2.5 cm)
    pieces

½ pound (225 g) jumbo prawns,
    shelled and deveined
1 tablespoon (15 ml) wine
2-4 tablespoons (30-60 ml) catsup
1 teaspoon (5 ml) soy sauce
½ teaspoon (2 ml) chili oil

1. Heat oil in hot wok over high heat. Add ginger and green onions, and stir for 30 seconds. Add prawns and stir-fry for 1-1½ minutes over high heat, or until they just turn pink and curl.
2. Add remaining ingredients. Mix well, stirring for another 30 seconds.
3. Transfer to a platter and serve immediately.

Remarks
- *Traditionally, the prawns are cooked and served with the shells intact, which makes them more challenging to eat. You have to use your lips, tongue and teeth to get to the tasty treat, but you can better savor the tasty sauce. It also takes more time, but is a lot more fun.*

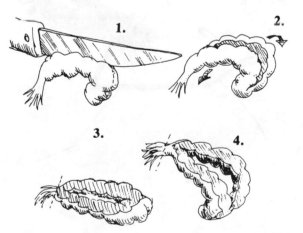

Stir-Fried Winter Melon with Prawns   CANTON

Here is another popular alternative for creative cooks. The contrasting colors of the vegetables make this dish a delight to the eye as well as a tasty treat.

2 tablespoons (30 ml) oil
1 clove garlic, minced
¼ pound (112 g) fresh or frozen prawns, shelled, deveined and diced
½ pound (225 g) winter melon flesh, diced
½ medium-size carrot, cut into ½" (1.5 cm) cubes
5 water chestnuts, quartered
2 tablespoons (30 ml) peas

4 fresh mushrooms, diced
¼ cup (60 ml) straw mushrooms, canned (optional)
¾ teaspoon (3 ml) salt
1½ teaspoons (7 ml) wine
½ teaspoon (2 ml) sugar
1 teaspoon (5 ml) oyster-flavored sauce (optional)
1/3 cup (80 ml) soup stock
½ teaspoon (2 ml) cornstarch solution

1. Heat oil and garlic in wok over high heat for 15 seconds. Add prawns and stir-fry for 1½ minutes. Remove and set aside.
2. Add remaining ingredients to wok, except cornstarch solution. Mix well, cover, reduce heat to medium-high and cook for 3-4 minutes. Return cooked prawns to wok and mix well. Thicken with cornstarch solution. Serve hot.

Remarks
- *Precooking this dish and reheating it does not affect the quality too much. Thus it would be a good choice for a big meal.*
- *If winter melon is not available, replace it with zucchini.*
- *Fresh Chinese winter melon can be purchased by the pound only in Chinese grocery stores. It keeps for several days in the refrigerator.*
- *Use chicken, pork or scallops in place of the prawns.*

Stuffed Fish Rolls with Velvet Corn Sauce   CANTON

One of my most-treasured recipes — I'm sharing it with you because you're worth it! A precious, light and delicate blend of fish and corn.

¾ pound (340 g) fish fillet, cut into 9 or 10 thin slices, 2″ x 4″ (5 cm x 10 cm)

Marinade:
1 teaspoon (5 ml) wine
¼ teaspoon (1 ml) salt
1 egg yolk, lightly beaten
1½ teaspoons (7 ml) cornstarch
dash of white pepper
½ teaspoon (2 ml) ginger juice

2 ounces (56 g) sliced cooked ham, cut into 1″ x 2″ pieces (2.5 cm x 5 cm)
4-6 stalks green onion, white part only, cut into 2″ long pieces (5 cm)
3 dried black mushrooms, soaked and cut into 3 slices
3 tablespoons (45 ml) oil

Velvet Corn Sauce:
½ cup (125 ml) cream style corn
½ teaspoon (2 ml) salt
¾ teaspoon (3 ml) sugar
dash of sesame oil
1/3 cup (80 ml) soup stock
½ teaspoon (2 ml) cornstarch solution
1 egg white

1. Marinate fish fillet for 30 minutes.
2. Place one piece of ham, green onion, and mushroom on each fillet and roll up. Secure with a toothpick.
3. Heat oil in wok or frying pan over medium-high heat and brown fish rolls 3-3½ minutes, turning several times to brown evenly.
4. While browning the fish rolls, combine all sauce ingredients, except cornstarch solution and egg white, in a sauce pan. Bring to a boil over medium-high heat. Add cornstarch and thicken. Remove from heat and slowly stir in egg white.
5. To serve, place fish fillet rolls on a platter and pour corn sauce over top. Serve hot.

Remarks
- *Fish rolls may also be deep-fried over medium heat for 2 minutes. They will cook faster, more uniformly and be more golden in color.*

Sweet and Sour Fish Rolls

Tender fish rolls served in an appetizing sweet and sour sauce are great for the whole family. Prepare them at home for a sensational dish not found in any restaurant.

1¼ pounds (562 g) cod fillet, cut
    into about 12-2" x 4" (5 cm x
    10 cm) thin slices
½ teaspoon (2 ml) salt
2 slices Virginia ham, cut into 1"
    x 2" (2.5 cm x 5 cm) thin strips
½ carrot, cut into 1" x 2" (2.5 cm x
    5 cm) strips and parboiled
½ cup (125 ml) flour for dry-coating
4 cups (1 L) oil
Lettuce (for garnish)

Sweet and Sour Sauce:
1/3 cup (80 ml) white vinegar
1/3 cup (80 ml) brown sugar
½ cup (125 ml) water
3 tablespoons (45 ml) catsup
¼ teaspoon (1 ml) salt
pinch of white pepper
¼ cup (60 ml) peas
½ teaspoon (2 ml) Tabasco sauce or
    chili oil
1 tablespoon (15 ml) cornstarch solution

Batter Mix:
1 cup (250 ml) flour
¾ teaspoon (3 ml) baking powder
1 cup (250 ml) flat beer
dash of oil
dash of sugar

1. Marinate fish with salt for 30 minutes.
2. Place ham and parboiled carrot slice in fillet and make rolls. Secure with toothpicks.
3. Combine ingredients for batter and mix well.
4. Combine ingredients for sweet and sour sauce, except cornstarch solution. Bring to a boil, then thicken with cornstarch solution.
5. Coat rolls with flour; dip in batter. Deep-fry in oil over medium to medium-high heat (350°F, 180°C) for 3-4 minutes or until golden brown. Remove and drain well. Remove toothpicks and arrange rolls on a lettuce-lined platter. Pour the sauce over the fish rolls and serve immediately.

Remarks
- *Chinese sausage can be used in place of the Virginia ham.*

"Always follow precise measurements, . . . approximately . . ."

Hi, Protein: Eggs and Bean Curd

Don't curdle at the thought of eating eggs and soy bean curd (tofu). They are both rich in protein and make excellent supplements for a low-meat diet. In China, eggs are sold in stores and by sidewalk vendors, individually or by the pound. You can choose any size or color, and when you buy them, the owner will personally check the quality of each egg under a light bulb (if the inside blinks, it's too old!). Preserved eggs, such as salted duck egg or thousand year eggs, are also available in the Chinese stores.

The Chinese are typically ingenious with their eggs, which they can stir-fry, deep-fry, smoke, scramble and steam. They also add them to soups and numerous other dishes. A charming traditional custom is to offer friends and relatives hard-boiled eggs that are dyed red to show good wishes and happiness at birth announcements. When an odd number is presented (9 or 11 eggs), a baby boy has been born; an even number of eggs (8 or 10) means a baby girl.

Soy bean curd—the velvety-smooth 'cheese' made from soy beans, has long been an important part of Oriental cuisine. Containing 40 percent protein (by dry weight), bean curd is the poor man's meat and the rich man's delight. And they make no beans about that! Because bean curd is essentially tasteless, it goes well with many ingredients and flavors and is easily prepared in many different dishes. For the health and budget-conscious cook, it is the best and most natural meat substitute. Soy bean curd—either fresh, dried, fermented, or fried, will make your favorite dishes more enjoyable without worrying about too little protein, too many calories, or too much cholesterol.

Watch your curds and the whey you prepare them!

All About Beans:

Perhaps it's hard these days to find something that amounts to a hill of beans, but if you *had* a hill of beans, you could sure make a lot of soybean curd! For centuries, soybean curd (tofu) has been a staple food in China, but only in recent years has it begun to gain recognition in America. Vegetarians and meat-eaters alike enjoy this nutritious, protein-packed and highly versatile food. In addition to the pluses just mentioned, bean curd is low in calories and inexpensive — a rare combination when a food tastes good, too! You can purchase bean curd in several different forms: fresh, dried, canned, fried or fermented.

All the recipes in this book that call for bean curd use it in the fresh form, which can be either firm or soft. The firm type has a consistency similar to Monterey Jack cheese, while the soft type is more like custard. If you can't find the firm one, just place the soft bean curd squares in cheesecloth, place them under a heavy object (2-4 pounds) like a large book, brick or breadboard and leave it for several hours or overnight. Placing the squares of curd on a large platter with high edges or on a board over the sink will take care of all that water you're going to squeeze out.

Have a look at the following chart — I think you'll find it interesting, maybe even amazing! Once you see how bean curd stacks up against some common animal protein sources, you'll see why it's sometimes called the "boneless meat."

Foods, 100 gms	Firm Bean Curd	Chicken Egg	Ground Beef	Cottage Cheese
Calories	147	180	268	95
Protein, gms	17.6	13	17.9	12.9
Carbohydrates, gms	5	0.8	0	2.6
Fats, % total	8.8	11.6	21.2	4.2
Saturated fats, %	15	33	48	52
Unsaturated fats, %	80	50	47	37
Cholesterol, mgs	0	500	63	13.7
Calcium, mgs	316	54	11	86

Making Bean Curd

It's time to learn to use your bean and make some curd! The process is very simple, a lot like making cheese from milk, but much faster!

In making bean curd, a solidifier of some kind is required to hold the stuff together. Here are some of the more common ones: Epsom salts, gypsum, magnesium chloride, calcium chloride, Nigari (a sea water extract available at health food stores). The following recipe gives you a choice of solidifiers. You can pick whichever one you want. Don't be afraid to experiment! Try two or three different ones, until you find the one you like the best. Now . . . get ready, set, curdle!

Bean Curd
1½ cups soy beans, soaked overnight in enough water to cover
5 cups water
1 teaspoon Epsom salt
1 cup water, more if needed

1. Drain beans. Put beans in blender with 3 cups fresh water. Blend about 2 minutes. Put into jelly bag, squeeze out as much of the milk as possible and set aside.
2. Return beans to the blender with the remaining 2 cups of water, blend again. Remove milk and add to the first milk.
3. Pour milk into a saucepan, bring to a boil, stirring constantly to prevent scorching. Reduce heat and boil gently for 5 minutes. Remove pan from heat.
4. Dissolve Epsom salt in 1 cup water. Add half of the solution into the milk and stir vigorously. Slowly add the remaining Epsom salt mixture, a little at a time, until mixture begins to curdle and the whey separates (about ¼ cup).
5. Line colander with a double thickness of cheesecloth. Place curds and whey into the colander and strain, pressing gently to get all the water out. Let stand 15-20 minutes to solidify. Rinse gently with cool water.
6. Store in water in the refrigerator. Keep covered to avoid off flavors. Change clean water every one or two days.

Conclusion

Now that you have your fresh homemade bean curd, you are no doubt anxious to try some tempting recipes. Those given in this book are merely an introduction. You will find the uses of bean curd are almost unlimited. Try it in salads, soups, or appetizers, or main dishes. Fry it, stuff it, braise it in sauces — the sky's the limit!

Braised Stuffed Bean Curd

This is a widely known dish of Cantonese origin. It might take a couple of extra minutes to prepare, but it's worth trying! The mild flavor of bean curd is perfectly contrasted with the flavorful pork-shrimp stuffing and complemented with garlic and oyster-flavored braising sauce.

Stuffing Mixture:
3 ounces (84 g) ground pork
2 ounces (56 g) fresh or frozen shrimp, finely mashed
1 water chestnut, finely chopped
½ dried black mushroom, soaked and finely chopped
1 teaspoon (5 ml) soy sauce
1/3 stalk green onion, finely chopped
sesame oil to taste

3 squares bean curd, 1½ pounds (675 g), each cut into 4 smaller squares
¼ cup (60 ml) cornstarch for dry-coating
4 cups (1 L) oil

Braising Sauce:
1 clove garlic, chopped
1 tablespoon (15 ml) soy sauce
¾ teaspoon (3 ml) sugar
1 teaspoon (5 ml) oyster-flavored sauce
¾ teaspoon (3 ml) cornstarch solution
¾ cup (200 ml) soup stock

1. Combine ingredients for stuffing mixture. Mix well and let stand for 30 minutes.
2. Make a small indentation on top of each small square of bean curd. Sprinkle lightly with cornstarch. Place ½ teaspoon (2 ml) stuffing mixture on indentation and press to make a smooth surface. Drain on paper towels for 5-10 minutes. Pat dry. Set aside.
3. Heat oil in wok over medium-high heat (350° F-375° F, 180° C-190° C). Deep-fry stuffed bean curd for 2½ minutes. Remove, drain well and set aside. Remove oil from wok.
4. Heat wok with 2 teaspoons (10 ml) oil over medium-high heat. Add braising sauce ingredients and bring to a boil. Return fried bean curd to wok. Cook over medium-low heat for 4-5 minutes, turning bean curd occasionally to ensure uniform braising.

Braised Szechwan Bean Curd Sandwiches   SZECHWAN

*Tasty and nutritious, this is one of those 'do ahead' dishes which fits well
into any menu. Distinctly-flavored pork provide a savory filling for these
Chinese-style sandwiches. Try these instead of ham and cheese!*

4 ounces (112 g) ground pork

Marinade:
¼ teaspoon (1 ml) salt
1 teaspoon (5 ml) wine
1 teaspoon (5 ml) cornstarch
1 egg yolk, lightly beaten

2 stalks green onion, finely chopped
2 slices ginger, finely chopped
2 water chestnuts, chopped
4 squares bean curd (2 lbs, 1 kg)
¼ cup (60 ml) flour
¼ cup (60 ml) oil

Braising Sauce:
4 teaspoons (20 ml) soy sauce
¾ teaspoon (3 ml) sugar
1 cup (250 ml) soup stock
½ teaspoon (2 ml) sesame oil
2 teaspoons (10 ml) cornstarch solution

1. Marinate ground pork for 30 minutes.
2. Combine marinated pork with half of the green onion, ginger and
   water chestnuts. Place in a large bowl, mix well and set aside.
3. Slice each square of bean curd horizontally into 2 thinner squares.
   Then cut in half and let drain on paper towel.
4. Spread 1¼ teaspoons pork mixture evenly over half of bean curd
   squares, placing the rest of the squares on top of the mixture to form 8
   sandwiches.
5. Coat bean curd sandwiches with flour and brown in frying pan with
   1-1½ tablespoons (15-22 ml) oil over medium heat until light brown,
   about 2 minutes on each side. Move pan constantly while frying. Turn
   sandwiches carefully as bean curd crumbles easily.
6. Combine ingredients for braising sauce, except cornstarch solution, in
   a bowl. Mix well and pour over bean curd sandwiches. Cover and
   simmer for 12-15 minutes over low heat, moving pan occasionally.
   Remove to a platter and thicken remaining sauce with cornstarch.
   Serve hot. Garnish with remaining green onions.

Remarks
• *Add extra stock during braising, if needed.*
• *If it is convenient, prepare sandwiches ahead. Refrigerate and reheat
  when ready to serve.*

Colorful Steamed Eggs

This is a meatless, yet high protein dish. Simple and nutritious, this is a good dish for a balanced vegetarian diet. It is also one of the most traditional and popular dishes in many southern regions of China.

4 medium-size eggs, lightly beaten
1 cup (250 ml) water
1 preserved egg, cut into 8 wedges
1 salted egg, break yolk apart

Dressing:
½ teaspoon (2 ml) oil
pinch of salt
pinch of white pepper
1 teaspoon (5 ml) dark soy sauce
1 teaspoon (5 ml) chopped green onion
½ teaspoon (2 ml) sesame oil

1. Combine all the eggs and water in a mixing bowl. Blend well. Transfer to an 8" (20.5 cm) pie pan or pyrex dish.
2. Steam egg mixture for 8-10 minutes over medium to medium-high heat or until it becomes a smooth pudding. Don't overcook or it will lose its fine smooth texture.
3. Pour dressing mixture over top of egg pudding and serve hot.

Remarks
- *This is not one of my favorite dishes, but it may be one of yours.*
- *Preserved egg (thousand year old egg) and salted egg are only available in Oriental stores. They can be kept in a dry, cool place for several months. Please don't try to keep them for the rest of your life!*
- *Open preserved eggs in the privacy of your own kitchen or you will lose all of your friends!*

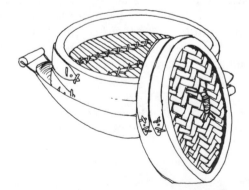

Red Cooked Bean Curd with Chicken

In the past couple of years, everyone has been talking about natural, healthy foods and searching for new sources of protein to substitute for high priced, high cholesterol animal products. All of a sudden, soy beans have become a rising star in the consumer market. Here, soy beans are used in a delicious, nutritious dish that will soon be on your list of favorite recipes!

1½-2 squares (1 pound, 450 g)
   bean curd
4 cups (1 L) oil
2 ounces (56 g) boneless chicken
   breast, cut into 2" (5 cm)
   thin strips
2 dried black mushrooms, soaked
   and shredded
½ stalk celery, cut into 1½" (4 cm)
   thin strips
2 ounces (56 g) ham, cooked and
   shredded
2 tablespoons (30 ml) shredded carrot
1 teaspoon (5 ml) cornstarch solution

Red Cooked Sauce:
1 tablespoon (15 ml) oyster-flavored
   sauce
2 teaspoons (10 ml) dark soy sauce
1 teaspoon (5 ml) chopped green onion
½ teaspoon (2 ml) sugar
½ teaspoon (2 ml) sesame oil
¾ cup (180 ml) soup stock

1. Cut each piece of bean curd diagonally into 4 small triangles. Drain well and pat dry. Set aside.
2. Heat oil over high heat. Reduce heat to medium-high (350°-375° F, 180°-190° C) and deep-fry bean curd for 4-5 minutes or until golden brown. Remove, drain on paper towels, and set aside. (Have a grease screen or lid handy to safeguard against splashing oil.)
3. Combine sauce ingredients and set aside.
4. Heat wok with 2 tablespoons (30 ml) oil over medium-high heat. Stir-fry chicken for about 1 minute. Add mushrooms, celery, ham, and carrot and stir-fry for 1-1½ minutes.
5. Return fried bean curd to wok. Add red-cooked sauce and mix well. Cover and cook over low to medium-low heat for 5 minutes. Thicken with cornstarch solution. Serve immediately.

Remarks
- *If you don't want to deep-fry the bean curd, blanch it for 3-4 minutes.*

Special Egg Foo Yung

This is a well-known recipe — like many Chinese dishes, it has an interesting and poetic name. Foo Yung is a rare and extremely pretty flower grown in southeastern China. This foo yung is a rich omelet filled with a bouquet of goodies.

Omelet:
3-4 large eggs, lightly beaten
1 cup (250 ml) bean sprouts
2 tablespoons (30 ml) chopped
   BBQ pork (optional)
1 cup (250 ml) chopped cooked
   ham
1 cup (250 ml) fresh or cooked
   shrimp
2 stalks green onions, chopped
2 tablespoons (30 ml) peas and
   carrots
½ teaspoon (2 ml) sugar
dash of white pepper
1 tablespoon (15 ml) flour
salt to taste

4 teaspoons (20 ml) oil

Foo Yung Sauce: (optional)
½ cup (125 ml) soup stock
½ teaspoon (2 ml) sugar
2 teaspoons (10 ml) soy sauce
¼ teaspoon (1 ml) sesame oil
1½ teaspoons (7 ml) cornstarch solution

1. Combine omelet ingredients in a large bowl; mix well.
2. Heat a 6"-7" (15-17.5 cm) skillet with 2 teaspoons (10 ml) oil over medium-high heat. Pour ½ of omelet mixture in skillet, spreading to an even thickness. Cook for 1½ minutes on one side until lightly brown. Turn and cook for another 1½ minutes. Remove to a platter. Cook remaining half of mixture in the same way.
3. Bring sauce ingredients to a boil and keep warm. Serve over egg foo yung.

Remarks
- *Any ingredient can be substituted or omitted — try an original vegetarian foo yung!*
- *Add 2 teaspoons cornstarch to the omelet for a thicker mixture.*
- *Foo Yung will quickly turn watery as a result of a physical process, osmosis. Cook immediately after preparing omelet mixture.*
- *Foo Yung sauce is optional. In fact, the traditional recipe never calls for it.*

Szechwan-Style Spicy Omelet

This is an exotic dish for those with discriminating tastes. A fluffy omelet topped with a delicious hot sauce — spicy and nutritious. It's a wonderful choice for those who relish good quality protein and a long-lasting hot lip!

5 eggs
¼ teaspoon (1 ml) salt
2 teaspoons (10 ml) cornstarch
2 tablespoons (30 ml) oil
2 slices ginger, finely chopped
2 cloves garlic, finely chopped
4 ounces (112 g) ground pork
2 stalks green onion, chopped
6 water chestnuts, sliced

2 tablespoons (30 ml) hot bean paste
   or chili sauce
2 tablespoons (30 ml) soy sauce
1½ teaspoons (7 ml) sugar
½ teaspoon (2 ml) salt
2 teaspoons (10 ml) white vinegar
1 teaspoon (5 ml) sesame oil
¼ cup (60 ml) soup stock
1½ teaspoon (7 ml) cornstarch solution

1. Combine eggs, ¼ teaspoon (1 ml) salt and cornstarch in a mixing bowl. Beat until foamy. Set aside.
2. Heat an 8" (20.5 cm) non-stick frying pan or skillet with 1½ tablespoons (22 ml) oil. Pour in beaten eggs and cook over medium to medium-high heat to make a fluffy omelet. Don't overcook. Remove and place on a platter.
3. Heat wok with 1½ teaspoons (7 ml) oil, ginger and garlic over high heat for 10 seconds. Add pork, onion, and water chestnuts, stirring for 1 minute. Add the remaining ingredients except cornstarch solution. Mix well and cook for 1½-2 minutes.
4. To serve, thicken pork mixture with cornstarch solution and pour in center of golden, fluffy omelet. Roll up the omelet and slice into four sections. Serve hot.

Remarks
• *For the avid, spicy food fan, double the amount of hot sauce. For the less enthusiastic, use half as much or none at all.*

Upside-Down Bean Curd Cake NEW DISCOVERY

"Light", "delightful", and "nutritious" are the words you can use to describe this particular dish. Steamed to perfection, try something different, and you will find that Chinese cooking has a whole array of choices for everyone's taste. Experiment with this dish, and it may become a regular addition to your diet.

2 squares (1 lb, 450 g) bean curd
4 cups (1 L) soup stock
¾ teaspoon (3 ml) salt
3 dried black mushrooms, soaked and shredded
2 ounces (56 g) thinly shredded Virginia ham
2 ounces (56 g) fresh or canned crab meat, shredded

4 ounces (112 g) broccoli flowerets
1 teaspoon (5 ml) oil
1 teaspoon (5 ml) sesame oil
2 teaspoons (10 ml) soy sauce
pinch of white pepper
1 teaspoon (5 ml) sugar
1½ teaspoon (7 ml) cornstarch solution

1. Cut each bean curd square into quarters. Simmer bean curd over low heat in a saucepan with soup stock and salt for 10-15 minutes. Remove bean curd, reserving stock. Drain bean curd and mash with a fork, into a paste. Drain in a fine colander.
2. Arrange shredded mushroom, ham and crab meat in separate rows in a greased 9" (22.5 cm) pie pan. Cover with mashed bean curd. Press lightly and steam over high heat for 15-20 minutes. Drain excess liquid from dish after steaming.
4. While mixture is steaming, blanch broccoli in boiling water with ½ teaspoon (2 ml) oil for 2-2½ minutes; set aside.
5. In a small saucepan, combine ¾ cup reserved stock, ½ teaspoon oil, and remaining ingredients, except cornstarch solution. Bring to a boil over high heat. Thicken with cornstarch solution; keep warm and set aside.
6. Place serving platter upside down on pie pan and invert, so that mushroom, ham and crab are facing up. Cover with sauce and arrange blanched broccoli around the edges of the platter.

Remarks
- *Other vegetables can be substituted for the broccoli.*
- *Serve this dish immediately after cooking or it will become too watery due to the bean curd which is over 90% water.*
- *If canned crab meat is used, drain and rinse the crab in cool water to remove excess salt.*

Garlands from the Garden

The Chinese didn't need Popeye to tell them that vegetables were good for them, but they could have told Popeye a thing or two about cooking spinach. Forget about mushy, icky greens that have been cooked to death. The Chinese have developed the art of vegetable cookery to the point of perfection, and both the stir-frying technique and steaming are particularly well-suited to the nature of vegetables. The application of high temperature and short-time cooking yields a fresh crispness and vivid color, while the maximum nutritional value is retained. Whether leafy or tuberous, most vegetables require only a few minutes to prepare.

Even so, plain vegetable dishes are rarely served at formal banquets, since they are considered to be too common. Many vegetable dishes contain meat or seafood. The Confucian precept is that one-fourth of the dish should consist of meat (soy bean curd and wheat gluten for strict vegetarians), and the other three-fourths consist of vegetables. Once again, I strongly recommend that you shop for the freshest produce. Frozen vegetables are simply not as good; since they are excessively high in water content, when heated, they will produce a disappointing mushy mess, instead of a rejoicing crispness. But other than that, there are no tricks to becoming a superlative vegetable cook. Simply take root, branch out, and break new grounds!

CHUNG KWONG CHEUNG

Broccoli with Crab Meat Sauce CANTON

This dish is suited for lavish dinners. The fresh and crunchy broccoli with a delicate crab meat topping will please the most critical palate. Out of this world!

¼ pound (112 g) crab meat, shredded

Marinade:
2 teaspoons (10 ml) wine
1 teaspoon (5 ml) cornstarch
dash of salt
dash of sesame oil

¾ pound (340 g) broccoli
4 teaspoons (20 ml) oil
2 teaspoons (10 ml) finely chopped ginger
¼ cup (60 ml) soup stock
¼ teaspoon (1 ml) salt
¼ teaspoon (1 ml) sugar
dash of white pepper
1 teaspoon (5 ml) wine
¾ teaspoon (3 ml) cornstarch solution
1 egg white, lightly beaten

1. Marinate crab meat for 30 minutes.
2. Wash broccoli and peel off tough skin on stems. Remove flowerets from stem and cut into bite-size pieces. Cut stem diagonally into thin slices.
3. Heat wok with 2 teaspoons oil and add 1 teaspoon finely chopped ginger. Add broccoli and stir for several seconds. Add soup stock and salt, cover and cook over medium to medium-high heat for 2-2½ minutes, until tender-crisp. Remove and arrange broccoli on a platter with stems in the center and flowerets around the edge.
4. Heat wok over medium-high heat with 2 teaspoons oil. Add 1 teaspoon finely chopped ginger and stir for 10-15 seconds. Add crab meat, mix well and stir for 1 minute more. Add sugar, pepper, and wine; simmer for one minute.
5. Thicken with cornstarch solution. Remove from heat and slowly pour in egg white. Mix well and pour over broccoli stems. Serve immediately.

Remarks
- *If canned crab meat is used, wash well and drain before marinating.*
- *It is also popular to substitute spinach for broccoli.*

Cabbage with Chinese Sausage

CANTON

This is a typical dish of southern China — simple and yet exotic. It uses Chinese sausage which can only be purchased in Chinese grocery stores. It has a strong taste and a high percentage of fat. When I was little. my Mom used to add several slices of sausage to the rice as it was cooking. When it was done, the sausage was cooked to perfection. A good meal in a hurry.

2 teaspoons (10 ml) oil
1 clove garlic, chopped
2 whole Chinese sausages, sliced
    thin diagonally
1 pound (450 g) cabbage, cut into
    1½″ x 2″ pieces (4 cm x 5 cm)

¾ cup (200 ml) soup stock
½ teaspoon (2 ml) sugar
¾ teaspoon (3 ml) salt
1 teaspoon (5 ml) cornstarch solution

1. Heat wok over high heat with oil. Add garlic and Chinese sausage, stirring constantly for one minute.
2. Add remaining ingredients except cornstarch solution. Stir well, cover and cook for 4 minutes, stirring occasionally. Thicken with cornstarch solution and serve.

Remarks
- *Any fresh vegetable can be used to replace the cabbage. Good choices are eggplant, lettuce, Chinese mustard green, Chinese cabbage, bok choy or zucchini.*

Cauliflower and Broccoli in Sweet Cream Sauce

Using your imagination to create something new is an exciting experience. Snow white cauliflower contrasts nicely with the bright green broccoli, and the white cream sauce makes it refreshing and unique.

6 ounces (168 g) cauliflower flowerets	*Cream Sauce:*
	1 teaspoon (5 ml) oil
1 teaspoon (5 ml) salt	**5 teaspoons (25 ml) sugar**
4 ounces (112 g) broccoli flowerets	**2 tablespoons (20 ml) soup stock**
1 teaspoon (5 ml) oil	**½ cup (125 ml) half and half**
	¼ teaspoon (1 ml) cornstarch solution

1. Cut cauliflower and broccoli into bite-size flowerets.
2. Blanch cauliflower in boiling water with ½ teaspoon salt for 3½ minutes. Drain and rinse with cool water; set aside.
3. Blanch broccoli in boiling water with ½ teaspoon salt and 1 teaspoon oil for 2-2½ minutes. Drain, cool and set aside.
4. Put cauliflower in the center of a round platter, with flowerets facing up. Arrange broccoli around cauliflower with broccoli flowerets facing out.
5. Combine all ingredients for cream sauce, except cornstarch solution, in a saucepan and bring to a boil over medium heat, stirring constantly. Thicken with cornstarch solution. To serve, pour sauce over vegetables.

Remarks
- *When boiling cream sauce, be sure to stir continuously, as milk tends to stick to the bottom of the pan and burn. Do not cook milk over high heat because it will easily boil over.*

Eggplant with Black Beans CANTON

Here is a simple dish — light and low in calories. The spongy texture of the eggplant absorbs liquid easily, so the pungent flavor of the black beans soaks right in. Wonderful over rice!

1 large or 2 small eggplants
   (1-1¼ pound) (450-560 g)
1½ tablespoon (22 ml) oil
½ onion, sliced
2 cloves garlic, finely minced
1½ tablespoon (22 ml) salted black
   beans, washed and mashed
   into a paste

¼ teaspoon (1 ml) sugar
1 tablespoon (15 ml) soy sauce
¾ teaspoon (3 ml) salt
½ cup (125 ml) soup stock
1 teaspoon (5 ml) cornstarch solution

1. Cut the eggplant lengthwise into quarters; cut each quarter into ¼ ″ (0.75 cm) slices.
2. Parboil eggplant in boiling salted water for 2-3 minutes. Remove and drain well. Set aside.
3. Heat wok with 1½ tablespoons oil over medium-high heat. Add onion and stir-fry for 10-15 seconds; add garlic and black bean paste. Stir-fry for 10-15 seconds.
4. Add blanched eggplant and remaining ingredients, except cornstarch solution; mix well. Reduce heat to medium-low, cover and simmer for 3-3½ minutes. Stir the mixture several times while cooking. Thicken with cornstarch solution and serve immediately.

Garden Vegetable Platter

If you love fresh, wholesome garden vegetables, this dish is designed for you. Carefully chosen ingredients form a delectable combination of colors and textures.

8 dried black mushrooms, soaked
1 cup (250 ml) soup stock
½ teaspoon (2 ml) sugar
1 teaspoon (5 ml) oyster-flavored
    sauce
2 medium-size tomatoes
1 cup (250 ml) broccoli flowerets
1 cup (250 ml) 3″ (7.5 cm)
    pieces asparagus
1 teaspoon (5 ml) oil
1 teaspoon (5 ml) salt
1 cup (250 ml) cauliflower flowerets
½ cup (125 ml) canned baby corn

Sauce:
½ teaspoon (2 ml) salt
¾ cup (200 ml) vegetable broth
1 teaspoon (5 ml) sesame oil
¾ teaspoon (3 ml) sugar
dash of white pepper
1½ teaspoons (7 ml) cornstarch solution

1. Simmer mushrooms in stock with sugar and oyster-flavored sauce over medium-low heat for 15-20 minutes. Cut each tomato into 8 wedges and set aside.
2. Blanch broccoli and asparagus in boiling water for 2½ minutes with ½ teaspoon oil and ½ teaspoon salt; drain. Blanch cauliflower separately for 5-6 minutes with ½ teaspoon oil and ½ teaspoon salt; drain.
3. Arrange all vegetables on a platter.
4. Combine all ingredients for sauce, except cornstarch solution, in a saucepan. Heat over medium-high heat until mixture comes to a boil and thicken with cornstarch solution. Serve hot over vegetables.

Remarks
- *The arrangement of the vegetables gives you a chance to create something unique. A floral design would be very eye catching.*
- *Vegetable broth is available in most health food stores, and vegetarian bouillon cubes are available in many grocery stores.*

Green Beans with Preserved Bean Curd   CANTON

*Here is a superb example of an everyday meal — simple and economical.
It uses preserved bean curd, a fermented soy bean cake which is salty and
has a strong taste and aroma. It could be called Chinese cheese.*

¾ pound (340 g) fresh green beans   ½ cup (125 ml) soup stock
1½ tablespoons (22 ml) oil   ½ teaspoon (2 ml) sugar
2 cubes preserved bean curd,   1½ teaspoons (7 ml) wine
   mashed into a paste

1. Wash and trim ends of green beans. Cut into 2-3″ lengths (5-7.5 cm).
2. Heat wok with oil over medium-high heat; stir in bean curd paste and
   continue stirring for 15 seconds. Add green beans and stock. Cover
   and cook for 4-5 minutes over medium-high heat until beans are tender. Add extra soup stock, if necessary.
3. Mix in sugar and wine. Stir for several minutes, until well blended.
   Serve hot.

Mushrooms in Two Sauces NEW DISCOVERY

This is a creative masterpiece. Two types of mushrooms, with two distinct, tasty sauces, give this dish a classy look. Don't be afraid to add other ingredients to create your own mushroom dish.

Mushroom A:
1 tablespoon (15 ml) oil
6 ounces (168) fresh mushrooms
   with stems trimmed
¾ cup (200 ml) cream of mushroom
   soup, unreconstituted
2-3 tablespoons (30-45 ml) soup
   stock
¼ teaspoon (1 ml) sesame oil
dash of white pepper
¼ teaspoon (1 ml) salt
½ stalk green onion, chopped

Mushroom B:
2 ounces (25 g) dried black mushrooms
   (uniform in size)
1 teaspoon (5 ml) oil
1 tablespoon (15 ml) oyster-
   flavored sauce
1 teaspoon (5 ml) dark soy sauce
½ teaspoon (2 ml) sugar
¾ cup (200 ml) soup stock
½ teaspoon (2 ml) cornstarch solution

1. ***For Mushroom A:*** Heat wok with oil over medium-low heat and add all ingredients. Cover and simmer for 2-3 minutes. Arrange in center of a platter.
2. ***For Mushroom B:*** Soak dried mushrooms in warm water for ½ hour, remove and drain. Heat wok with oil over medium-high heat. Stir in all ingredients, except cornstarch solution. Cover and simmer for 15-20 minutes, or until tender. Thicken with cornstarch solution. Arrange around edges of the same serving platter with Mushroom A. Garnish with green onion.

Remarks
- *Clean fresh mushrooms with a brush or damp paper towel. If water is used, the sauce may become too thin and watery.*
- *For Mushroom A, use milk instead of soup stock for a thicker and smoother sauce.*

Potato Curry and Onion

Curry always goes well with potato. With the aromatic scent of onion, this is a delicious alternative for potato lovers.

1 medium-size onion	½ teaspoon (2 ml) 5-spice powder
2 cups (500 ml) or 2 small potatoes	1 cup (250 ml) soup stock
2 tablespoons (30 ml) oil	½ teaspoon (2 ml) salt
1 clove garlic, minced	1 tablespoon (15 ml) soy sauce
2 teaspoons (10 ml) curry powder	1 stalk green onion, cut into 1″ (2.5 cm) lengths (optional)

1. Wash and cut onion and potatoes into ½″ (1.25 cm) cubes.
2. Heat wok with oil and garlic over medium-high heat for 15 seconds.
3. Add curry powder and 5-spice powder stirring constantly for 10-15 seconds.
4. Put in onion, stirring for a few seconds. Add potato cubes and the remaining ingredients. Reduce heat to medium. Cover and cook for 18-20 minutes, stirring occasionally. Add extra soup stock if needed.

Remarks
- *One extra step for those who love french fries: deep-fry potato cubes in hot oil before adding to wok. If french fry potato is used, only stir-fry potato for 1-2 minutes.*
- *For a burning sensation, add a touch of chili powder along with the curry powder.*
- *You can thicken the dish with cornstarch solution if too watery.*

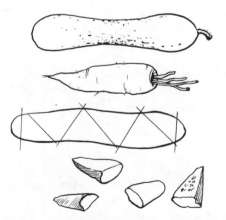

Cut vegetables into cubes by roll-cutting.

Preserved Pork with Chinese Broccoli

Similar to regular bacon, Chinese preserved pork is a cured, sweet-tasting and waxy-looking pork belly, sold in Chinese stores. It has a very firm texture, a distinctively strong aroma and keeps well in the refrigerator for a couple of months. Steamed with rice or stir-fried with vegetables—it adds an exotic and traditional Cantonese flavor.

2 teaspoons (10 ml) oil
¼ pound (112 g) Chinese preserved
   pork, thinly sliced
1 pound (450 g) Chinese broccoli,
   cut into bite-size pieces

½ cup (125 ml) soup stock
½ teaspoon (2 ml) sugar (optional)
¾ teaspoons (3 ml) cornstarch solution

1. Heat wok with oil over medium-high heat. Add preserved pork slices and stir-fry for 30-45 seconds. Remove pork and drain oil, reserving 1 tablespoon in wok.
2. Add the broccoli and pork and stir-fry for 30 seconds. Add soup stock and sugar. Cover and cook for 4½ minutes. Thicken with cornstarch solution and serve.

Remarks
- *Preserved pork can also be steamed over rice or served by itself.*
- *Any vegetable may be used. Preserved pork also goes well with soy bean curd.*

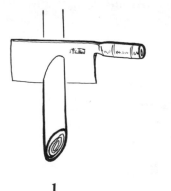 

1	2	3

Slicing technique

Refreshing Celery Salad

An extraordinarily simple and tasty salad. A great side dish for any menu.

10 ounces (280 g) celery stalks
½ teaspoon (2 ml) salt
4 cups (1 L) water

Dressing:
2 cloves garlic, minced
2 teaspoons (10 ml) sesame oil
2 teaspoons (10 ml) sugar
2 teaspoons (10 ml) vinegar
2 teaspoons (10 ml) soy sauce
pinch of pepper
1 teaspoon (5 ml) chili oil or paste

1. Wash stalks of celery and trim off fibrous portion with a paring knife. Cut into ½" x 2" (1.25 cm x 5 cm) pieces.
2. Bring 4 cups of water to a boil; add salt and blanch celery for 3 minutes. Remove and rinse with cold water. Drain well and set aside.
3. Combine dressing ingredients in a mixing bowl and mix well. Add blanched celery and transfer to the refrigerator. Serve cold anytime.

Remarks
- *In my opinion, the Chinese style chili paste with garlic is the best choice for this dish. It is only available in Chinese grocery stores.*

Shoot Some Nuts

You do not have to be good to shoot these nuts, just a good appetite and a desire to go on a healthy diet.

1 teaspoon (5 ml) oil
2 cloves garlic, minced
8 ounces (225 g) bamboo shoots, cut
    into ½″ (1.25 cm) cubes
4 ounces (112 g) unsalted roasted
    peanuts
4 ounces (112 g) cucumber, peeled
    and cut in ½″ (1.25 cm) cubes

1 teaspoon (5 ml) soy sauce
1 teaspoon (5 ml) sesame oil
¼ teaspoon (1 ml) sugar
¼ teaspoon (1 ml) salt

1. Heat oil in hot wok. Add minced garlic and stir for 10 seconds. Put in bamboo shoots, stirring for 1 minute.
2. Add remaining ingredients and mix well.

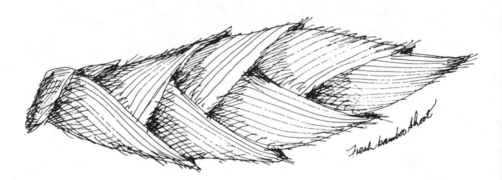

Fresh bamboo shoot

Sprouting (Your Beans) in Style!

Sprouting your own seeds is an easy, delicious and nutritious way to beat ever mounting food costs. Its extraordinary food value provides a tasty, healthy alternative to expensive meats. They are a most inexpensive addition to your diet. Mung Bean sprouts have exceptional nutritional value and very few calories (approximately 150-160 per pound). These sprouts are very low in carbohydrates (about 30 grams per pound). One pound of mung bean sprouts can contain as much as 4.0-4.5% protein higher than most other vegetables. Its vitamin content rivals that of many fruits, with vitamins A and C and large amounts of thiamine (B1), riboflavin (B2), and niacin. You will also find all kinds of minerals, including calcium, phosphorus, potassium and lots of iron.

Aside from the practical value, growing bean sprouts is also an exciting hobby for all ages, particularly when you first notice the delicate beans cropping up after a very short while. The average harvest costs only 5 cents per pound and takes 4-5 days. It is under your complete control — you can grow it when you want and grow as much as you want.

The germination of seed requires water, light, and the right temperature. For many types of bean sprouting, a room temperature of 68-75° F (20-22° C) is ideal. No light is required to yield white and tender sprouts, therefore, they should be grown in a covered pot or placed in a dark corner. Try your bedroom closet, if no other place is available. Just remove your whole wardrobe and use the entire closet for your sprouting!

How to grow (mung or soy beans)

- Wash ½ cup of the tiny green mung beans (usually available in Chinese stores or any health food store and sold by the pound in plastic bags) to get rid of broken beans and any foreign matter. Soak overnight with 4 times as much water as beans. Beans will hydrate and swell.
- Pick a large clay pot (12″ x 10″). Place a stainless screen or cheesecloth on top of drainage hole. Put soaked mung beans into pot and sprinkle water over beans. Place the pot in a dark area (yes, your closet!).
- Water beans 3-4 times a day. If you can't sleep some night, give your beans a couple of extra waterings! The idea is to insure the moisture content of the beans and to keep the temperature low. Germination gives out heat — it is an exothermic process. Too high a temperature will promote the rotting of seeds and will yield uneven growth.
- Continue the same procedure for 4-5 days without disturbing the seeds. You will see wonders towards the fifth day.
- Harvest when the white stems reach about 2-2½″. Don't wait until they grow and become a tree!
- To harvest, pick them all up from the pot, transfer into a large bowl and cover them in cold water in the sink. Agitate the water to allow the bean hulls to surface. Skim off all the hulls and discard them. Only keep the nice, white, tender bean sprouts. Store them in a plastic bag with holes and refrigerate for freshness. Serve them raw in salads or use them in stir-fried dishes, in soups or in anything you can dream of.

Tomato Soy Beans

Now you don't have to spend a fortune to buy a can of your favorite beans! Here is a simple, delicious, yet exceptionally nutritious dish to prepare for your family.

2 tomatoes	¼ cup (60 ml) hot catsup
8 ounces (225 g) soy beans	¾ cup (200 ml) soup stock
2 teaspoons (10 ml) oil	¼ teaspoon (1 ml) salt
1 ounce (28 g) pork fat (optional)	1 teaspoon (5 ml) wine
	2 teaspoons (10 ml) sugar

1. Peel one tomato and cut into small chunks. Cut the other into 8 wedges for garnishing.
2. Wash and soak soy beans for 8-10 hours or overnight. Transfer beans to a large bowl. Cover with water and agitate the beans to remove the loose skins of the beans. Drain and set aside.
3. Heat oil in hot wok or saucepan over medium-high heat. Add pork fat and brown for 2-2½ minutes, stirring well. Put in beans and toss for 1 minute.
4. Add remaining ingredients, including tomato chunks. Cover and cook over medium-low heat for 12-13 minutes, until most of the liquid has evaporated. Stir frequently to insure even cooking. Garnish with tomato wedges. Serve hot or cold. Prepare ahead and serve as a snack or side dish.

Twin-Colored Vegetable Plate

An attractive and simple dish you can prepare everyday. The combination of cauliflower and bright green broccoli complement each other in color and texture. It is a superb vegetable dish for a weekend dinner party.

2/3 pound (160 ml) cauliflower	¼ teaspoon (1 ml) salt
2/3 pound (160 ml) broccoli	½ teaspoon (2 ml) sugar
4 teaspoons (20 ml) oil	¼ teaspoon (1 ml) sesame oil
1 cup (250 ml) soup stock	2 teaspoons (10 ml) cornstarch solution

1. Wash and cut cauliflower and broccoli into bite-size flowerets. Save stems for other dishes.
2. Heat 2 teaspoons oil in hot wok over medium-high heat. Put in cauliflower and stir for 30 seconds. Add ½ cup soup stock. Cover and cook for 2½ minutes.
3. Pour in remaining 2 teaspoons oil. Add broccoli and stir well. Put in remaining soup stock and ingredients except cornstarch solution. Cover and cook for 2½ minutes. Add extra stock if needed. Thicken with cornstarch solution.
4. To serve, arrange cauliflower in center of a platter with broccoli around the edges. Serve hot.

Remarks
- *Cook cauliflower separately for 3-3½ minutes to avoid the green color of broccoli mixed in with the cauliflower. Then remove cauliflower from wok and cook broccoli for 2-2½ minutes. Combine both vegetables, add remaining ingredients and thicken with cornstarch.*

"Reading while you cook can be a burning experience."

"Lots of rice to bowl you over"

Oodles of Noodles and Rice to Bowl You Over

Rice is the main bulk in a Chinese diet. The blandness of rice is a perfect complement for savory rich or hot and spicy dishes, and a meal is given unity with the addition of rice. No one should attempt to pour spoonfuls of soy sauce onto steaming, fluffy white rice (hide those soy sauce bottles!), as it would eliminate the purpose of serving something neutral in flavor (that's rice!) to accompany your meal.

Long grain or medium grain rice are the most common types of rice available in the local markets. When boiled or steamed, long grain is drier and fluffier compared to the medium grain which is more tender and moister when cooked. (For making fried rice, long grain rice is the better choice.) You will also find short grain rice or glutinous rice in the Oriental markets. These two types (with a stickier consistency) are used mainly for stuffings and desserts.

Rice can be prepared in numerous ways, and most are very simple. For most Chinese meals, rice is usually prepared by boiling or steaming. Leftover rice can be used to prepare fried rice; further boiled (with water or broth) into porridge (congee); or can be simply reheated for your next scrumptious meal. So you can prepare enough rice to last you through several meals.

Noodles are eaten throughout the day in both northern and southern regions of China. Aside from rice, noodles and steamed buns (Chinese bread) are the most popular and important bulk in the Chinese diet. This is particularly true in Northern China, where abundant harvest of wheat are available. Of course, the legend goes that Italian pasta has its origin from the Great Wall and was introduced in the 14th century by none other than Marco Polo. (so, perhaps you should really be eating your spaghetti with a pair of chopsticks!)

In China, you can find a wide assortment of different kinds of noodles—wheat flour noodles, egg noodles, rice flour noodles, or bean thread noodles (made from mung bean flour). All noodles, whether fresh or dried, should be steamed or boiled before they are prepared in other ways. Then, you can enjoy your noodles in soup or as tossed noodles, noodles in sauce or fried noodles. With the infinite ways of cross-cooking, noodles can be combined with almost any type of meat, seafood or vegetable. Chow mein (fried noodles) is perhaps the best known Chinese noodle dish—boiled noodles are stir-fried in a small amount of oil and then garnished with meat and vegetables in a generous amount of sauce. (Think I'll take a break and go have some, right now!)

It is a popular tradition that a noodle dish be served at weddings, anniversaries or birthday parties as a symbol of longevity (now you know why noodles are so *long!*) But you don't have to wait until your best friend gets married to try some—that might be a long time!

Beef with Fresh Rice Noodles

Rice noodles have a soft, smooth texture which most people enjoy. They go well with various meats and vegetables, in soups or in stir-fried dishes. Rice noodles make this a great dish for lunch or for a midnight snack. Look for the fresh ones in Chinese grocery stores.

2 tablespoons (30 ml) oil
1 tablespoon (15 ml) salted black
   beans, rinsed and made into
   a paste
1 teaspoon (5 ml) crushed chili
   pepper
2 slices ginger, shredded
¼ pound (112 g) flank steak, sliced
2 stalks green onion, cut into 1"
   (2.5 cm) strips

1 cup (250 ml) bean sprouts
2 tablespoons (30 ml) dark soy sauce
½ teaspoon (2 ml) sugar
¼ teaspoon (1 ml) sesame oil
dash of white pepper
1 pound (450 g) fresh rice noodles, cut
   into 3" (7.5 cm) strips

1. Heat wok with oil, black bean paste, chili pepper and ginger, over high heat. Add beef and green onion, stirring for 1-1½ minutes. Add remaining ingredients except rice noodles. Stir well.
2. Add rice noodles and continue to stir for 1-2 minutes. Stir continuously to prevent rice noodles from sticking to the wok.

Remarks
- *In Chinese stores, you may find dry rice noodles. They are not the thread-like ones. To use, soak in water for 30 minutes, rinse with hot water until tender, then stir-fry with other ingredients.*

Curry Fried Rice with Beef

This fried rice dish will become a new star on your dinner table. You won't find it in a restaurant, but it's a great dish for an everyday meal.

2 tablespoons (30 ml) oil
2 slices ginger, finely chopped
1 clove garlic, chopped
½ onion, diced
¼ pound (112 g) lean ground beef
¼ cup (60 ml) peas and carrots
2 stalks green onion, chopped
2 teaspoons (10 ml) curry powder

1 teaspoon (5 ml) sesame oil
1 teaspoon (5 ml) salt
1 tablespoon (15 ml) dark soy sauce
dash of white pepper
1 teaspoon (5 ml) chili sauce
4-5 cups (1-1¼ L) cooked rice
3-4 tablespoons (45-60 ml) soup stock
    for steaming

1. Heat wok with oil, ginger and garlic over high heat for 10 seconds. Add onion, stir-fry for 1 minute. Add beef and stir-fry for another minute. Add remaining ingredients except rice and soup stock; stir for 30 seconds.
2. Separate and fluff rice.
3. Reduce heat to medium-low, add rice and cook for 1½ minutes, sprinkling in 2 tablespoons stock and stirring continuously until hot. Add more stock if needed.

Remarks
* *If cold rice is used, add about ¼ cup (60 ml) stock, cover and simmer for a few minutes extra until rice is tender.*
* *Any fried rice dish can be prepared ahead and reheated. (Bake at 350° F (180° C) for 15 minutes or stir-fry on low heat for a few minutes).*

Mandarin Style Noodles

This dish is traditionally served at birthday parties. Hot bean paste gives it a spicy and salty taste which goes perfectly with noodles. The bean paste can be purchased in Chinese stores. Don't make this dish without it since it's the bean paste that gives the dish its character. A great treat for lunch, breakfast or a midnight snack.

½ pound (225 g) fresh egg noodles
1½ teaspoon (7 ml) sesame oil
4 teaspoons (20 ml) oil
1 tablespoon (15 ml) dried shrimp, soaked and chopped (optional)
2-3 tablespoons (30-45 ml) hot bean paste

¾ teaspoon (3 ml) salt
¼ pound (112 g) ground pork
1 cup (250 ml) shredded cabbage
½ cup (125 ml) shredded cucumber
dash of sugar
1-2 tablespoons (15-30 ml) soup stock

1. Bring a large pot of water to a boil. Blanch fresh noodles for 1½ minutes in boiling water. Remove, run under cold tap water for 30 seconds, drain and mix well with sesame oil. Set aside.
2. Heat wok with oil over high heat. Stir-fry shrimp, hot bean paste and salt for 10 seconds; add ground pork, stirring for 1-1½ minutes. Add cabbage and cucumber, stirring for 1 minute. Add sugar and 1 tablespoon (15 ml) stock, stirring constantly. Add remaining tablespoon of soup stock if needed.
3. To serve, place everything, including noodles in a large bowl and mix well. Serve hot or cold.

Remarks
- *Traditionally, this dish calls for northern style thick noodles.*

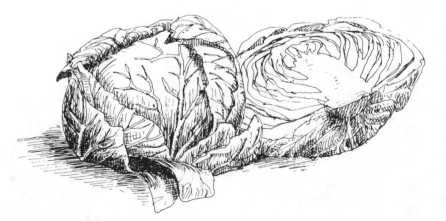

Pan-Fried Noodles with Shrimp   CANTON

If you have never tried chow mein, you must have never eaten in a Chinese restaurant! The noodles in this recipe are not deep-fried crispy noodles, but stir-fried fresh egg noodles. It is great for lunch or as a last course in a dinner if everyone is still hungry.

½ pound (225 g) fresh egg noodles
2 tablespoons (30 ml) oil
½ pound (225 g) fresh or frozen
    shrimp, shelled, deveined and
    sliced in half lengthwise
½ onion, shredded
½ small carrot, shredded
1 celery stalk, shredded
1 stalk bok choy, shredded, without
    leaves (optional)
2 ounces (56 g) shredded zucchini
2 ounces (56 g) bean sprouts
1 stalk green onion, cut into 1" (2.5 cm)
    pieces
1½ teaspoons (7 ml) cornstarch solution

Sauce:
2 tablespoons (30 ml) soy sauce
¾ teaspoon (3 ml) sesame oil
½ teaspoon (2 ml) salt
¼ cup (60 ml) soup stock
¾ teaspoon (3 ml) sugar (optional)

1. Bring 2 quarts of water to a boil in a large pan. Add fresh noodles to water, return to a boil and cook for 1½ minutes. Remove and rinse with cold water; drain and set aside. Mix noodles with 1 tablespoon (15 ml) oil to prevent sticking.
2. Heat a large non-stick frying pan with 1 teaspoon (5 ml) oil over medium-high heat. Spread blanched noodles evenly in pan. Cook 2½-3 minutes on each side or until golden brown, lightly pressing noodles during browning. Rotate pan over burner in a circular motion to cook evenly. Add more oil if needed.
3. Combine ingredients for sauce, mix well and set aside.
4. Stir-fry shrimp in wok over high heat with 1 teaspoon (5 ml) oil until pink. Remove and set aside.
5. Add onion and carrot to wok and fry for 1 minute. Add remaining vegetables and stir-fry for 30 seconds. Add shrimp and sauce mixture; mix well. Thicken with cornstarch solution and spoon over noodle pancake. Serve.

Remarks
* *Save the bok choy leaves for soup.*

Plain Cooked Rice

Rice is the main staple in China. A meal without rice is like not eating at all. A good pot of rice is tricky to make. This recipe guarantees perfect results.

2 cups (55 ml) long grain rice
3 cups (750 ml) water

1. Wash and drain rice several times until water is somewhat clear. Drain well.
2. Combine rice and 3 cups of water in a saucepan. Bring to a boil over high heat, uncovered.
3. Reduce heat to low, and simmer until almost all water has evaporated and crater-like holes appear in the rice. Cover saucepan and simmer for about 20 minutes to achieve total gelatinization.
4. Remove from heat and let stand 8-10 minutes to complete final cooking. Fluff the rice and serve hot.

Remarks

- *The purpose of washing the rice is to get rid of excess starch powder and broken rice kernels which make the cooked rice mushy and sticky.*
- *Cooking time and rice texture are affected by the amount of water used and by storage time. Old rice requires more cooking and more water. Only experience will give the best results.*
- *Even though the Chinese never use ingredients other than water when cooking rice, you may use soup stock or add salt and butter.*
- *Cooked rice can be stored in the refrigerator and reheated with a little bit of water.*

Singapore Rice Noodles

Rice noodles are thin, thread-like dry noodles made from rice flour. They can be soaked and used in stir-fried dishes or deep-fried and used as a garnish. Stir-fried rice noodles with meat and vegetables are often served at lunch as a meal by itself.

½ pound (225 g) rice noodles
2 tablespoons (30 ml) oil
1 slice ginger, finely chopped
2-3 tablespoons (30-45 ml) shredded
    pork
3-4 fresh or frozen shrimp, diced
¼ small onion, sliced
1-2 stalks green onion, cut into 1"
    (2.5 cm) strips
¼ bell pepper, shredded
2 ounces (56 g) bean sprouts

2 teaspoons (10 ml) soy sauce
½ teaspoon (2 ml) sesame oil
dash of sugar
dash of white pepper
1-2 tablespoons (15-30 ml) soup stock
½ teaspoon (2 ml) salt
2 teaspoons (10 ml) curry powder
¼ teaspoon (1 ml) chili powder
¼ cup (60 ml) soup stock, if needed

1. Bring a large pot of water to a boil. Add noodles and boil for 30-45 seconds. Remove from stove and let soak for 15-30 seconds. Rinse immediately with cold water. Remove all the hard noodles that did not completely rehydrate. Drain well and set aside to cool.
2. Heat wok with oil and ginger over high heat for 10 seconds. Add pork; stir-fry for 1-1½ minutes. Add shrimp and both types of onions; stir-fry for 1 minute. Add remaining ingredients and stir for 1 minute.
3. Reduce heat to medium-low. Add blanched rice noodles to wok, mix well and stir for 1-2 minutes. Sprinkle occasionally with stock to prevent sticking. Serve with hot sauce, if desired.

Spiced Peanut Noodles

This type of dish is not common in Chinese cooking. It is served cold and is absolutely refreshing on a hot, muggy summer day. Do try this gastronomic adventure!

1 teaspoon (5 ml) salt
½ pound (225 g) fresh egg noodles
1 teaspoon (5 ml) sesame oil
¼ pound (112 g) cooked pork or
   chicken, thinly shredded
1 cup (250 ml) bean sprouts, roots
   snapped off
2 stalks green onions, cut into 1½"
   (4 cm) strips

Dressing:
2 tablespoons (30 ml) ground peanuts
2½ teaspoons (12 ml) sesame oil
2 tablespoons (30 ml) white vinegar
2 teaspoons (10 ml) chili oil or Tabasco
   sauce
1 teaspoon (5 ml) sugar
2 tablespoons (30 ml) peanut butter
2 teaspoons (10 ml) soup stock

1. Add salt to a large pot of water and bring to a boil. Stir in noodles; return to a boil and cook for 1½ minutes. Remove and drain noodles in running water. Toss with 1 teaspoon (5 ml) sesame oil and chill in the refrigerator.
2. Combine dressing ingredients in a bowl. Mix well and set aside.
3. To serve, place noodles in a large salad bowl. Toss with cooked meat, bean sprouts, green onions and dressing until well blended. Place on a serving platter and enjoy.

Remarks
- *Mix dressing well before serving over noodles.*

Steamed Pork Dumplings

(Siu Mai)

Here is a completely different use for wonton wrappers — dumplings! Siu Mai is one of the most well known and popular dim sums in Cantonese restaurants — delicious, tiny bite-sized morsels of savory meat steamed to perfection in exotic bamboo steamers.

½ pound (225 g) wonton wrappers, trimmed to circular shape

Filling:
½ pound (225 g) boneless pork butt, finely minced
1 green onion, minced
¼ pound (60 ml) fresh or frozen shrimp, shelled, deveined and minced
2-3 tablespoons (30-45 ml) chopped bamboo shoots or water chestnuts
1 tablespoon (15 ml) soaked and minced dried shrimp (optional)
¾ teaspoon (3 ml) salt
½ teaspoon (2 ml) sugar
1½ teaspoon (7 ml) cornstarch
dash of white pepper (optional)
dash of MSG (optional)

1. In a large bowl, combine filling ingredients and mix well. Let stand for 20 minutes.
2. Form dumplings by placing ¾ tablespoon of filling mixture in the center of each wrapper, gather sides and squeeze toward the center. Continue forming remainder of dumplings in the same way.
3. To cook, place dumplings in a bamboo steamer or in an aluminum pie pan with many holes to allow the steam to reach the food. Steam for 10-12 minutes over high heat. Add water, if necessary.

Remarks
- *Siu Mai can be made ahead of time and stored in the refrigerator or freezer; cover with plastic wrap to avoid dehydration. When ready to use, steam for 12-14 minutes over high heat. Steam 3-4 minutes longer if frozen.*
- *Before placing wrapped Siu Mai in bamboo steamer or pie pan, lightly grease surface to prevent dumplings from sticking.*
- *Dumplings can be steamed, then stored in the freezer. Resteam when ready to serve.*

Yang Chow Fried Rice GENERAL

Fried rice is a fascinating wonder of Chinese cooking. Varying the ingredients will give you a new rice dish. This recipe is special. You will never see so many goodies used to make fried rice!

2½ tablespoons (37 ml) oil
2 slices ginger, finely chopped
1 clove garlic, finely chopped
¾ teaspoon (3 ml) salt
2 stalks green onion, chopped
¼ onion, chopped
2 dried black mushrooms, soaked
    and shredded (optional)
½ Chinese sausage, thinly sliced
    (optional)
3 tablespoons (45 ml) peas and
    carrots
2 ounces (56 g) fresh or cooked
    shrimp, diced (optional)

1 slice cooked ham, diced
¼ cup (60 ml) diced BBQ pork
1 ounce (28 g) bean sprouts
2 eggs, lightly beaten and made into thin
    omelet (cook until firm), then finely
    shredded
1 tablespoon (15 ml) dark soy sauce
2 tablespoons (30 ml) light soy sauce
1½ teaspoons (7 ml) sesame oil
dash of white pepper (optional)
¼ cup soup stock, if needed
6 cups (1½ L) cooked rice

1. Heat wok with oil, ginger, garlic, and salt over high heat for 10 seconds.
2. Add green onion, onion, black mushrooms, Chinese sausage, peas and carrots and shrimp; stir for 2½ minutes. Add a bit of stock if too dry.
3. Reduce heat to medium-low. Add remaining ingredients and stir for 2-2½ minutes or until well blended and hot. Serve hot.

Remarks
- *When refrigerated rice is used, add ¼ cup soup stock in Step 3 to soften rice; cook it a bit longer.*
- *Six cups of rice is a lot. You may eat fried rice all week!*
- *When fresh rice is used, it may be too sticky. Spread out and let dry briefly before preparing fried rice.*
- *Use only medium to medium-low heat to stir-fry after rice is added to avoid burning and sticking. Stir rice continuously.*
- *Any of the above meats and vegetables can be substituted with other ingredients or simply omitted.*
- *Prepare ahead and reheat when time to serve.*

Exotic Excesses

From the rich cultural heritage of China emerges succulent dishes that will stimulate a gourmet's tastebuds. The term 'gourmet' is not meant to frighten, but to enhance creativity and curiosity. Anyone can enjoy these dishes, and they are not necessarily trickier or more expensive to prepare. There is a vast variety of everyday ingredients that you can choose from to make delicious and delectable dishes.

Also included in this chapter are many favorite recipes from Japan, Korea, Indonesia, the Phillipines and Malaysia. So take a chance and explore these many culinary delights. Then you, too, can be like Admiral Perry or Captain Cook in your own kitchen.

Aromatic Fish

Most Vietnamese dishes are light and refreshing. They are as pleasing to the eye as they are to the stomach. They should never be overpowering, each dish having just the right amount of seasoning and condiments to bring out the flavors of the main ingredients. Fish sauce is the most common seasoning in most Vietnamese dishes. Try this very simple and flavorful fish, and you will want to move to Vietnam.

10 ounces (280 g) white fish fillet
1 egg white, lightly beaten
1 tablespoon (15 ml) cornstarch
3 tablespoons (45 ml) oil
1 medium-size onion, sliced
3 cloves garlic, crushed
¾ teaspoon (3 ml) roasted fennel
    seeds, crushed

1 dried red chili, crushed
2 tablespoons (30 ml) lime or lemon
    juice
2 teaspoons (10 ml) sugar
½ cup (125 ml) water or stock
1 tablespoon (15 ml) fish sauce
sprigs of mint (optional)

1. Cut fish fillet into approximately 2″ (5 cm) squares. Brush egg white over fish, then coat lightly with cornstarch. Heat 2 tablespoons oil in a non-stick frying pan and cook fish to golden brown, about 1½ minutes on each side. Remove and drain well. Keep warm. Save oil in frying pan for next step.
2. Stir-fry onion, garlic, fennel seeds and dried chili in 1 tablespoon oil for 1-2 minutes over medium high heat in same pan. Add lemon or lime juice, sugar and water; bring to a boil. Cover and simmer over low heat for 1½-2 minutes. Return fish slices to sauce mixture; splash in fish sauce and simmer for another 3-4 minutes. Garnish with mint leaves.

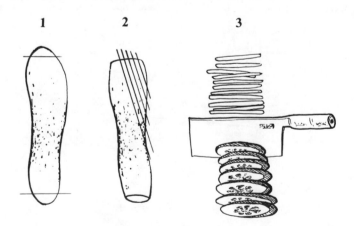

1   2   3

Slicing technique

Beef and Cabbage in Coconut Sauce   THAILAND

Eating Thai food is a multiple gourmet experience. Heady aromas, brilliant colours, sweet, sour, pungent and stingingly hot tastes often jumble together in one single dish. The aroma from coconut and the stingingly hot chili will offer you the experience of a lifetime.

10 ounces (280 g) lean beef
½ teaspoon (2 ml) salt
1 tablespoon (15 ml) dark soy sauce
1¼ cups (310 ml) thin coconut milk
3 dried chilis, crushed
1 slice ginger, shredded
3 cloves garlic, minced
1 medium-size onion, sliced

2 tablespoons (30 ml) roasted,
   unsalted peanuts, crushed
2 teaspoons (10 ml) brown sugar
1¾ teaspoons (8 ml) cornstarch
   solution
¾ pound (340 g) Chinese cabbage
¼ teaspoon (1 ml) salt
½ cup (125 ml) sliced carrot (optional)
2 red chilis, chopped (for garnish)

1. Cut beef into thin strips. Marinate with salt and soy sauce for 10 minutes.
2. Combine ¾ cup coconut milk, chilis, ginger, garlic and sliced onion in a saucepan. Bring to a boil; add marinated meat. Reduce heat, cover and simmer for 2-3 minutes. Stir in roasted peanuts and brown sugar; thicken with cornstarch. Remove and set aside; keep warm.
3. Cut cabbage into 2″ (5 cm) pieces. Cut carrots into thin slices. Cook carrots in boiling water for 2-3 minutes and drain. Put cabbage in a saucepan with a little salt and ½ cup coconut milk. Cover and simmer over low heat for 4-5 minutes.
4. To serve, arrange cabbage in a serving dish, top with carrots and cooked beef. Pour sauce over and garnish with chopped red chilis. (There should be plenty of coconut sauce for your rice to bowl you over!)

Bird's Nest Soup

This may be a once-in-a-lifetime gastronomic experience to try something very exotic and expensive, which has no distinctive taste by itself—the bird's nest, an edible gelatinous substance, produced by tiny swifts living around the South Pacific. The smooth velvet chicken and flavorful Smithfield ham in a rich soup stock give a marvelous compliment to the delicate bird's nest.

1 cup (250 ml) loosely-packed ground
    bird's nest
3 slices ginger
1 cup (250 ml) clear soup stock
2 teaspoons (10 ml) wine
dash of white pepper
dash of sugar (optional)

3½ cups (875 ml) rich soup stock
salt to taste
dash of white pepper
1¾ tablespoons (26 ml) cornstarch
    solution
2½ tablespoons (37 ml) minced
    cooked Smithfield ham

Velvet Chicken:
4 ounces (112 g) boneless chicken
    breast
½ teaspoon (2 ml) salt
1 teaspoon (5 ml) wine
2 teaspoons (10 ml) cornstarch in 2
    tablespoons (30 ml) water
2 egg whites, beaten until foamy

1. ***To prepare bird's nest****:* Soak bird's nest in lukewarm water for 3-4 hours; rinse and drain well; pick out the down or any impurities. (This step requires tremendous patience, and it may take years to finish!) In a saucepan, place cleaned bird's nest and ginger slices in 2 cups (500 ml) water. Parboil in bubbling hot water for 3-4 minutes. Discard ginger; remove nest, drain and squeeze to dry. Return parboiled nest to a saucepan with 1 cup clear soup stock, wine, pepper and sugar. Simmer over medium-low heat for 15-20 minutes. Set aside and keep warm.
2. ***To make velvet chicken:*** (This can be prepared ahead of time.) Ground chicken into a paste. Add salt, wine and cornstarch solution; mix and stir in one circular motion for 2-3 minutes. Put in egg white and continue to stir in same motion until mixture becomes visibly smooth and fluffy. Keep in refrigerator.
3. Bring 3½ cups rich soup stock to a boil in a pot. Add prepared bird's nest, reduce heat to medium-low and simmer for 4-5 minutes. Put in salt, pepper and cornstarch solution; stir until thickened. Reduce heat to low and slowly pour in velvet chicken, stirring constantly until soup is smooth.

4. To serve, pour soup into tureen or individual soup bowls and serve with minced ham.

Remarks
- *Parboiling bird's nest in water serves to remove its faint fishy taste.*
- *Bird's nest is an exotic and fairly expensive item; its price varies from US$40-$100 per pound. It is normally served at formal dinners.*
- *A popular and traditional sweet bird's nest soup is sometimes served at the end of a banquet.*
- *For a rich soup stock, cook regular soup stock for a longer period of time to reduce liquid and achieve a more concentrated flavor.*

Cabbage Pickles (Kim Chi)   KOREA

Korean food is as robust and warming as her climate. Most dishes have a rich spiciness with the generous use of hot chili, and a pungent aroma of garlic and sesame seeds. No meal is considered complete without rice and Kim Chi. In Korea, the vegetables are cut up, seasoned with salt, hot pepper, garlic and sealed in large jars for use. Kim Chi ranges in taste from quite bland to very hot, depending on the length of fermentation and the amount of chili used.

1½ pounds (675 g) Chinese cabbage	2 stalks green onion, minced
1 tablespoon (15 ml) salt	2 cloves garlic, minced
8 ounces (225 g) watercress (optional)	1 slice ginger, minced
2 teaspoons (10 ml) sesame oil	2 tablespoons (30 ml) soy sauce
1½ teaspoons (7 ml) ground toasted	2 tablespoons white wine vinegar
sesame seeds	1 tablespoon (15 ml) sugar
1½ teaspoons (7 ml) chili powder	

1. Wash cabbage and drain well. Cut into 2″ (5 cm) squares and sprinkle with salt. Let stand for 4 hours; toss and lightly squeeze occasionally. Squeeze cabbage as hard as you can to get out the excess moisture; set aside.
2. Wash watercress, shake out water and break into sprigs. Put cabbage and watercress in a large bowl and sprinkle with sesame oil.
3. Combine remaining ingredients and pour over vegetables. Toss to blend well. Transfer contents to large jars, seal and allow to stand overnight. Flavor will improve as seasoning prolongs. It will keep for months in the refrigerator.

Remarks
- *The process of squeezing the water out of the cabbage is the best exercise you can get; be prepared—you may be exhausted afterwards!*

Coconut Rice Cakes

This unique Thai sweet is easy to prepare and absolutely out of this "kitchen" world. The artificial color of the cakes give an interesting eye-appeal.

2½ cups (625 ml) thin coconut milk
3½ ounces (88 g) rice flour
3 eggs
4 ounces (112 g) sugar
4 ounces (112 g) grated coconut

green and pink food coloring
¼ teaspoon (1 ml) salt
3 tablespoons (45 ml) oil
¼ cup (112 g) grated coconut

1. Combine coconut milk, rice flour, eggs and sugar to make a thin batter. Beat for 5 minutes, then sprinkle in grated coconut. Divide the batter into 3 portions, color one pink, one bright green and leave one plain. Add a little salt to each and beat well. Let stand for 15-20 minutes.
2. Heat a non-stick pan with 1 teaspoon oil, slowly pour a thin layer of batter and swirl pan to thinly cover the bottom. Cook pancake over medium heat until brown. Flip over and cook the other side until brown. Roll up and slide into a plate. Cook remaining pancakes and arrange the different colors in whatever way you wish.
3. Serve warm or cold, with grated coconut.

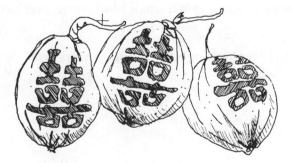

Malay Chicken MALAYSIA

In Malaysia, there are three races—Malay, Chinese and Indian, living side by side in harmony, thus they enjoy three major culinary styles. We will pick only one. The following is a traditional Malay curry. Like many dishes in southern India, creamy coconut milk is used to achieve a smooth sauce and to temper the hot chili.

1 whole chicken, approximately 3-3½ pounds (1575 g)

Curry Paste:
6-8 dried chilis, soaked
1 teaspoon (5 ml) cumin
2 teaspoons (10 ml) curry paste or powder
1 teaspoon (5 ml) turmeric powder
4 stalks green onion, chopped
2 cloves garlic, chopped
1¼ teaspoon (6 ml) salt

2 tablespoons (30 ml) oil
1½ teaspoons (5 ml) sugar
1 cup (250 ml) thick coconut milk, canned
½ tomato, sliced (optional)
½ onion, sliced
3-4 sprigs coriander (fresh Chinese parsley)
½ cucumber, thinly sliced (for garnish)
1 tomato, thinly sliced (for garnish)

1. Trim off all chicken fat, then cut chicken into 12-14 pieces.
2. Combine curry paste ingredients in a blender; blend to a paste. Remove and set aside in a bowl.
3. Heat oil in a wok over medium-high heat. Put in curry paste; stir for 1½ minutes. Add chicken pieces and brown for 1-1½ minutes, stirring frequently. Reduce heat to medium-low; add sugar and coconut milk. Blend well, cover and cook for 22-25 minutes, until chicken is tender.
4. Add tomato, onion and coriander, simmer for another 3-4 minutes, stirring occasionally.
5. Transfer chicken to a platter and garnish with cucumber and tomato slices. Pour extra sauce into a small bowl; serve over rice or noodles.

Remarks
• *There should be plenty of curry sauce to serve over rice or noodles.*

The Legend of the Mongolian Fire Pot

During the 13th century, a period existed in the western civilization known as the Middle Ages. On the vast prairie of Eastern Asia, outside the Great Wall of China, lived a nomadic tribe.

Besides the delicious Mongolian Barbeque, the Mongols invented the exciting and exotic Mongolian Fire Pot. This is another excellent cooking technique that insures the tenderness, nutrition and superb taste of fresh food. At night, the nomadic Mongol tribes gathered around their fires where slices of meat were speared and cooked in a large kettle of bubbling stew. Over hundreds of years, the Chinese transformed the simple Mongolian cauldron into the festive Mongolian Fire Pot we know today.

Sitting together around the table, you and your guests share a pot of bubbling broth in which each person cooks his (her) own meat, vegetables, bean threads, bamboo shoots, bean curd, green onion, and Chinese greens. Add meat and vegetables to the hot broth. Cook until meat is done and vegetables are tender, using small wire baskets, chopsticks or tongs to retrieve the food you cooked in the pot. Dip the cooked food in the desired sauces. Repeat with remaining ingredients until all are cooked.

Toward the end of the meal, the remaining broth which is now well seasoned serves as a delicious soup.

Mongolian Fire Pot

Here is a dish that is ideal for a cozy, winter evening. Everyone sits around and participates in the cooking. The idea is similar to the fondue and the Japanese Sukiyaki. The number of guests you invite is of no limit, it just depends on how big your fire pot is. The following are just some of the common ingredients used. The amount will depend on the number of people.

10-14 cups (2½-3½ L) broth, more if required.

A. *Meat:* Chicken, beef, lamb, fish balls, shrimp, scallops — sliced into thin pieces and placed in different small plates.

B. *Vegetables:* Lettuce, napa cabbage, spinach, bean curd, cellophane noodle — all washed and cut to convenient size.

C. *Dipping Sauce Mixture:*
(in one large bowl)
½ cup (125 ml) sesame oil
½ cup (125 ml) red vinegar
½ cup (125 ml) red bean curd sauce
½ cup (125 ml) sesame paste
¼ cup (60 ml) sugar
¼ cup (60 ml) soy sauce
chili oil to taste

D. *Other Extra Seasonings:*
(in small separate bowls)
Minced garlic
Chinese parsley
Fish sauce
Chopped green onion
Salt
Soy sauce

1) In an authentic Mongolian fire pot or an electric wok, bring 8-10 cups broth to a boil, reduce heat and set at bubbling medium heat.
2) Place all meats and vegetables on platters and set around the cooking vessel, thus everyone has access to them. Cook meat or vegetables in bubbling broth until done (one piece at a time in a small wire basket).
3) To serve, each guest should help himself to the various dipping mixtures. Use anything that suits your fancy.

Pork Adobo with Coconut Milk PHILLIPINES

Filipino cuisine is a magical mixture of East and West. It combines the characteristics of Chinese, Indonesian, Thai, Malaysian and Spanish cuisines. The Adobo, a marinated meat mixture with the pungent flavors of vinegar, garlic and black pepper, is among many exciting Filipino dishes.

1½ pounds (675 g) pork shoulder

Pork Marinade:
1/3 cup (80 ml) white vinegar
4-5 cloves garlic, finely chopped
¾ teaspoon (3 ml) black pepper

½ cup (125 ml) soup stock
½ cup (125 ml) thick coconut milk, canned
2 tablespoons (30 ml) oil

1. Cut pork into large 1¼″ (3 cm) chunks. Marinate pork for 2 hours.
2. Heat wok over medium-low heat. Add marinated pork to wok, cover and simmer until almost all the liquid has evaporated. Then slowly stir in stock and continue to cook, covered, over low heat until most of the liquid has evaporated, turning meat frequently.
3. Pour in coconut milk, cover, and continue to cook over low heat until most of the juice is absorbed by the meat. Be careful not to burn the meat.
4. Add 2 tablespoons oil and stir-fry over medium-high heat until meat is browned and crispy. Serve hot.

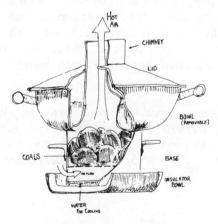

How Mongolian Fire Pot works

Shark's Fin Soup

To the Chinese, shark's fin is caviar—one of the most expensive and elegant ingredients in Chinese cuisine. It is not served in everyday meals, but rather, in the most lavish, formal dinners and banquets. Here is a somewhat simplified recipe which you can prepare in your own kitchen.

4 ounces (112 g) prepared dried
    shark's fin
3 slices ginger
4 stalks green onion, kept in a bunch
2 ounces (56 g) cooked crab meat,
    shredded

Crab Meat Marinade:
1 teaspoon (10 ml) beaten egg white
½ teaspoon (2 ml) cornstarch
¼ teaspoon (1 ml) salt

4½ cups (1060 ml) soup stock
3 dried black mushrooms, soaked
    and finely shredded
2 teaspoons (10 ml) Shaoshing wine
    or dry sherry
dash of white pepper
salt to taste
2 teaspoons (10 ml) soy sauce
    (optional)
2¼ tablespoons (34 ml) cornstarch
    solution
2½ tablespoons (37 ml) finely
    shredded cooked Smithfield ham

1. *Preparing shark's fin*: Soak dried shark's fin in cold water until softened, about 6-8 hours. Drain well and set aside. Bring 4 cups (1 L) water to a boil; add ginger, green onion, and soaked shark's fin. Reduce heat to low and simmer for 1 hour. Let cool and drain; discard ginger and green onion. Set shark's fin aside.
2. Marinate crab meat for 10 minutes.
3. Bring 4½ cups soup stock to a boil; add cooked shark's fin, shredded mushroom, wine, pepper, salt and soy sauce. Reduce heat to low and simmer for 20-30 minutes. Put in marinated crab meat, stirring to separate meat. Thicken with cornstarch solution.
4. To serve, pour soup into tureen or individual soup bowls; sprinkle ½ teaspoon (2 ml) shredded ham into each bowl and serve hot.

Remarks
- *Cooked chicken, finely shredded, can be used in place of crab meat.*
- *These dried, transparent needlelike gelatinous protuberances from the shark's fin are available in Chinese stores, sold by the pound. For more information, refer to 'Chinese Spice and Everything Nice!'*

Spiced Fish Fillets (Ikan Pecal) INDONESIA

Most Indonesian foods are seasoned with a great variety of spices. The regions of Sumatra and Java use savory combinations of spices with onion, chili, garlic, ginger, and creamy coconut milk in their dishes. Fresh green chilis are often served as a side dish or are chopped with garlic, onion, tomato, dried shrimp paste, sugar, and vinegar or soy sauce to make "sambal" which accompanies every meal. The following recipe has true Indonesian flavor and can be prepared on the stove or on your favorite outdoor barbecue.

1 pound (450 g) white fish fillet
2 tablespoons (30 ml) oil
1 lime or lemon, cut into 4-6 wedges

Spicy Marinade:
3 cloves garlic, chopped
1 medium-size onion, chopped
1½ teaspoons (7 ml) crushed chili pepper
½ teaspoon (2 ml) sweet basil leaves
3 slices ginger, shredded
¾ teaspoon (3 ml) dried shrimp paste (optional)
1 teaspoon (5 ml) crushed tamarind
1¼ teaspoons (6 ml) salt
1 cup (250 ml) thick coconut milk, canned

1. Cut fish into 2" x 3" pieces (5 cm x 7.5 cm); pat dry and set aside.
2. Combine spicy marinade ingredients in a blender and whir until smooth.
3. Marinate fish for 30 minutes; drain and set aside.
4. Heat oil in hot skillet or frying pan over medium-high heat. Brown 4-5 fish fillets at a time for 1½-2 minutes on each side, basting frequently with remaining marinade. Transfer fish to a large platter when done.
5. Bring remaining marinade sauce to a boil in a saucepan. Reduce heat to medium-low and simmer until slightly thickened, about 4-5 minutes.
6. Pour sauce over fish and serve with lime or lemon wedges.

Remarks
- *Shrimp paste is a traditional and popular seasoning ingredient in most southeast Asian cuisines. It has a strong and distinctive fermented fish aroma which you may have to develop a taste for. Try just a little the first time.*
- *Most of the spices in this recipe are available in the supermarket spice section.*

Spiced Seafood

A very quick and simple dish to prepare for any occasion. You will love it.

¼ pound (112 g) fish fillet
1 egg, lightly beaten
1 teaspoon (5 ml) salt

1 teaspoon (5 ml) white sesame
   seeds, ground
1 teaspoon (5 ml) chili powder
1 tablespoon (15 ml) sesame oil

1. Cut fish fillet into 1" x 2" pieces.
2. Combine beaten egg, salt, ground sesame seeds and chili powder in a bowl. Coat fish in this mixture. Heat oil in a shallow pan and fry fish until dark brown, crisp and quite dry.
3. Serve cold, as a side dish with Korean BBQ. Prepared in large quantities and stored in the refrigerator. Re-fry before serving.

Sukiyaki

This is one of my most prized Japanese recipes because it can be prepared right at the dinner table — I do not get stuck in the kitchen while everyone else is eating!! Meat and vegetables prepared in a savory, soy-flavored sauce is a perfect choice for a group of hungry people.

1-1½ pounds (450-675 g) beef,
    sliced paper thin
1 pound (450 g) bean curd, cut into
    1" cubes (2.5 cm)
¼ pound (112 g) mushrooms, sliced
1 stalk green onion, cut into 2"
    (5 cm) strips
¼ pound (112 g) asparagus
¼ pound (112 g) green beans, cut into 2"
    pieces (5 cm) (ends removed)
¼ pound (112 g) spinach, washed
    carefully to remove sand
1-3 ounces (84 g) can bamboo shoots,
    sliced
1 large onion, sliced
2 ounces (56 g) yam noodles (optional)

Sukiyaki Sauce:
2½ cups (625 ml) water
1-1/3 cups (330 ml) soy sauce
½ cup (125 ml) wine
½ cup (125 ml) sugar

1. Arrange beef and vegetables attractively on a large platter.
2. Combine sukiyaki sauce ingredients and set aside.
3. Heat an electric skillet, electric wok or a large frying pan over medium (300° F, 150° C) heat. Add sauce and bring to a boil (only add about 2/3 of sauce to begin with). Add about 1/3 of the meat, cook slightly, then add 1/3 of each vegetable and noodles, keeping each separate. Cook to desired doneness, turning gently while cooking. Serve immediately. Replenish sauce, meat, vegetables and noodles as needed.

Remarks
- *Ideally, sukiyaki is cooked in an electric skillet right at the dinner table, so that each person can choose and cook whatever he or she wants.*
- *Traditionally, the skillet is greased with a small amount of suet (meat fat) or oil, then the meat is added and cooked slightly before adding the sukiyaki sauce.*
- *You can use any vegetables you wish in this dish.*
- *Sweetness of the sukiyaki sauce can be adjusted to your own taste.*
- *Sukiyaki can be served with a raw egg on the side to be used as a dip.*
- *With these ingredients, you can actually feed an army!*
- *Don't throw away extra sauce; it can be stored in the refrigerator and used again.*
- *Ask your butcher to slice the meat extra thin for you.*

Tempura

Tempura is a selection of vegetables and seafood which are dipped in batter and deep-fried until light and crispy. The combination of fresh ingredients, a light coating, oil at a constant temperature, and a tasty dipping sauce make an unforgettable Japanese meal. Sometimes simple things are better — our 10,000 ingredient recipe for batter did not come out so I selected 4 simple recipes to choose from. They all come out restaurant-perfect!!

flour for dry coating
4 cups (1 L) oil
6 prawns, shelled with tails intact
4-6 onion rings
½ zucchini, cut into ¼" (0.75 cm) diagonal slices
1 small carrot, cut into 3" (7.5 cm) thin slices
8-10 mushrooms
2 ounces (56 g) broccoli flowerets, parboiled
¼ pound (225 g) green beans, cut into 2" (5 cm) pieces (ends removed)
¼ eggplant, cut into ¼" (0.75 cm) thick diagonal slices
½ sweet potato or yam, cut into ¼" (0.75 cm) diagonal slices

Batter mix choice #1: (very crispy)
1¼ cups (310 ml) cake flour
1 cup (250 ml) flat beer

Batter mix choice #2:
1¼ cup (310 ml) cake flour
1 cup (250 ml) flat beer
1 egg, beaten

Batter mix choice #3:
1¼ cup (310 ml) cake flour
1 cup (250 ml) water
1 egg, beaten

Batter mix choice #4:
1¼ cup (310 ml) cake flour
1 cup (250 ml) water

Dipping Sauce: (optional)
1 cup (250 ml) stock (dashi-no-moto)
¼ cup (60 ml) soy sauce
2 tablespoons (30 ml) wine
2½ teaspoons (12 ml) sugar
grated ginger or white radish (optional)

1. Combine ingredients for dipping sauce and reserve. Keep warm.
2. Place shrimp and vegetables in separate groups on a' platter.
3. Combine batter mix ingredients and stir just until blended. (Make batter mix just before deep-frying.) Don't beat.
4. Sprinkle flour over prawns and vegetables to dry-coat. Cook prawns and each type of vegetable separately. Deep-fry in hot oil over medium to medium-high heat (350°-375° F, 180°-190°C) until golden brown. Cooking time depends on type of vegetable. Drain well. Serve hot.

Remarks
- *The selection of vegetables is up to you. Vary the amount of ingredients according to the number of people.*
- *For variation of batter consistency, adjust amount of water used.*

Teriyaki Chicken

In Japanese cooking, the term, "teriyaki" refers to a sweet soy sauce-flavored glaze, used as a marinade or as a sauce for meats and seafood. "Teri" means gloss or luster, describing the sauce which is poured over broiled ("yaki") foods or serves to marinate them. My personal favorite is teriyaki fish. I order the extra-large size fish at the restaurant and can eat the whole thing by myself — extra large bones and all!! This teriyaki chicken dish is almost as good!

1 whole chicken, cut up

Teriyaki Marinade:
1 cup (250 ml) soy sauce
2/3 cup (160 ml) sugar
¼ cup (60 ml) wine
2 cloves garlic, mashed
2 teaspoons (10 ml) grated ginger

1. Marinate chicken for 1-2 hours
2. Bake chicken at 350° F (180° C) for 40-50 minutes, turning and basting occasionally with marinade.
3. Arrange on a platter and serve.

Remarks
- *To prepare chicken: Cut chicken in half; cut off legs, wings and thighs. Cut remaining portion into 4 pieces.*
- *Save leftover marinade for future use.*
- *Sweetness of marinade can be adjusted to your own taste.*

Udon (Japanese Noodles)

Let's take a break from Chinese cuisine and focus on another. Japanese noodles, udon, in a delicate fish broth is a sensational choice for a light meal or a snack. You can whip it up in no time!

1 pound (450 g) udon (Japanese
   wide noodles)
½ pound (225 g) cooked chicken or
   BBQ pork, cut into thin pieces
4 hard-boiled eggs, halved or 1
   (2-egg) omelette, cut into 2″
   (5 cm) thin strips
1 stalk green onion, chopped
6 ounces (168 g) fish cakes, sliced
   (optional)

Soup Broth:
6 cups (1½ L) water
1 bag (about 0.4 ounces (11 g))
   dashi-no-moto (fish stock)
4 dried black mushrooms, soaked and
   cut into thin strips
2 tablespoons (30 ml) soy sauce
1 teaspoon (5 ml) sugar
1 teaspoon (5 ml) salt
2 teaspoons (10 ml) wine

1. Bring a large pot of water to a boil. Add noodles and return to boil, stirring slowly to keep noodles from sticking to bottom of pan. Add 1 cup (250 ml) cold water and continue to cook until noodles are tender. Drain and rinse with cold running water. Drain again and set aside.
2. **For Soup Broth**: Combine water, dashi-no-moto and black mushrooms in a saucepan; bring to a boil. Reduce heat to low and simmer for 10 minutes. Stir in soy sauce, sugar, salt and wine. Mix and keep warm.
3. Place noodles in individual serving bowls. Top with meat, eggs, green onion and fish cake. Ladle soup broth into bowls and serve.

Remarks
- *Noodles can also be served cold.*
- *For added variety and visual appeal, use 2 hard-boiled eggs and a 2-egg omelet, together.*
- *Other combinations of meat and vegetables can be substituted.*

Fanciful Finales

My friends want to know why the Chinese didn't invent apple pie—I don't know. There's no Chinese chocolate cake, either. Come to think of it, it's hard to find anything resembling desserts on a typical everyday Chinese menu. It's just that dessert, served at the end of a meal, is another one of those inscrutable western customs that the Chinese don't understand.

On the other hand, the Chinese do serve sweet pastries as interludes or as snacks between meals. They just don't have any place as part of a daily meal. As for baked pastries, we run up against the traditional Chinese stove, with its lack of an oven, that tends to make baking an uncommon activity. The pastries that the Chinese prefer are either steamed or deep-fried and are always served with tea. Many traditional Chinese desserts are entirely liquid, such as sweet soups made from peanut, almond or roasted sesame seeds, which are often served warm or hot. Aside from the sweet soups, fresh or sweetened fruits and vegetables, nuts and rice and wheat flour pastries are common enough, as found in Chinese bakeries. The sweetened paste of black and red beans and lotus seeds are among the most popular and traditional fillings for most cakes, puddings, steamed buns and a great variety of other pastries. Actually, one of the most traditional Chinese ways to conclude a meal is to present a plateful of fresh, succulent fruits. I suppose that's one way of saying that it's hard to improve upon nature, but we keep trying. And so, the following recipes include some of the rarest of all Chinese dishes: *dessert*.

Almond Float

On a sweltering summer evening, a taste of this cool and refreshing dessert will start you thinking of icebergs and glaciers!! Snow white cubes of almond pudding floating lightly in a sea of fruit—a feast for the eyes and taste buds!

¼ cup (60 ml) cold water
1 pkg unflavored gelatin
¾ cup (200 ml) boiling water
2 teaspoons (10 ml) sugar
2/3 cup (160 ml) low fat milk
1¼ teaspoons (6 ml) almond extract

Syrup:
1 cup (250 ml) water
1/3 cup (80 ml) sugar

8 ounces (225 g) or 1 cup (250 ml)
   fruit cocktail

1. Pour ¼ cup cold water into a shallow rectangular dish. Sprinkle with gelatin and allow to soften for 5 minutes.
2. Add ¾ cup boiling water and stir to dissolve gelatin completely. Add sugar; stir well. Blend in milk and almond extract. Refrigerate until set.
3. **To make syrup**: Combine sugar and water in a saucepan; bring to a boil and cook for 1 minute. Cool and refrigerate.
4. To serve, cut set gelatin diagonally to form diamond-shaped cubes. Pour in syrup and loosen cubes gently from the dish with a spoon. Mix fruit cocktail into jello.

Remarks
- *To change the taste, use different flavors of extracts.*
- *Sweetness should be adjusted to your own taste.*
- *Add lychees to fruit cocktail, if available.*
- *This recipe should be enough to serve a party of four. Double the recipe if you wish to try it again the next day.*

Butterflies Are Free!

Holding on to butterflies is difficult, especially these butterflies! They are so delicious, your kids will be begging for more. Butterflies may be free, but these are far from being free of calories! A light dessert smothered with caramelized sauce.

12 egg roll wrappers
3 cups (¾ L) oil

½ cup (125 ml) sugar
1 tablespoon (15 ml) toasted sesame
    seeds (optional)

1. Cut egg roll wrappers in half. Place 2 wrappers on top of each other. Cut one 3½″ (9 cm) long slit in the center of each. Make a butterfly by lifting one end and placing it through the center cut and flipping over to the other side. Don't pull all the way through or you will be right where you started.
2. Deep-fry butterflies in hot oil over medium-high heat (350°-375°F, 180°-190°C) until golden brown. Set aside and drain well.
3. Make syrup by heating sugar and 1½ tablespoon (22 ml) oil in a heavy skillet over medium-low heat until completely melted. Keep hot.
4. To serve, coat fried butterflies with hot, running syrup by placing the butterflies in the skillet and turning them until coated. Sprinkle with sesame seeds.

Remarks
- *You can use powdered sugar instead of syrup — it tastes just as good.*

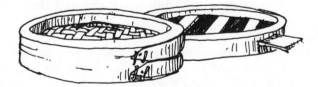

Candy Apple Fritters

This is a popular dessert of Peking origin. The batter-fried apple is coated with a caramelized sugar syrup. When the apple is plunged into ice water, the syrup forms a shiny, brittle glaze. The crackly outside and succulent, tender inside make a novel dessert to finish your dinner.

2 apples
2 teaspoons (10 ml) fresh lemon juice
2 tablespoons (30 ml) flour for
   dry coating

3 cups (¾ L) oil
1 teaspoon (5 ml) toasted sesame
   seeds
1 big bowl of ice water

Batter:
¼ cup (60 ml) flour
¼ cup (60 ml) cornstarch
1 large egg
4-5 (20-25 ml) teaspoons water

Syrup Glaze:
½ cup (125 ml) sugar
2½ tablespoons (37 ml) oil

1. Peel and core the apples. Cut into large, bite-size chunks. Add lemon juice to a large bowl of water. Drop apples in to prevent browning.
2. Combine the batter ingredients in a bowl and mix until smooth. Set aside.
3. Remove the apples from the water. Drain well and dry-coat with flour. Dip each piece of apple into batter and coat well.
4. Heat oil in a wok over medium-high heat (350°-375°F, 180°-190°C). Deep-fry 5-6 apple chunks at a time for 1½-2 minutes or until lightly browned, turning apples during frying. Remove and drain well.
5. To make syrup glaze, pour 2½ tablespoons oil into a hot saucepan or heavy skillet. Reduce heat to medium-low and add sugar. Stir constantly until sugar melts and begins to foam and caramelize. Keep glaze over low heat.
5. While making syrup, refry apple chunks in hot oil over high heat for about 1 minute. Remove, drain and immediately place into syrup. Turn to coat apple chunks as well. Transfer chunks to a greased platter and sprinkle with toasted sesame seeds.
7. To serve, dip apple chunks into ice water and then bite!

Remarks
- *For a crisper apple, deep-fry the pieces a second time while you are making the syrup and dip pieces of apple in syrup just before serving.*
- *Unless you intend to make burnt, carbon-flavored caramel, be sure to keep the heat low and stir frequently while melting the sugar.*

Eight Treasures Rice Pudding GENERAL

Here is a classic dessert, frequently served at banquets in Northern China. The moist, tender glutinous rice (sweet rice) is boiled and then steamed to a perfect tenderness with a combination of colorful ingredients. It is surprisingly rich, smooth and sweet.

1 cup (250 ml) glutinous rice, rinsed
   and drained
1 cup (250 ml) water
4 teaspoons (20 ml) oil
2 tablespoons (30 ml) sugar
4 dates
2 tablespoons (30 ml) raisins
8-10 lotus seeds (optional)
4 red cherries
4 green cherries
2/3 cup (160 ml) red bean paste

Syrup:
1 cup (250 ml) water
¼ cup (60 ml) sugar
1-¾ teaspoon (8 ml) cornstarch solution

1. Cook rice with 1 cup water over high heat until boiling. Reduce heat to low, cover and simmer for 25-30 minutes. Fluff rice. Add oil and sugar to cooked rice and mix well.
2. Arrange fruits artistically around the bottom and sides of a greased 1-quart (1 L) bowl. Spread 1/3 of the cooked rice over fruits and press lightly to form a layer. Place 1/3 cup (80 ml) red bean paste on top of rice and spread evenly. Then place another 1/3 of the rice and remaining 1/3 cup (80 ml) of red bean paste to form alternate layers. Cover with the remaining 1/3 of rice. If you can, prepare this in advance, and refrigerate.
3. Steam for 35-40 minutes over medium heat for 1 hour. Replenish water in the steamer, if necessary.
4. While rice is steaming, combine syrup mixture in a saucepan. Cook over medium heat until thickened. Keep warm.
5. To unmold, invert the bowl of pudding over a deep platter. Slice the pudding, then pour the syrup over it and serve.

Ginger-Ale Melon Balls

I'll tell you the truth — I've never tried this before. Be bold and adventurous! Mellow melon balls saturated in slightly sweet ginger ale is definitely a winner! This dessert should be served at your most elaborate dinners.

1¼ cup (310 ml) water
1/3 cup (80 ml) sugar
4 large slices ginger

2 cups (500 ml) ¾″ (2 cm) cubed
  watermelon, chilled
2 tablespoons (30 ml) shredded
  Chinese pickled ginger
4 cups (1 L) ice cold ginger ale

1. Bring water, sugar and ginger to a boil. Reduce heat to medium-low. Cover and simmer for 12-15 minutes until syrup lightly reduces to thicken. Remove and discard ginger slices. Chill.
2. To serve, place 4-5 melon cubes, 3-4 shreds of Chinese pickled ginger and 1 tablespoon (15 ml) ginger-flavored syrup into each sherbet glass. Fill with chilled ginger ale!

Remarks
• *Use a melon baller to cut watermelon into uniform balls.*

Golden Crispy Cashews

I am a nut who loves nuts and sweet things. If you are a nut, too, this will be just right for your taste buds. It's a simple and amazingly versatile snack.

2 cups (500 ml) water   1/3 cup (80 ml) honey
1 cup (250 ml) raw cashew nuts   4 cups (1 L) oil

1. Bring water to a boil. Add honey and reduce heat to low. Add the nuts and blanch for 7-8 minutes or until tender. Remove and let cool. Be sure they are completely dry.
2. Deep-fry the nuts in hot oil over medium-low to medium heat (300° F-325° F) (150° C-160° C), stirring frequently for 4-5 minutes, or until light brown. Avoid high temperatures and prolonged frying. Remove and let cool before serving.

Remarks
- *These nuts can be prepared ahead of time and stored up to a week in a cool, dry place. Don't keep them until you retire!*
- *Raw cashews may be purchased at most health food stores.*

Iced Lychees

The lychee is a sweet, succulent fruit grown in most parts of the Kwang-tung province. It is also found in Taiwan. The lychee has a thin rugged, strawberry-red shell. Occasionally, you will find aged fresh lychees in Chinese stores. However, the fresh ones are more delicate and naturally sweet. Lychees can be served fresh or chilled, as a dessert, or as an ingredient in many great dishes.

**2 cups (500 ml) strawberry or
    vanilla ice cream**
**1 can (20 ounces) lychees,
    chilled (approximately 25
    lychees)**

**4-6 large, fresh strawberries,
    washed (optional)**

1. Fill 4-6 sherbet glasses with a scoop of ice cream.
2. Drain lychees, arrange approximately 5 around the ice cream. Top each with a whole berry.

Remarks
- *If you can't get strawberries, substitute your favorite berry or add more ice cream.*
- *Be creative! Try layering ice cream, lychees and berries in a parfait glass.*

Open Mouth to Laugh

This sweet Chinese pastry will tickle your fancy. A delightful golden sesame seed ball that breaks into a smile as it is fried. It can be served as a dessert or as a snack. Try it; it will surely make you laugh, too.

Dough Mixture A:
2/3 cup (160 ml) sugar
1 tablespoon (15 ml) lard or
    shortening
1 egg, beaten
3 tablespoons (45 ml) water,
    more if needed

¾ cup (200 ml) sesame seeds
4 cups (1 L) oil

Dough Mixture B:
2 cups (500 ml) flour
1¼ teaspoon baking powder

1. Place ingredients for Dough Mixtures A and B in separate mixing bowls and mix well. Combine the two mixtures and knead to a soft, smooth dough.
2. Roll into a long roll and cut into approximately 20 equal pieces. Roll each piece into a round ball, dampen the surface with water and coat with sesame seeds. Set aside.
3. Heat oil over high heat (375°F, 190°C) then reduce heat to low and wait 30 seconds. (Oil should be about 350°F, 180°C for frying.) Carefully drop sesame seed-coated balls into oil. Deep-fry 4 at a time over low heat until ball cracks open. Continue frying, turning frequently, until golden brown. Drain well and cool before serving.

Remarks
- *Store in a container in a cool dry place. They will stay fresh for one week.*
- *If any of these do not open up and laugh, say goodbye and eat it quickly so no one else will see.*
- *Be sure oil is not too hot, or the balls will not crack and open and you will have sad balls. Too high a heat will cause them to burn before they get a chance to smile.*
- *Use a fine strainer to skim sesame seeds off the surface of the oil during frying to prevent burning.*
- *Sometimes these balls not only open one mouth, but crack up and open all over! If too many balls are fried at one time, they will all open their mouths at once, and the result will be a noisy kitchen!*

Sweet Almond Soup CANTON

This recipe is similar to Sweet Sesame Soup. It is much simpler and just as soothing and refreshing. The distinctive almond flavor makes a delicious end to a satisfying meal.

6 cups (1½ L) water
½ cup (125 ml) sugar (round cup)
1 cup (250 ml) ground almonds

½ teaspoon (2 ml) almond extract
5 tablespoons (75 ml) cornstarch
   solution

1. Bring water to a boil over high heat. Add sugar and ground almonds. Reduce heat to medium-low and cook for 2 minutes. Avoid over-boiling.
2. Add almond extract and stir well; thicken with cornstarch solution.
3. Serve hot in individual serving bowls.

Remarks
- *Sweetness and thickness can be adjusted to taste.*
- *In Chinese grocery stores, you can purchase ground almond powder in a can or a plastic bag. The powder will give the soup a smoother consistency.*

Sweet Sesame Soup CANTON

If the Chinese serve a sweet after meals, this is most likely what it would be — a thick, lightly sweetened, soothing soup to polish off the evening and delight your sweet tooth.

1 cup (250 ml) toasted sesame seeds
6 cups (1½ L) water

1 cup (250 ml) packed brown sugar
¼ cup (60 ml) cornstarch solution

1. Heat wok over high heat. Add sesame seeds and toast for 1 minute. Grind to a powder in a blender, then return to the wok.
2. Add water and bring to a boil; boil for 2 minutes. Stir in brown sugar. Reduce heat to medium-low and simmer for 2 minutes or until sugar is dissolved.
3. Thicken with cornstarch and serve hot.

Remarks
- *Reduce heat after adding cornstarch solution to avoid boiling over. Otherwise, you will have fun cleaning your stove.*
- *Be patient when grinding sesame seeds. Use a mortar to grind them first, then whir in a blender. Add some of the water if desired, to make a paste.*

Sweet Sheet Soup

This is perhaps one of the most traditional family-style desserts in Cantonese cooking—simple, nutritious and light. It is something very different from ice cream and forest cake.

1 whole sheet dried bean curd, soaked	**7 cups (1 ¾ L) water**
2 eggs, lightly beaten	**½ cup (125 ml) sugar (rounded cup)**

1. Break the whole dried bean curd sheet into 3-4 pieces. Soak in water for 1 hour. Cut into approximately 2″ (5 cm) squares.
2. Beat the eggs lightly and set aside.
3. Bring 7 cups of water to a boil in a large pot and dissolve the sugar in it. Add bean curd pieces and reduce heat to low. Simmer for 20-25 minutes, or until bean curd is tender.
4. Remove from heat; slowly pour in beaten eggs, stirring constantly. Serve hot in individual bowls.

Remarks
- *Four ounces (112 g) of Chinese rock sugar may be substituted for sugar.*

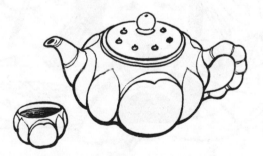

*"You may think everything's getting out of hand
just when things are really falling into place . . ."*

LET'S WRAP IT UP!

Cheers! A Toast to You — Tea and Wine

Some Tea Leaf Reading

The Chinese have been drinking tea for so long that they can't remember when they started. (The same thing happened with wine, but for a different reason.) If you search Chinese literature, you'll find one ancient writer, about 5000 years ago, who said that tea "quenches thirst. It lessens the desire for sleep. It gladdens and cheers the heart." Those are still among the best reasons to drink tea. But another, more practical reason probably has to do with the spread of tea drinking.

In more modern times, about 2500 years ago, it became common to boil water as a means of preventing disease. Perhaps a leaf accidentally fell into the boiling water, and so the first cup of tea was invented. I rather like that one, but the historians really begin to date tea drinking back to the Han Dynasty (about 206 B.C.). Within a matter of only a few short centuries, there existed about 8000 different grades of tea, which were classified by their manufacturing process, its quality, the quality of the leaf itself, and its place of origin (which numbered about 200 and were scattered over 16 provinces).

Even today, there are hundreds of different kinds of Chinese teas; and a true connoisseur savors each variety for its special properties. You might drink jasmine tea while reading poetry or sip Keemun tea during a chess match. Wu-I, a black tea from Yunnan, is said to cure a cold, and many other teas are considered valuable medicinal aids for improving digestion, relieving headaches and ulcers, even as an antidote for hangovers.

Most of all, though, the Chinese drink tea for pleasure. Despite the enormous variety available, most Chinese tend to stick to one or two kinds that are grown in or near their native village or region. But if you have access to a well-supplied tea shop or Chinese markets, you can build your own tea collection. There are four major categories and you might try to find one tea from each.

1. *The unfermented or green tea.* In this case, fresh tea leaves are steamed to stop the fermentation process and to make them pliable. They are then rolled and dried to prevent oxidation. Unfermented green tea has a natural bouquet, a pale colored brew, and a pure and refreshing taste. The flavor is mild, but with a full body.

2. *Fermented or black tea.* Fresh tea leaves undergo an initial evaporation stage called withering, which reduces the moisture without drying the leaf completely. They are then rolled to release their juices and broken up by mesh sieves. The leaves are then spread out to oxidize in a fermentation room until they change to a bright, copper color, after which they are dried a final time before shipping. When brewed, the infusion gives a clear red liquor with a full body and a strong flavor. The best-known black tea is Keemun, but other Chinese favorites include Lychee Red Tea and The Iron Goddess of Mercy. (If you have no "Mercy," try Eyebrows of Longevity for a quick pick-me-up.)

3. *Semi-fermented tea*. This compromise between green and black teas offers a pleasant aroma and full body, with a tawny color. Probably the most popular is Oolong tea, which comes from Fuijian (Fukien) province, or Taiwan, where it is often used as the base for Jasmine tea.
4. *Scented tea*. You begin with choice green tea leaves, or semi-fermented oolong, and add fresh, fragrant flowers and fruits. These are blended naturally, without artificial flavors or essential oils. In the best quality jasmines, for example, you will find whole jasmine blossoms, which add a real bouquet to your teapot. Such scented teas have a pleasant aroma with a long-lasting after taste.

Tea Storage:

Keep your teas in air-tight containers in a cool, dry place, well away from spices and other strong-flavored foods. If you store them properly, teas should retain their flavors for one to two years, while some black tea varieties last much longer.

How to brew a perfect cup of tea:

If you believe the TV commercials, you may think that it takes a combination chemist and magician to make a decent cup of coffee. Tea is much easier, but a few tips may still help. Start with freshly-drawn cold water, and boil till the water rolls, but no more, or you'll boil away the oxygen, making the water flat. For best results, porcelain or earthenware teapots and teacups should be used because they do not distort the natural flavor of tea. Scald the teapot with hot water, swish it around and empty it before adding the tea and more water. Some tea packages recommend using one teaspoon per cup, but the Chinese generally prefer lighter teas, using only one or two spoonfuls per pot. You should experiment and decide what's best for you. After pouring the freshly-boiled water over the tea leaves, allow them to brew for three to four minutes.

In authentic Chinese restaurants, you won't find a sugar bowl or milk served with the tea. For one thing, mainland Chinese aren't accustomed to milk and have difficulty digesting it, and they prefer their tea "black." For that matter, green oolong and scented teas are best appreciated with nothing added that might mask their delicate flavors. Black teas, however, are more robust and may be enjoyed with milk or lemon and sugar. At home, of course, you are free to do as you please (although adding milk to the finest jasmine would make me weep); but in a Chinese restaurant, don't be surprised if your waiter gives you a funny look if you ask for sugar.

Chinese Spirits—The Bottled Kind

I am not really qualified to discuss this topic, because my tolerance of alcohol is so low that if I were to have even two sips of Chinese wine, I wouldn't be able to find my chopsticks. The Chinese have been making wine for about 4500 years, but according to some of my western friends, they still haven't gotten it right. The Arabs are supposed to have brought grapes to China by the second century B.C., but earlier alcoholic beverages were distilled from sorghum (and some are still being made from Kaoliang and range from 50 to 100 proof). Just the smell of some could have you feeling 'tipsy' in seconds.

Grape wines were popular among poets and mandarins in the 11th century, but in the 14th century, an emperor destroyed the local vines and replaced them with cereal crops. Some grape wines continued to be made (Marco Polo enjoyed some), but they never commanded the agricultural importance of wine-making as it developed in France and Italy.

The traditional Chinese rice wine, called Shaohsing, is made by fermenting sweetened glutinous rice or millet. This Chinese invention (approximately 12% to 18% alcohol) dates from the 3rd century B.C., and it also continues to be popular today, under a number of different brand names, such as Chia Fan, Hua Tiao, Yen Hung, and Hsiang Huseh.

In Chinese, there is only one word for both wine and spirits: *Chiu*. That covers the dry sherry-like Shaohsing and the white Kaoliang, which resembles gin or vodka, and ultimately includes the notorious Mao-Tai. I say 'notorious' because my western friends, who pride themselves on their cellars, regard Mao Tai as one of those 'acquired' tastes (like the Hong Kong delicacies of stir-fried bird's tongue, fish lips soup or braised duck feet) that most westerners never manage to acquire. Reaching a potency of 150 proof, Mao Tai can knock your socks off (even if you keep your shoes on). At a formal Chinese banquet, it would be drunk straight, with no water or ice to dilute its flavor (or its kick).

The Chinese drink their wines at dinner, with food, rather than before dinner. If you are at a Chinese banquet, and if it's your turn to toast the host (and if you can still stand), raise your glass and say, "Kan Pei!" That means, "Bottoms up." If you are invited to a banquet among North American Chinese, you may be surprised to find that whiskey or brandy has replaced rice wine as the Chinese alcoholic beverage of choice. Of course, part of this may have to do with the difficulty of obtaining a good selection of Chinese wines in this country. Some big city liquor stores in Canada stock a few brands, and some of the Chinese specialty stores in the U.S. carry some, but with alcoholic beverages, I've found that suitable substitutions are usually graciously received. Try Wan Fu (translated 'a million blessings'), which is actually a French light wine that is specially bottled and intended to complement a Chinese meal. There are also the California white wines, dry French Graves or Chablis, Italian Soave Bolla, Rhine wine or German Liebfraumilch. Red wines can be served with the heavier dishes, such as duck or beef. Incidentally, there's a very popular Chinese beer that's recently come on the market in North America, and it works quite well with most Chinese dishes.

Just remember that the principle activity at a dinner is eating, not drinking. Too much drink numbs the palate, which means that all those delicious dishes just go to waste.

If wine were not favoured by Heaven
No Wine Star would shine in the sky;
If wine were not loved by the Earth,
No Wine Spring would gush from her breast.
The blessing of Heaven, Earth's cordial stream
No man in his senses would deny.

Li Po

Leave the Wokking to Them

If you choose to entertain at a Chinese restaurant (most Chinese celebrate their birthdays, welcomings, weddings, anniversaries, and, oddly enough, even gatherings after a funeral at a restaurant), selecting a menu for a large group of people can be a difficult task. As a rule of thumb, choose dishes that are appropriate for the occasion and dishes that will most likely be enjoyed by your guest of honor. (Surely, you won't want a grumpy guest of honor, so feed him/her well!) Of course, if you are dining with your own family, it would be much easier to decide on a menu. (then, you can include the 'thousand year old egg' appetizer without any questions asked!)

As a common practice, order the number of dishes equivalent to the number of guests, plus soup and rice. The majority of Chinese restaurants in North America serve mainly quick stir-fried or deep-fried dishes, thus limiting the selections on the menu. However, you can still choose a great variety of dishes, particularly if you order in advance. (If the chef knows beforehand, he may be able to prepare something that is not on the menu.) Strive to select a dish from each food category—one chicken-, one pork-, one beef-, one seafood-, and one vegetable dish (or more than one, depending on the number of people). Choose a combination of flavors, colors, and textures (different ingredients as well as cooking methods) to get the most satisfaction out of a meal. (And if you smile nicely to the waiter, perhaps he'll even give you some extra fortune cookies!)

At a formal Chinese banquet, each dish is served individually to savor the characteristic flavor of each dish. No waiter should rush you through an eleven-course dinner (unless he promises to supply the alka-seltzer for everyone afterwards). To begin with, you are usually served a selection of cold dishes, followed by several quick stir-fried dishes, which can be rich, dry, crispy or aromatic, and each with different main ingredients. The dinner continues with a delicious (and most likely, expensive) soup, a roast or simmered duck, fried chicken, and sweet and sour whole fish. A few lighter or plain dishes conclude this feast, with rice or noodles as fillers. (By this time, you should excuse yourself to loosen your belt or take a 5-mile jog!)

Dining out should be a memorable experience. Do not limit your imagination—try something new and different each time. Here are a few humble suggestions for your dining pleasure.

Cantonese (Southern) Cuisine

Dinner for two:

A. Chicken cream of corn soup
    Sweet and sour pork
    Oyster beef
    Rice and tea

B. Bean curd and crab meat soup
    Paper wrapped chicken
    Beef in greens
    Rice and tea

Dinner for four:

A. Bean curd and eight treasure soup
    Pork cashew nuts
    Steamed garoupa
    Chicken liver with greens
    Rice and tea

B. Chicken and mushroom soup
    Stuffed crab claws
    Chicken and ginger with black bean sauce
    Fried fish balls
    Rice and tea

Szechwan (Western) Cuisine

Dinner for two:

A. Scallion with beef
   Dry cooked carp
   Bean curd soup
   Rice and tea

B. Deep-fried eight pieces of chicken
   Sauteed mushroom and bamboo shoots
   Ham and winter melon soup
   Rice and tea

Dinner for four:

A. Drunk chicken
   Szechwan preserved vegetable with pork
   Sizzling shrimp with tomato sauce
   Hot and sour soup
   Rice and tea

B. Vinegar sauce chicken
   Scallions with sliced pork
   Sauteed mixed vegetables
   Abalone and chicken soup
   Rice and tea

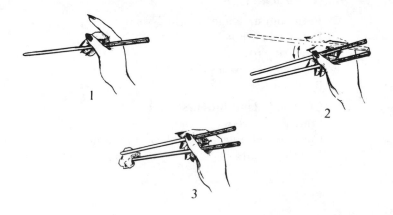

Shanghai (Eastern) Cuisine

Dinner for two:

A. Pork spareribs with salt and pepper
    Stewed yellow fish
    Meat and preserved turnip soup
    Rice and tea

B. Sliced pork with bamboo shoots
    Chicken with bean sprouts
    Shredded chicken, ham and pork soup
    Rice and tea

Dinner for four:

A. Fried chicken, abalone and prawn
    Shredded beef with green pepper
    Shanghai cabbage with chicken fat
    Yellow fish soup
    Rice and tea

B. Fried shrimp
    Braised meat and vegetables
    Diced chicken with chili sauce
    Sliced chicken soup
    Rice and tea

Peking (Northern) Cuisine

Dinner for two:

A. Bean curd with chili sauce
    Shredded pork with green pepper
    Chicken with mushroom soup
    Rice and tea

B. Fried shrimp or cold chicken
    Twice cooked pork
    Sliced chicken, abalone and prawn soup
    Rice and tea

Dinner for four:

A. Spiced beef with quick fried shrimps
    Diced chicken with chili sauce
    Stewed mixed vegetables
    Chicken and asparagus soup
    Rice and tea

B. Sizzling shrimps with tomato sauce
    Sliced fish with brown sauce
    Fried shredded beef with chili sauce
    Hot and sour soup
    Rice and tea

Chopsticks for two, three . . .

When entertaining (Chinese-style, of course!) at home, you should enjoy yourself—regard the event as a pleasure rather than a production. Plan your menu, organize your time and be realistic about your own skills and experience. You should be able to serve the dishes in sequence or simultaneously and still be able to dine with your guests (or there will be one hungry cook left in the kitchen!).

First, I suggest you quickly glance through pages 41-42, and become familiar with the recipes in this little booklet. Sit down and plan your meal, draw up the most feasible menu, depending on the availability of time, ingredients, cooking utensils, etc. Selecting the appropriate dishes for a Chinese dinner may require some thinking—even for this humble cook.

Most Chinese select the dishes simply out of habit or personal taste. For special occasions, simply add a few extra dishes which may be appropriate for the occasion or those you feel will be most appreciated by your honored guests. (Better think twice about those 'braised chicken feet'.) Avoid any repetition of dishes; variety is what you should strive for—the contrast of subtle and strong, soft and crisp, light- and richly-colored, cool and spicy, sweet and sour. The choice of ingredients, the cooking methods and the type of occasion should all be taken into consideration.

For a daily meal, the Chinese serve all the dishes simultaneously. How do they accomplish such a feat? The Chinese prepare everything in advance—wash and cut up the vegetables, slice and marinate the meats, measure seasonings and assemble all sauces. Then, when you start cooking, everything is ready to go and within easy reach. As each dish is cooked, it will be transferred to a plate or bowl, covered with foil and kept warm, while the next dish is being prepared. No time is wasted. Try not to tie up your cooking space. Prepare any dishes which can be cooked ahead of time and simply reheated just before serving. Plan to cook something on top of the stove, another dish in the oven and yet another dish that is steamed. Have only a minimum of stir-fried dishes which have to be cooked in the very last few minutes.

To help you get started, here are a few menu suggestions. You will probably find that the best menu for your next dinner party will be the one that excites you the most. Choose a menu that you can handle—one that allows you and not only your guests—to have a good time. (don't be left wearing your apron, embedded with soy sauce and sesame oil stains!)

Menus for a Party of Four

Singing Rice Soup
Tomato Beef
Hot Pot Lemon Chicken
Stuffed Pork Rolls and Broccoli
Plain Cooked Rice
Tea

Seafood and Bean Curd Soup
Cauliflower and Broccoli in Sweet Cream Sauce
Broiled Beef Shish Kebobs
Almond Chicken Crisp
Singapore Rice Noodles
Tea

Winter Melon Soup
Eggplant with Black Beans
Spicy Shredded Vegetables and Beef
Chicken Stuffed Pineapple
Yang Chow Fried Rice
Tea

Cucumber Soup
Honey Garlic Ribs
Sweet and Sour Fish Rolls
Eggplant with Black Beans
Curry Fried Rice with Beef or Anything
Tea

Creamy Chicken Corn Soup
Spicy Ginger Beef
Stir-Fried Winter Melon with Prawns
Special Egg Foo Yung
Plain Cooked Rice
Tea

Menus for a Party of Six

Winter Melon Soup
Almond Chicken Crisp
Mongolian Beef
Singing Shrimp Surprise
Spiced Minced Pork with Bean Curd
Garden Vegetable Platter
Yang Chow Fried Rice
Ginger Ale Melon Balls
Tea

Bird's Nest Soup
Chinese BBQ Pork
Lover's Prawns
Heavenly Honeydew Chicken
Mushroom in Two Sauces
Broccoli with Crab Meat Sauce
Curry Fried Rice with Beef
Almond Float
Tea

Seafood and Bean Curd Soup
Green Pepper Beef
Moo Goo Gai Pan
Sweet and Sour Pork
Braised Stuffed Bean Curd
Eggplant with Black Beans
Plain Cooked Rice
Iced Lychees
Tea

Special Effects—Garnishes

Like Hollywood special effects, the garnish should never be mistaken for the star. Of course, for the beginner, you may already have your hands full just getting the dish cooked. In that case, garnishing should be ignored because the food itself is clearly more important. When the cooking becomes second nature, then you can afford to devote your spare time to making what you cook look even better. Before you try it, though, here are a few pointers:

- Garnishes should always be simple and complement the food.
- It is not necessary to garnish every dish. Garnishing is like eye glasses—not everyone needs to wear them. Even without a garnish, your guests will still eat the food.
- Garnish with contrasting textures and colors to give a striking appearance.
- Garnishes should be a reflection of your imagination and personality.

Basic Tools

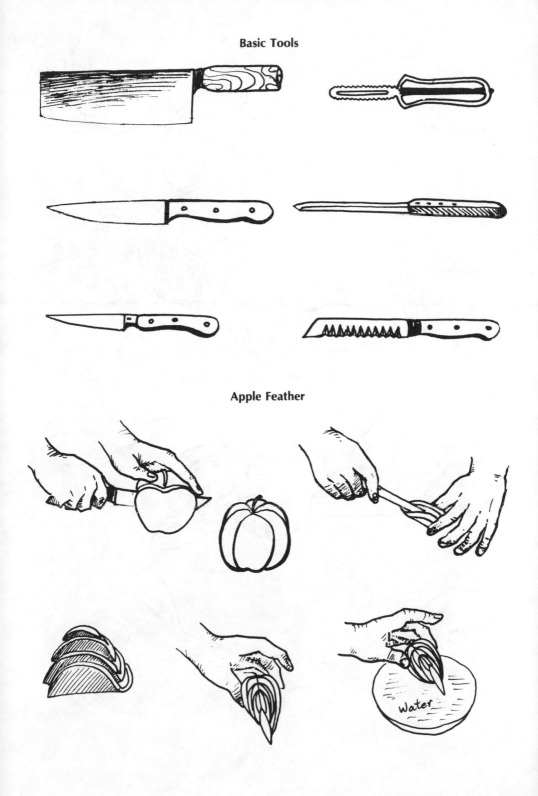

Apple Feather

Orange Loops

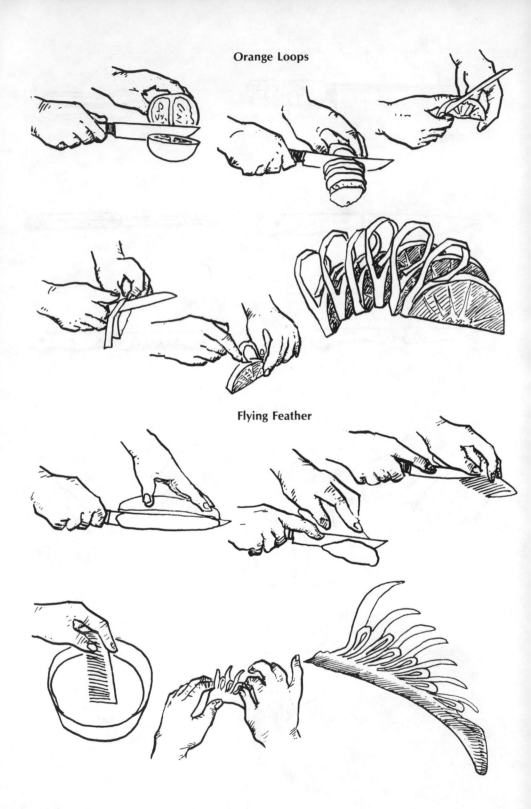

Flying Feather

272

Extended Cucumber Fan
(Cucumber)

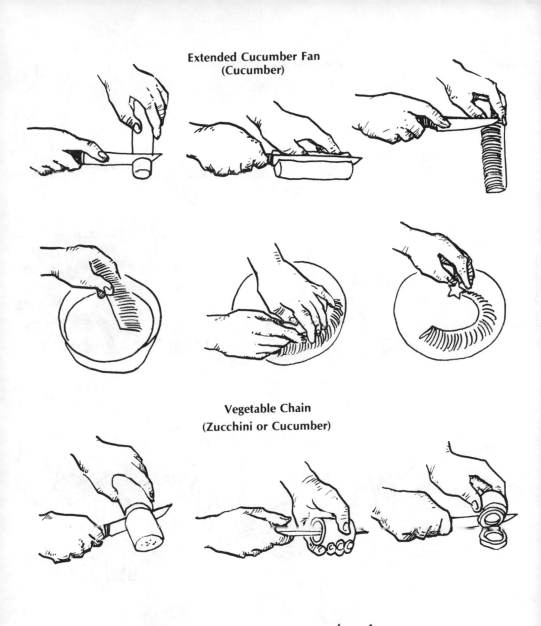

Vegetable Chain
(Zucchini or Cucumber)

Vegetable Spring (Cucumber)

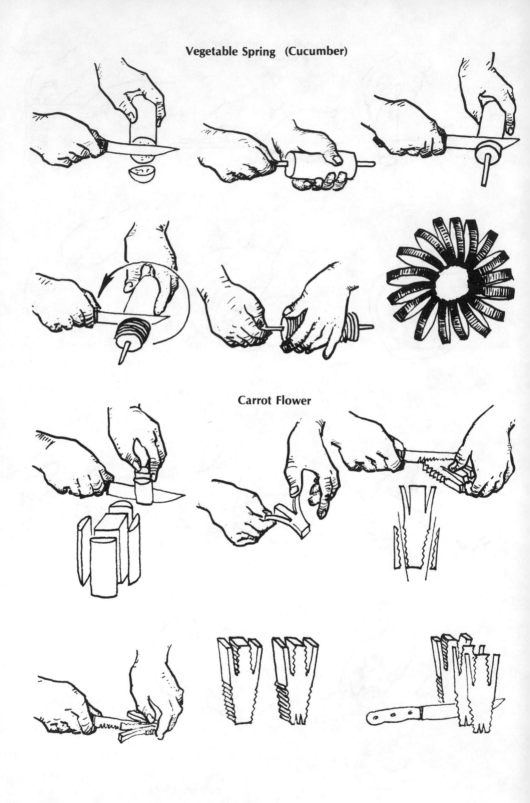

Carrot Flower

274

A Twist of Carrot

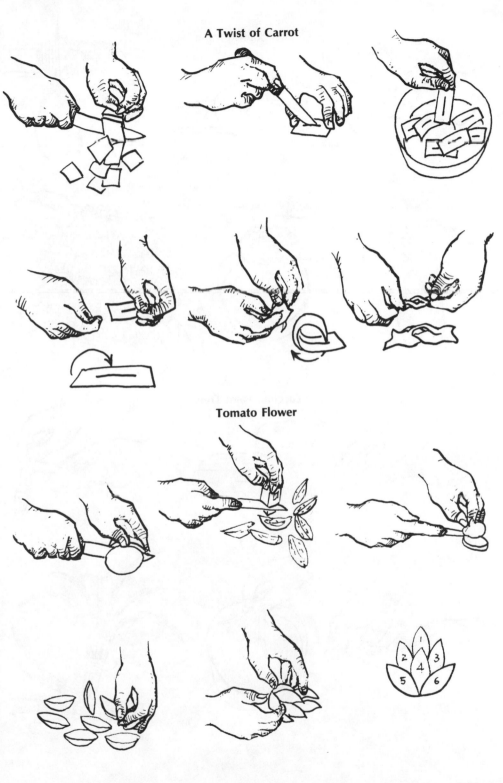

Tomato Flower

Red Radish Mum

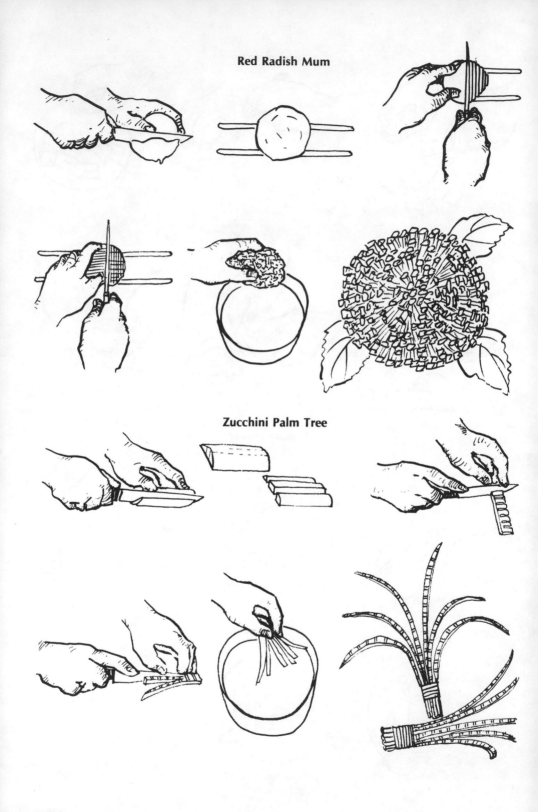

Zucchini Palm Tree

Chinese Roots—
Chop Suey and Chow Mein

People used to say that a plateful of bits of this and that was nothing but 'chop suey'. Actually, chop suey does mean 'miscellaneous odds and ends' in Chinese, and when people wonder whether it's truly an authentic Chinese dish, I have to say, "Yes and no."

There are many stories about the origin of chop suey, but most attribute its creation to the early Chinese immigrants who came to North America to build the railroads. In a foreign country, without many of their familiar ingredients, they improvised and put together whatever was at hand, creating many simple and practical dishes. Today, chop suey generally consists of quick fried bean sprouts, cabbage and other vegetables and a minimal amount of meats, served with plenty of sauce.

You may say "chow mein" in the same breath as chop suey, and in fact, it's sort of a sister dish. (Or, maybe more correctly, it's the half-sister who's legitimate, while the other one isn't quite.) Chow mein means 'pan-fried noodles' and is a genuine Chinese dish (as opposed to the kind with deep-fried noodles sometimes served in restaurants, which isn't genuine). Different regions of China have their own methods of cooking noodles, but generally, parboiled noodles (previously drained dry) are pan-fried and then combined with meat and vegetables. The noodles are first soft-fried in oil and then removed from the wok. Various meats and vegetables are then stir-fried until tender-crisp. The soft-fried noodles are returned to the wok before serving to reheat and to blend flavors.

Does that solve the great Chinese restaurant mystery? I hope so because chow mein is really a very casual and spontaneous dish that can incorporate any combination of ingredients with good cheer. Like spaghetti, it can be a one-dish meal for a very satisfying lunch, snack or as a final filler in a formal dinner. While the type of chow mein served in most North American restaurants with crispy deep-fried noodles is not traditional, no need to feel betrayed—all that really matters is if you like it.

Chung-Kwong Cheung

Chinese Spice and Everything Nice

Spices from the Orient used to come by camel caravan (not an old timey radio show!) and were associated with mystery, intrigue and great riches. Nowadays, many formerly exotic Oriental spices can be found in your corner supermarket, while a few may require a special trip to your local Chinatown markets. To the Chinese, of course, these are not exotic, but rather, the basic ingredients of cooking. For the average North American, though, they include many traditional and curious items that the average person is not likely to see in his lifetime. Fortunately, many of these are processed and preserved that can be kept for quite a while, if properly stored. For a fairly small investment, you can stock an extensive Chinese spice shelf that should be more than sufficient for the recipes in this book.

Seasonings and Condiments

Black Bean, Salted
A salted, fermented black bean with a strong, pungent aroma and flavor, used along with garlic to make into a paste as a seasoning in many Cantonese dishes. It goes well with beef and seafood. It is sold in cans or plastic bags in Chinese stores. Keep it in a covered container in the refrigerator or in a cool, dry area.

Brown Bean Sauce
A very thick, brownish sauce made from fermented soy beans, flour and salt. It is quite a popular item used as a seasoning sauce in many everyday dishes, such as steamed fish. It is only in Chinese stores, sold in bottles or tin cans. Store in the refrigerator.

Chili Oil
Available at most Oriental groceries in various sized bottles; however, you can also prepare chili oil at home. Heat one cup of oil in a saucepan until it begins to smoke. Turn off heat and wait 15-20 seconds. Put in 4 tablespoons of crushed or powdered red pepper, stirring well. Let stand until cool and transfer to a bottle.

Cooking Wine

In gourmet Chinese cooking, different type of wines are selected for different recipes. Some typical wines used are Shaoshing, Rose wine, Fun Chin or rice wine. Wine induces a desirable aroma and allows the different flavors to penetrate into the foods. In some cases, wine also reduces undesirable flavors and aromas in food. With its slight acidity, it also helps to tenderize meat and fish. For stir-frying, wine is introduced just before thickening to serve, thus retaining the delicate aroma. In stewing, simmering, or casserole dishes, wine can be used during the cooking process. In marinating meat, excessive amounts of wine should not be used since it will mask the natural flavor of the meat. If Chinese wine is not available, common dry sherry can be substituted. Use liberally for any dish if you wish to have an "instant hangover."

Five-Spice Powder

A blend of five different powdered spices — cloves, fennel, cinnamon, anise seeds and Szechwan peppercorns. It is usually sold in small bottles or plastic bags in Chinese stores. Though some types consist of more than five spices, it is basically an all-purpose seasoning, commonly used in various BBQ dishes. To make your own five-spice powder: place fifty to sixty Szechwan peppercorns, four whole star anise, two and one-half teaspoons fennel seeds, three to four one inch pieces of cinnamon bark and twelve to fourteen whole cloves in a blender to produce a fine powder. It will yield approximately five teaspoons of powder. Keep it tightly sealed in a cool, dry area, and it will keep forever.

Garlic

One of the very important ingredients in the flavoring of almost all Chinese dishes. It is usually sauteed in the wok in hot oil, along with ginger slices, before adding other ingredients. Garlic has many acclaimed medicinal functions. Use a great deal if you want to get rid of your social life! Whether it is left in the wok and served with the dish or removed prior to serving, is entirely up to the discretion and taste of the cook.

Ginger, Fresh

Ginger, is one of the most frequently used ingredients in all Chinese dishes. It imparts a delightful flavor and aroma to all foods, and of course, it helps to eliminate undesirable odors as well. The flavor and aroma help to elevate any ordinary dish into the sublime. It can enhance the character of any meat or vegetable dish. You can even make ginger tea or ginger desserts. Hot and nippy, only a few thin slices are needed to achieve the desired purpose. Ginger root can be sliced, shredded or grated, depending on the dish. If ginger juice is required, a garlic press can be used. Cut only enough to be used immediately, and store the rest in the refrigerator in a plastic bag. For prolonged storage, keep in a glass jar with a lid in the freezer. Ginger root is available in most supermarkets — just look for a knotty, ugly root in the produce section. Always pick the ginger that is firm and slightly shiny. Dry ginger or ginger powder are not satisfactory substitutes.

Green Onion

Its strong flavor and color will brighten all your dishes. To use, cut into varying lengths, then chop or mince depending on the particular dish.

Hoisin Sauce

A dark brown thick sauce with a delightful sweet and spicy flavor made from fermented soy beans, flour, sugar, garlic and spices. Along with plum sauce, it is mostly used for seasoning BBQ dishes and is also used as a dip. Sold in bottles or tin cans. Keep in the refrigerator.

Hot Bean Paste

A special seasoning sauce frequently used in the dishes from Szechwan. It is made from the regular bean paste and crushed chili peppers. Its spiciness gives any dish a muted hotness. If kept in the refrigerator, it can be stored for a long time.

Hot Chili Peppers, Fresh or Dried

Chili peppers come in many colors, shapes and sizes, but one thing they all are is…"hot stuff!" Fresh ones are available in most Oriental, Italian and Spanish stores all year round. Some varieties are hotter than others. Regardless of the extent of the hotness, they all add excitement to a great variety of dishes whether on cold winter nights or hot, muggy summer days. Manor varieties include Caribe, Floral Gem, Fresno, Jalapeno and the tiniest and hottest of them all — the Serrano Chilies. They can burn your heart out! Be especially careful when preparing fresh chilies; their juice is something else! It is not only hot enough to light a fire and generate smoke from your hair, it will also cause a great deal of discomfort if accidently rubbed from your hands into your beautiful eyes. So watch out, always use the amount to suit your taste. Some of your guests may love to fire themselves red-hot, some may not. Fresh peppers will keep in the refrigerator for several weeks. Crushed, dried peppers are available in most supermarket spice sections.

Mono-Sodium Glutamate (MSG)

This crystalline white powder ($C_5H_8O_4NaN$), extracted mostly from soy bean or other high protein cereal grains, is basically a flavor enhancer. In Chinese it is called "wei-ching" which literally translated, means "essence of taste." It is commonly sold under the trade names Aji-no-moto (Japanese) or Accent. A good Chinese cook does not use MSG in every dish. With high quality, fresh ingredients, the right seasonings and proper cooking, a recipe should not require the use of MSG. Some people use it on certain dishes with very bland tastes, such as bean curd or frozen vegetables.

"Chinese restaurant syndrome," refers to a group of symptoms including headache, dizziness, skin rashes, feeling of pressure on the temples, pressure on muscles around the neck, and extraordinary desire to drink 5 gallons of water, experienced by some people who are allergic to this chemical. It is interesting to know that MSG is present in most processed foods, particularly meat and soups. There is nothing to worry about! Do not use it in your recipe if you are worried that your neck might get stuck. Personally, I prefer homemade soup stock or even bouillon cubes to MSG. The amount of MSG used varies from chef to chef since most Chinese restaurants usually employ several cooks. For those who may experience such reactions to MSG, may I suggest that you tell the waiter to skip MSG in your dishes when you order in any Chinese restaurant.

Mustard, Chinese

This hot and pungent mustard is used mostly in condiments. It is not the same as French mustard. If the Chinese types are not available, mix 2 tablespoons of English mustard and 3-3½ tablespoons cold water, stirring to form a paste. Let it sit for 30 minutes to an hour to mellow the harsh, bitter taste. It can be kept for several weeks.

Oyster Sauce

A dark brown sauce made from oyster extract, salt and modified starch. It is a very strong-flavored and tasty sauce with varying consistencies. Thickness is not the measure of quality. There are many brand names with a great range of prices. Try them out, and see which one you prefer. As a seasoning or as a dip, it goes well with practically any meat and vegetables. Keep in the refrigerator.

Parsley, Chinese

A delightful, aromatic herb, it is green and parsleylike. It is also called cilantro and coriander and is widely used in Mexican and Far Eastern cooking. The flavor is strong, zesty and absolutely exciting. The taste often lingers on your tongue for quite a while. Its main uses are as a garnish to give a touch of color and flavor in soups, stews, poultry and fish dishes. It is an excellent addition for those who enjoy its distinctive flavor. Chinese parsley is sold in Oriental, Mexican and Italian specialty stores and in some supermarkets. Always pick the fresh, green color of unwilted bunches. Keep in a plastic bag in the refrigerator for up to five days.

Peppercorn Salt, Roasted

This is one of the few seasonings used in the different regions of China. It adds a distinctive touch of spiciness to deep-fried meats. To make your own, combine 1 teaspoon of Szechwan peppercorns with 3 tablespoons salt in a frying pan. Brown mixture over low heat, shaking the pan continuously. Stir occasionally with spatula until the salt browns slightly. Turn off heat and crush the mixture with a rolling pin or the handle of a cleaver or mortar. Put the mixture in a tightly sealed jar and store it in a cool, dry area.

Plum Sauce

A yellowish brown sauce with a sweet, pungent flavor made from salted plums, vinegar, sugar, sweet potato, hot chili pepper and spices. Plum sauce is commonly used as a seasoning sauce and as a dipping sauce. It is a great accompaniment to hot or cold meats and is served with egg rolls in some local restaurants. Sold in cans or glass jars in Chinese stores. Keep in the refrigerator. If ready made plum sauce is not available, prepare your own by refering to the recipe in sassy sauces.

Rock Sugar

This crystallized sugar, also known as rock candy, is pale brown in color and less refined than the common white rock sugar. Its sweetness and rich color give a dish a unique flavor and glossy appearance. Crush it before measuring.

Sesame Paste

This paste is commonly used in meat marinades and dressing sauces for cold dishes because of its strong aroma and rich flavor. The Middle Eastern "taheeni or tahini" is less flavorful but an acceptable substitute if the Chinese paste is not available. Before using, dilute one part paste with an equal part of water or oil.

Sesame Oil

This is not the kind of sesame oil you may find in most health food stores, which is lighter in color and is used for cooking and frying. Instead, this is a concentrated, strong nutty-flavored oil from toasted sesame seeds, used widely all over China in marinades, in soups, and as a last-minute touch of flavor. To prolong storage, keep in the refrigerator. A small bottle will last you a couple of generations.

Soy Sauce

No Chinese kitchen is complete without soy sauce. It gives Chinese dishes their characteristic flavor. Various regions in China produce their own types of soy sauce differing in color, aroma and flavor, yet the ingredients (soy beans, wheat, salt and water) fermentation processes are basically similar. In Cantonese cooking, there are two common types: light soy (thin soy) — lighter in color and saltier, used mostly for marinating and seasoning in stir-fried dishes, and dark soy (black soy) — much darker in color and sweeter, used mostly for stewing and sauteing dishes to add color. It should be pointed out that *not* every Chinese dish calls for soy sauce because soy sauce usually darkens food, whether it is light or dark soy. When the natural colors of the food are to be retained, salt is used instead of soy sauce. In this book light soy sauce is implied when a recipe simply calls for "soy sauce" without specifying the type.

Star Anise

This licorice-flavored ingredient is available either whole, with an eight-point star shape, or powdered. It is often used as a seasoning in stewed or BBQ dishes.

Starch

A. For thickening — In most cases, tapioca, corn or arrowroot starch can be used for thickening at the end of cooking. Simply mix one part of starch with one to two parts of cold water or broth and slowly add to the boiling liquid, stirring continuously. Starch solution tends to settle to the bottom, so be sure to stir well before adding to the wok. Most starches, particularly tapioca starch, when used in thickening a dish or making lots of sauce, will give a clear, shiny sauce.

B. For coating and holding in meat marinades — Cornstarch gives the meat a light coating, helping to seal in the natural juices to make the final product more tender and juicy. It also helps to hold onto the surface moisture, making the meat smoother and avoids spattering during deep-frying.

C. For coating meat in deep-fried dishes — Chinese chefs not only use starch to eliminate excess liquid in the meat, they also mix it with wheat flour, baking powder and water to give a batter of different thickness for coating deep-fried foods.

D. In gourmet Chinese cooking, water chestnut powder is frequently used in thickening because of its sweetness and its ability to give a more adhesive consistency.

Sugar

Like many great cuisines, a small amount is often used to give a contrast of flavor in most dishes. In China, brown sugar is often used.

Szechwan Chili Paste

Widely used as a basic seasoning for most hot Szechwan and Hunan dishes, it is made from hot peppers, salt and garlic.

Szechwan Peppercorn

Seeds from berries of Zanthoxylum plants. It has a strong aromatic flavor and is used frequently in specially prepared spicy dishes. When used, it is first browned in a frying pan, then crushed and used as a seasoning. They will keep forever in a sealed container.

Tangerine Peel, Dried

The sundried, tangerine skin is commonly used in soups or stewed dishes to add special fragrance and flavor. Wash before using.

Vinegar

There are white, red and black vinegars available in Chinese stores. The white one is used in preparing sweet and sour dishes; the red one is used mostly as a dip for crab and fried dishes; the black one is used in braising dishes and as a table condiment.

White Pepper

Both white and black pepper are produced by the same plant. Pepper is the berry of a perennial vine; white pepper has had the black hull removed to expose the cream colored core. White pepper, having a more delicate aroma, is less pungent than black pepper. It is often used in meat marinades or to add zest to soups and various dishes. White pepper is available in the spice section of supermarkets.

Dried and Other Preserved Ingredients

Agar-Agar

This is processed seaweed, used frequently in cold dishes with meats and vegetables. It can be used in place of gelatin in jellied dishes. When dissolved in hot water it melts into a gelatinous substance. Agar-agar is sold in three forms — powder, solid rectangular sections, and fine strips. The powdered and solid forms are generally used for desserts, while the fine strips are used in salads.

Bean Curd

Custard-like squares of about 3½″ x 2½″ x 1″ size and made from soy beans, it has long been a favorite in the Orient. Inexpensive, nutritious, low in calories and with no cholestrol, soy bean curd blends well with many foods and many flavors. It is sold fresh daily and should be kept in water and refrigerated, changing the water every two days to avoid souring. It can be served cold alone or combined and cooked with countless meat and vegetable dishes. Many places sell bean curd (tofu) in plastic sealed containers which usually indicate the last day of freshness and should be left sealed in the container until ready to use.

Bird's Nest

A semi-translucent gelatinous substance from the nests of tiny swallows of the South China Sea. Scarcity, labor and the difficulty involved in preparing it as a marketable product makes this an expensive delicacy. Bird's Nest is mostly served in soup and also is prepared as a dessert in formal banquets. It is sold in boxes and is available only in Chinese stores. Many Chinese believe bird nests prolong life and are a good source of energy, and, most of all, is good for the complexion.

Lily Buds

Dried buds from the tiger-lily flowers, yellowish-gold in color and about 3½″ long. They are often called "golden needles" by the Chinese and are used as a symbolic food in dishes at ceremonial and festive occasions. It will be exciting to serve a plate full of gold needles while the price of gold is sky-rocketing. Soaked before use, it goes well with other ingredients in many dishes. Sold in plastic bags only in Chinese stores, it can be kept for a long time.

Mushrooms, black dried or fresh

Here I refer to the Oriental black mushroom (SHII-TA-KE). This type of mushroom, long known as "The Emperor's Food" in both China and Japan, has been recognized by gourmets worldwide as a precious delicacy. It is richer in flavor than most ordinary mushrooms and can be used virtually along with any ingredients in any dish. For centuries in the Orient, these mushrooms have been regarded as the "elixir of life" which will enhance human sexuality, slow down aging and keep men vigorous. These Oriental mushrooms contain a large amount of calcium, phosphorous and iron. They are also excellent sources of vitamin B and D. Dried black mushrooms are commonly available in Chinese or Japanese stores and come in various sizes and prices. Before use, they should be soaked in warm water for 30 minutes to soften. They are excellent in combination with most meat and vegetables. Store in air-tight containers in a dry, cool area. Fresh ones have a milder flavor, a much more superior texture and are only available in a few areas, such as Vancouver, Toronto and Los Angeles. For more information on growing or purchasing large quantitities of fresh black mushrooms, you may contact Royal Mushroom Co. Ltd. in Mississanga, ONT., Canada.

Salted Egg

These are duck eggs, soaked in brine for one to two months, or coated with a salt and mud mixture. Due to a chemical reaction, the egg proteins change their physical appearance and the white becomes watery and very salty, while the yolk firms up and reddens. When served, they are cooked either by hard boiling or with other ingredients. The hard-boiled salted eggs are very common in family meals, served along with rice, in congee (rice soup) or in vegetable soups. They are sold in Chinese stores only.

Sausage, Chinese

Chinese sausages are solid, flavorful little links (5½-6" long), made from pork, pork fat, or duck liver. They are sold individually or by the pound. They may be steamed or boiled before serving, or cut into thin slices and stir-fried with other meats and vegetables. The Chinese often cook several links along with their rice and then serve the sausages as a side dish. They can be kept in the refrigerator for several months and forever in the freezer.

Seaweed

Purple in color with a delicate flavor (from the iodine), seaweed combines well with other meat and vegetables and is a common ingredient in soups. Rinse with water in a bowl before using.

Shark's Fin

These are cartilages of the shark's fin, and are one of the most expensive Chinese delicacies. The time, labor, and the difficulty of cleaning and preparation make shark's fin costly. Thus, it is used mostly for formal parties. Shark's fin is available only in Chinese stores dried or in cans and is mostly prepared as soup.

Shrimp, Chinese Dried

These shrimps are sold in 4 or 8 ounce packages in Chinese grocery stores. They have a strong flavor which enhances many vegetable dishes and soups. Soak them in warm water for 30 minutes before using.

Shrimp Chips

Thin slices of dried dough made from dried shrimp powder, tapioca starch and food coloring. They are mostly used as garnish in deep-fried poultry dishes. To prepare, simply deep-fry in hot oil until they puff up. They are also great to serve as hors d'oeuvres at cocktail parties. With these sensational chips, everyone will drink twice as much and get drunk three times as fast! They can be deep-fried ahead of time and stored in a plastic bag in a cool, dry place for several days.

Soy Bean Sheets, Dried

When soy bean milk is boiled, the thin film on top is removed and dried forming soy bean sheets. The sheets are very brittle and should be handled with care. They are sold by the pound and are available in different shapes and sizes. Use them within one or two months because they turn rancid. Soy bean sheets are used in soups, vegetarian dishes, and desserts. They may also serve as an edible wrapping in steamed and deep-fried dishes. Soak soy bean sheets for about 30 minutes before using.

Thousand Year Old Eggs

These eggs are preserved in a coating of salt, lime and ashes and cured for about three months, producing eggs with a strong, pungent ammonia odor. The ammonium compound derived from the above mixture denatures the egg protein, turns the egg white into a dark amber color and the yolk into a darkish green cheeselike texture by the capillary action through the shell. It is a delicacy to the Chinese and is often served along with pickled ginger as an hors d'oeuvre. Sold only in Chinese stores. Try it. You might hate it!

Wood Ears (Cloud Ears)

This is actually a tree fungus. Most of them come from the Szechwan province and are widely used throughout China. You will find them in hot and sour soup and many vegetarian dishes. There is little taste to the wood ears, but the notable, crunchy texture combines well with most ingredients. They are sold only in Chinese stores, in small packages of 4 to 8 ounces. Soak in warm water for 15-20 minutes before using, and they will expand into resilient clusters of dark petals. The hard "eye" in the center of the petals should be removed aand discarded. Rinse the wood ears to remove sand and slice them according to recipe instructions. Recent medical research suggests that wood ears slow down blood clots and should be incorporated into the diets of people with heart problems.

Fresh and Preserved Vegetables

Baby Corn

These little corn cobs are a special variety that only grow 3-3½ inches in size. They are canned in water or are pickled and are found in Chinese stores, gourmet food shops and many supermarkets. Water-packed corn cobs are used to add color and flavor to Chinese dishes. Baby corn is so sweet and tender that you can eat the cob and all!

Bamboo Shoots

Several varieties of bamboo shoots are grown in different parts of China with usually 3 crops of shoots annually — the spring bamboo, the summer bamboo and the winter bamboo. Bamboo shoots have a mild taste and a desirable crispy texture that goes well with practically any ingredient and flavor. They are sold in 11 ounce or 15 ounce cans, whole or in slices. After opening, keep in water in a covered container and store in the refrigerator, changing water daily. They will keep for 5-6 days.

Bean Sprouts, Fresh

These crisp sprouts, cooked or raw, have a fresh, delicate flavor and unusual texture: In salads or main dishes, bean sprouts will add a new dimension. Sprouted from mung beans, they can be purchased by the pound in most local supermarkets. Choose fresh-looking, crisp sprouts which have tips that are not dry. Any sprouts that are bruised or discolored should be discarded. The shorter the sprout, the younger and more tender it is. They should be washed thoroughly before use to remove any loose particles such as skins of the beans. Like other fresh vegetables, bean sprouts should be bought fresh and used the same day. Although they are quite perishable, they will keep well for 3-4 days if kept in a plastic bag in the vegetable drawer of your refrigerator. For information on how to sprout your own and tips on preparation, refer to the vegetable chapter. Canned sprouts are an extremely undesirable substitute, because they are mushy, discolored and taste funny.

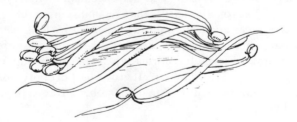

Bitter Melon

Bitter melon is also known as Foo Gwa, but it is actually not a melon. It is more squash-like and used as a vegetable marrow. This green vegetable with bumpy, shiny skin, resembles a "fat" cucumber. The young, light-green bitter melon darkens, and the interior turns red as it matures. Quinine gives the melon its cool, bitter taste. The flavor is tangy, but likeable. Don't peel it, but scoop out the seeds and pulp prior to use. It can be parboiled 2-3 minutes in salt water to reduce the bitterness, if desired. Bitter melon is used in stir-fry dishes or is cut into rings crosswise and stuffed with minced fish or pork. Look for it either fresh or canned in Chinese grocery stores. It will grow well in your backyard in hot, moist soil. Planting: March-June. Harvesting: June-September.

Bok Choy

Bok Choy is a popular Chinese green which belongs to the loose-leaf cabbage family. Inner leaves and hearts are tender and savory with a gentle hint of mustard flavor. With big, white stalks and large, dark green leaves, it can be used in many meat and vegetable dishes, in soups, etc. and is a good source of vitamin B & C. The stalks are crispy if not overcooked. It is sold in most supermarkets and you can try to grow it in your own garden quite easily; it grows best in cool, moist soil.
Planting: March-May. Harvesting: April-June.

Broccoli, Chinese (Gai Lan)

Chinese broccoli is dark green and leafy, with very small flowers — totally different from the regular supermarket broccoli. This vegetable is only available in Chinese stores. To identify look for a long stalk with big green leaves and a small flower bud on top. Choose fresh-looking, green stalks with the flower buds unopened. If you cannot find it in the store, it can be grown quite easily. Planting: March-April; August-October. Harvesting: May-June; October-November.

Buttercup Squash

This dark green squash has a knob on top and looks like a green brioche. It is available in the fall and has a starchy, sweet taste similar to Chinese pumpkin. Cook it in soups and stews or stir-fry it with black bean sauce. Buttercup squash goes especially well with beef. Banana squash is a good substitute.

Cabbage, Chinese (Napa)

Chinese cabbage (Siew Choy) is a sweet and succulent member of the cabbage family. It looks more like romaine lettuce than regular round cabbage. The leaves are crinkly with pale green and white coloring which form a long, slender head. Since it has no odor when cooked, it is great for stir-fry dishes, soups, casseroles, salads or as a vegetable by itself. It is normally available in the supermarket year-round, and is a good source of vitamin C. It grows best in cool climates in moist, rich soil. Planting: March-April; August-October. Harvesting: May-June; October-December.

Egglant, Chinese or Japanese

This type of eggplant, is smaller than the usual type you see in the store. They have dark purple, glossy skin and are much like a sponge in that they absorb a tremendous amount of liquid or sauce. It goes well with most meats or served by itself. In flavor, texture and cooking qualities it is similar to the big eggplants, but the skin is thinner and more tender. Eggplant can be stir-fried, deep-fried, or used in stewed dishes with strong flavorings such as oyster sauce or black bean paste.

Leeks

Sold fresh by the bunch in most supermarkets, this perennial plant has large green leaves. Leeks look like giant green onions but they have a milder flavor, and more fibrous texture. They are popular in Northern China as a vegetable and as a seasoning. Use them with beef, lamb and liver, in soups or in stir-fried dishes. Cut leeks in half, lengthwise, and wash carefully to remove sand and dirt before using.

Lotus Root

This tuber, the stem of the water lily, has 2-3 sections, each 2½-3 inches in diameter and about 6-8 inches long, linked together like sausages. 5-7 tunnels run through the vegetable forming interesting patterns when sliced. The potato-like, crisp texture adds variety when thinly sliced for stir-frying or in soups. It is available, fresh, canned or dried, only in Chinese groceries. Fresh ones are available between July and February. The dried ones must be soaked for at least 20 minutes before cooking. Lotus root can be served as a vegetable in most dishes or as a dessert in light syrup.

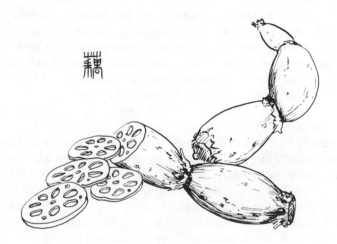

Mustard Greens, Chinese (Gai Choy)

A member of the cabbage family, mustard greens have a bittersweet taste. They have a much more pungent flavor than most Chinese vegetables. They are used mostly for soups, but can also be stir-fried. When buying this vegetable, choose the ones with fresh, dark green leaves that are not wilted. The younger and more tender leaves will have better flavor. Mustard greens are available fresh or pickled and are available all year round in Chinese groceries. They can be prepared fresh or cooked in pickled form. The Cantonese pickle them by parboiling the whole vegetable then pickling it in brine to ferment until sour. Rinsed sauerkraut may be substituted for pickled mustard greens.

Pickled Vegetables

Pickled vegetables, with sweet and sour tastes, are a delight all over China. Several kinds of vegetables, but mostly cucumber, carrot and turnip, are pickled at various stages of growth (most commonly at maturity). These pickled vegetables, packed in 6 ounce or 15 ounce cans, can be found in all Chinese groceries. After opening, transfer into a tightly sealed glass jar or plastic container and store in the refrigerator.

Snow Peas

Snow peas are edible pea pods, and are eaten for the delicate flavor and crisp texture of the pod itself. They are bright green, slightly sweet pods and are considered a delicacy in salads and main dishes. They are available in most supermarkets in the fresh produce section. Be sure to pick the ones that are dark green, flat, crisp and free from blemishes. Avoid droopy, wilted pods and ones that are plump, yellowish and big, as they tend to be overly-matured and too fibrous. They are available practically year round, but are most plentiful in the summer. Always keep in the refrigerator. To use, snap off the end to remove the stem and any string along each side. Stir-fry or blanch over high heat for 2-3 minutes. They grow best in a cool climate, with moist, non-acid soil and good drainage. Pick the pods when peas just become visible. Planting: March-May; August-October. Harvesting: April-June; October-December.

Straw Mushrooms

These dark brown little mushrooms with pointed caps have a texture and flavor completely different from other mushrooms. They go well with meat and vegetable dishes. Straw mushrooms come fresh, canned or dried and are found only in Chinese stores. After opening, canned mushrooms should be stored in water in a glass or plastic container and refrigerated. When the water is changed every couple of days, canned mushrooms will keep up to a week. The fresh straw mushrooms are very perishable and only keep for a few days.

Szechwan Preserved Vegetable

This hot and spicy canned pickled vegetable is widely used in many northern style dishes and soups. Wipe off some of the red chili powder if you cannot take it too hot, then slice it thin to use in various dishes. After opening, it will keep for many months in a covered jar in the refrigerator.

Water Chestnut, fresh or canned

Fresh water chestnuts, with dark brown scaly skins and white, crunchy, sweet and nutlike centers, are hard to find except in Chinese specialty stores. Watch out for the dried, bruised or shrivelled ones — they are good for nothing! The canned ones are widely available and are sold in cans of 8 or 15 ounces, sliced or whole. They remain crisp and crunchy even after cooking. Their delicate flavor never overpowers other ingredients in a dish. Water chestnuts marry well with the other flavors and are a good addition to many dishes. After opening a can, transfer to a covered container with water and store in the refrigerator; they will keep for several days.

White Turnip, Chinese

Also known as lobak or daikon (in Japanese), this is a crisp-textured white radish about 7-10 inches in length. It looks very much like an overgrown horse radish and has a subtle flavor, but strong "odor." White turnip goes well with beef, in soup and in stir-fried dishes and are available only in Chinese groceries and occasionally in some supermarkets.

Winter Melon

It is more or less like a large squash, with frosty but dark green skin and a white core with lots of seeds. It belongs to the muskmelon family and is the size of a large watermelon and is very succulent with a very mild taste. Winter melon is sold by the pound in most Chinese stores and is prepared in stir-fried dishes and soups. If kept in the refrigerator it will last up to a week. A whole melon can be stored up to several months. For banquet and formal dinners, the soup is prepared inside the scooped-out melon with lots of other goodies. The Chinese also make them into candies.

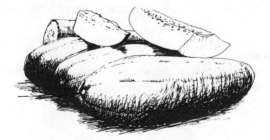

Yard Long Beans, Chinese

These are long, skinny, string beans that can be up to 20 inches long. They are crisp, tender and firm and the color of the skin ranges from light to dark green. The shorter and less "lumpy" the pod, the younger and more tender it will be. To prepare, trim the tips off an cut into 2-3 inch lengths. Cook for 3-4 minutes. They can be stored in the refrigerator for 7-10 days without spoiling.

Rice and Noodles

Cellophane Noodles

This translucent, thread-like noodle made from mung bean starch resembles stiff nylon fishing line. They are used in meat and vegetable dishes and soups and are deep-fried when used as a garnish. When using these noodles in stir-fried dishes or soups, first soak them in warm water for several minutes. Be sure to add enough liquid during cooking because the noodles will soak up a large amount of water. For deep-frying break them up inside a plastic bag, otherwise you might end up having noodles on the floor, in your bedroom and of course in your backyard because they will fly all over the place! They are sold in 4 or 8 ounce plastic bags in Chinese stores and some supermarkets.

Chinese Egg Noodles, Fresh or Dried

Fresh and dried egg noodles are parboiled for 1½-2 minutes, rinsed under cool water and drained before using in soups or stir-fried dishes. Fresh noodles are sold in 1 pound plastic bags and can be kept in the refrigerator for 3-5 days or can be frozen.

Rice, Long-grain

A daily staple in many parts of the Orient, it will be dry, separated and fluffy after cooking. This is the type you use to make fried rice. It is sold in 2 or 4 pound plastic bags. For more information, refer to the "Plain-Cooked Rice" recipe. It is also ground into rice flour to make different types of pastries and rice cakes in southern China.

Rice, Medium-grain

Mostly grown in California, it has the characteristic between long and short-grain. It has a great flavor and aroma when cooked. A good choice to serve as table rice.

Rice, Short-grain

A short-grain, pearly, slightly transparent white rice which yields a soft, moist and sticky final product when cooked. It is mainly used in preparing pastries, stuffings and desserts when ground to rice powder.

Rice flour, Long-grain or Glutinous

Whiter than wheat flour, these fine powders are made either from long-grain or glutinous rice. Rice flour is mainly used in pastries and dumplings as well as in wrappings for sweet or salty fillings. Glutinous rice flour is moister and stickier than long-grain rice flour.

Rice Noodles, Fresh or Dried

Made from long-grain rice flour, they are used exclusively in Cantonese dishes. Similar to bean thread noodles, these dried rice sticks are more brittle, but are easier to handle. Soak them in hot water for about 10-15 minutes before using in soups or stir-fry dishes. They can also be deep-fried in hot oil (when dried). They pop up in just a few seconds like a white nest when prepared this way. Fresh noodles can be kept in the refrigerator for 3-5 days and kept in the freezer for months. Stir-fried fresh Rice Noodles with Beef is one of the most popular lunch dishes in Cantonese restaurants.

Spring Roll Wrappers

White, pliable and paper-thin, these wrappers are soft flour and water, formed into 3″ rounds or squares. (They are often confused with those yellowish egg roll wrappers available in supermarkets. In China, there are no egg roll wrappers.) They are sold fresh or frozen only in Chinese stores. When deep-fried over high heat, they give a crispier texture than the common egg roll wrappers. These wrappers dry out extremely fast, so avoid prolonged exposure to air. Take out a few at a time to work on, and keep the rest covered with a damp cloth. When stored in the refrigerator, they will last 7-10 days. If frozen, they will stay fresh for several months, and should be defrosted inside the package before use.

Won Ton Wrappers

These thin pieces of dough, about 3½ inches square, are made from high-gluten flour, water and eggs. They are usually packed in air-tight plastic bags or waxed paper in 1 pound packages, and are available fresh or frozen in any Chinese store and in most supermarkets. You can fill them with a variety of fillings both sweet and salty. They can be deep-fried, steamed or cooked in soups. When preparing dishes made from won ton wrappers, take out a few at a time and cover the rest with a damp cloth to prevent them from drying out. Store them wrapped in several sheets of plastic wrap in the refrigerator for 7-10 days or in the freezer for up to 3 months. If frozen, defrost inside the package before using.

A Magical Metric Tour

I thought it was hard enough just being a cook; but now, with kitchens around the world switching to metric, I've got to be a mathematician as well. I don't even know how many millilitres are in one teaspoon! And I thought I was one confused cook before! But not to worry, everyone assures me. The most important thing to remember is not to switch back and forth from one system to another. You could end up adding a pound of salt to 25 grams of beef. Now, before you throw a metric tantrum, check at the back of this page for the conversion table. I've also included the metric equivalents in all the recipes. If you still end up with too much salt, don't blame me!

Approx. volume measure rounded to nearest 10.		Approx. mass measurements	
Conventional	**Metric**	**Conventional**	**Metric**
½ teaspoon	2 ml	½ ounce	14 grams
1 teaspoon	5 ml	1 ounce	28 grams
½ tablespoon	7 ml	2 ounces	56 grams
1 tablespoon	15 ml	4 ounces (¼ pound)	112 grams
¼ cup	60 ml	6 ounces	168 grams
1/3 cup	80 ml	8 ounces (½ pound)	225 grams
½ cup	125 ml	10 ounces	280 grams
¾ cup	200 ml	12 ounces (¾ pound)	340 grams
1 cup	250 ml	16 ounces (1 pound)	450 grams
1¼ cups	310 ml	1½ pounds	675 grams
1½ cups	370 ml		

Approx. Temperature Conversions

F	C
300°	150°
325°	160°
350°	180°
375°	190°
400°	200°

Conventional	Metric
1¾ cups	430 ml
2 cups	500 ml
4 cups	1 L
6 cups	1½ L

Other measurements

Ingredients	Conventional	Metric (app.)
rice	1 cup	220 grams
flour	1 cup	220 grams
sugar	1 cup	220 grams
chopped veg.	1 cup	220 grams
cornstarch	1 teaspoon	5 grams (5 ml)
cornstarch	1 tablespoon	15 grams (15 ml)
sugar	1 teaspoon	10 grams (5 ml)
sugar	1 tablespoon	30 grams (15 ml)
salt	1 teaspoon	(5 ml)
salt	1 tablespoon	(15 ml)

Puzzled? Let Me Straighten You Out!

1. How would you get ready for wok cookery? What should I keep in mind before I start?

    Line up a lot of help! Make a list to check if you have all the ingredients and utensils necessary. Organize your menu with respect to the order of preparation of dishes. Prepare those dishes first that can be kept warm without suffering any flavor loss. Then do the stir-fried dishes in the last few minutes. If you get into trouble, shout at the help you have lined up! Always remember to keep your composure.

2. Is there any advantage in using a wok to cook Chinese food? Is it healthier to "wok"?

    Yes, the unique shape of the wok gives several advantages for cooking. First, you need only a minimum amount of oil to cook a large amount of food. Secondly the high heat and short cooking times used permit quick searing, which retains vitamins, minerals and juices. This results, of course, in more nutritious food.

3. Since high temperatures are used in most of the stir-fried dishes, how do you stay cool over a hot wok?

    Don't get steamed up!! Do what I do — fill up your kitchen with Yan Can "fans"!

4. Once I have learned the Chinese way, how do I improvise my own dishes?

    First, open the refrigerator door and pick up anything that isn't dead or moving! Strive for contrast in color and texture in meat and vegetable dishes. There are no set rules, just use whatever pleases your palate.

5. Are all foods safe to eat after stir-frying for only a few minutes?

    Yes, because in Chinese cooking, the food is chopped or sliced into bite-size morsels. Oftentimes, these pieces are cut at an angle, exposing greater surface area to the heat. That means the food can be cooked in just a few minutes over high heat.

6. Do the Chinese put ginger, garlic, and soy sauce in everything they cook?

    For the uninspired, unimaginative and boring cook, these are the only "three musketeers" they know. But for the creative cook, the sky's the limit, and they are only used to enhance the flavors of certain dishes. If you used only these three in everything, all the dishes would taste alike — just like having a Big Mac every day!!

7. Does a fancy Chinese meal really have 25 or more dishes? Isn't that too much to cook and eat?

   In the past, traditional Chinese banquets did have that many courses as well as that many people. Today the number of dishes have been cut down, and banquets for large numbers of people are often held in restaurants. The general rule of thumb is to serve as many courses as there are people sitting at one table.

8. Are all the recipes that you present in your T.V. shows and cookbooks authentic Chinese dishes?

   Yes and no! The majority of the recipes are basically traditional dishes. Some were developed through teaching and personal experience. Others were suggested by students, friends and associates. And still others were created, depending on the availability of ingredients in North America.

9. After so many years of T.V. shows, are you running out of recipes and ideas?

   Yes, after 3 years on the air with a total of 390 shows, I've presented about 650 totally different recipes. Now I am one pooped cook! Life has been crazy here — they wok me to death! They won't give me time to change my apron. Fortunately, I set aside 4 months to go on promotional tours, meeting and talking with many of you and my professional friends from coast to coast. I also set aside 2-2½ months to relax and do some traveling around the country and all over the world to get new ideas and inspiration. Thanks to you — you are the ones that keep me going.

10. How can you be so young and so good? Where do you learn all this?

   I have been wokking for these past 62 years. I learned to wok even before I was born! Since practice makes perfect, wokking in the kitchen for so many years can make *you* wok just as well or even better.

A Little Spotlight on my
Friends Behind the Scenes

No one can accomplish a job without the help and support from many friends. Their's are the 'credits' who really deserve credit. They deserve all the credit for what little value this humble book possesses; any discredit should fall on my head (but not too hard, please).

I owe special gratitude to Janet Turnbull, my editor, who worked so hard that she collapsed with "Chinese cookbook Syndrome'. Many thanks to Professor and Mrs. Martin W. Miller, who introduced this book so graciously; Susan, whom I thank for everything, but especially for her patience with this wandering cook for a roommate; Janet Huddle, for her valuable assistance in all phases of this publication; Gerald Levitch, the best writer I know of who has the nerve to put words in my big mouth; Dorothy Louie, my former associate, for her sensitivity, knowledge and support; Mr. Noel Wagner of CFAC TV, for his confidence in me; Len Ross, Dan Parrish, Bruce Wardill and Lewis Manne, the dedicated and talented directors of my TV shows; the ever-hungry production crews at CFAC TV and VTR Studios who licked the plates clean; Marian Wallace, for her 'hard work' in typing up the recipes for "Yan Can" to please the fans before the book even came out of the oven; Wayne Lum, the most talented artist who designed the cover; Chung Kwong Cheung, who did all the artful illustrations; Howard Eng, for the fantastic cartoons to brighten up this book; my readers and audiences, who wrote and gave me all their ideas, suggestions and all my associates, who worked hard and sweated with me throughout the revisions of this new edition.

And, of course, this poor Chinese cook also wishes to thank *you*, for spending your hard-earned cash to buy this little book. I hope you enjoyed it.

Readers Strike Back!

I hope that you did not gain too much weight trying all my recipes. If you did, I hope you enjoyed yourself doing it. One of life's great pleasures is eating something that is not too bland and not too strong, not too raw and not too burnt, but is *just* right. I have always enjoyed sharing good cooking with my friends and anyone else who dares to try it. I hope that you, in turn, will experiment and share the happy results with your family and friends (any *un*happy results should be disposed of quietly).

Before publishing this book, we tested all the recipes. By 'we', I mean all my associates and my friends. By 'friends', I mean that, after swallowing all sorts of disasters, they don't blame me too much for my mistakes. If you have any problems or disasters, you can write me, and I'll try to help. I really do appreciate your suggestions and opinions, and I won't duck your complaints. (I won't 'chicken' out, either.) If I know what difficulties you have encountered, perhaps I can solve them in the future.

Mailing Address:

In the U.S.A.: Yan & Associates
           580 Allen Way
           Yuba City, Ca. 95991

In Canada: Yan Can & Company
          500 Keele St., Unit 206
          Toronto, Ont., M6N 3C9

Regarding recipe for: _____ Page: _____

Complimentary Comments: _____

_____

_____

Complaints _____

Name: _____

Address: _____

_____

Telephone number _____

"Never wake up a sleep wokker...."

本酒家歷史悠久，向以菜式上乘、價錢公道為宗旨。特由香港聘請四位名廚，創製新奇名菜。

❖八十元
▲酬賓席▼
鷄絲燕窩羹
當紅炸子鷄
脆皮掛爐鴨
海蔘會冬菇
雙菇滑鷄球
時菜牛肉球
清蒸海上鮮
甜酸古魯肉

❖九十元
▲喜慶席▼
鷄絲魚翅羹
脆皮炸子鷄
玉環扎大鴨
紅爐燒乳鴿
酥炸奶蝦球
碧綠蠔油鮑
香港樓牛球
香羅古魯肉

❖百一十元
▲豪華席▼
蟹王大生翅
金華玉樹鷄
北京片皮鴨
烘燒嫩乳鴿
緬省生龍蝦
金黃釀蟹拑
鮮菇會鮑片
百鳥齊歸巢
清蒸海上鮮
香港樓美點

週末午市供應

▲南北美點▼
火白粥　鮮炸油條

正宗粵菜　經濟和菜
白灼鮮蝦　保仔小菜
常備海鮮　粉麵雲吞
他名少參　全日供應

本廠富有多年經驗製造爐頭，叉燒爐和各式餐館用品，兼做建築工程，產品優良，工作精緻，價錢公道。　許全老好道好高好譽論公烤菜務讚

All My Favorites
—Index of Recipes

Poultry

Beef

Pork

Seafood

Eggs and Bean Curd

Desserts

All My Other Favorites—Recipes
from *The Yan Can Cook Book*

Fowl Plays

Holy cows and Little Lambs

Pork Out

Catch of the Day—Seafood

Bean Curd, Eggs and Other Protein-Rich Foods

Harvest from the Garden—Vegetables

To Martin Yan, Our Cook

Every day our hero cooks,
He knows what to do without (cook) books.

If you wonder, "Who is this man?"
Turn to your T.V. and meet Yan.

He cooks rice and everything nice in a wok,
All the time he jokes and talks.

If you need a few extra cooking clues
Turn on Yan Can for wokking news!

Brenda and Kathy
Oshawa, Ontario

"Some days I feel YAN-TASTIC!!"

魚与熊掌

皆不可兼得

中国古諺 仲光写

ABOUT THE HUMBLE COOK

"I am a serious, humble cook," says Martin Yan, "but people start to laugh when I pick up a cleaver." The ways of his inscrutable western audience still puzzle Martin, a "serious" chef from Kwongchow, China, who never expected to become a North American media star. His daily TV series, YAN CAN COOK, is seen by an audience of at least 500,000 Canadians, plus an unknown number of American viewers in border cities from coast to coast. With 527 TV shows to his credit, Martin has made YAN CAN COOK into the longest running Chinese cooking show in the English speaking country. Since 1978, THE JOY OF WOKKING has become a national best-seller with more than 100,000 copies in print. His latest book, THE YAN CAN COOK BOOK, has proven just as successful.

From the age of 13, Martin has cooked his way thru Hong Kong restaurants and earned a diploma from the Overseas Institute of Cookery in Hong Kong and a Master's degree from the University of California at Davis. Equally important, he has travelled extensively throughout China and Southeast Asia, from the waterfront markets of Hong Kong to the great restaurants of Taiwan, learning new techniques and studying under renowned chefs. Martin, in addition to his expertise and knowledge of foods and Chinese cookery, has taught classes since 1969 to thousands.

For the past 4 years, Martin has lived out of a suitcase, keeping a hectic schedule, that includes personal appearances at the Canadian National Exhibition, cross-country tours for department stores, national home shows, conventions, and seminars. He also serves as a consultant to the Food Stuff Research Centre in Hong Kong and writes feature articles for Food World Magazine (Hong Kong) and many other publications. Martin is a certified professional member of the International Association of Cooking Schools and the Institute of Food Technologists. Although Martin's formal credentials are formidable, he never loses sight of his basic goal to make classic Chinese cooking accessible to the broadest possible audience. As he often closes his show, "What the heck. If Yan can, so can you."

thank you